ISBN 0 85429 417 1

A FOULIS Motoring Book

This second edition published 1984
First published 1977

Published by:
Haynes Publishing Group
Sparkford, Yeovil, Somerset BA22 7JJ,
England

Distributed in North American by:
Haynes Publications Inc.
861 Lawrence Drive, Newbury Park,
California 91320 USA

Editor: Rod Grainger
Page layout: Barry Griffiths
Printed in England, by: J.H. Haynes &
Co. Ltd

Contents

Foreword
by Roger Clark

I must say that I was delighted when I heard that Graham Robson was preparing to write *The Works Escorts*. It was high time some permanent record of these great cars was published. I can personally vouch for the number of times an Escort has helped me to a big win where no other car in the world would have coped. I would not say they were indestructible, but it is nice to have the machine on *your* side at all times.

This book will appear when the factory cars are already tackling their tenth season. The miracle of it all is not that they are still in there, fighting, but that they are still winning. That magnificent RS1800 which gave me my second RAC Rally win in 1976 was the finest I have ever driven – and I have driven a few – and that was getting on for nine years after I had first driven a prototype Boreham-developed Twin Cam.

I know what sort of trouble Graham had in digging out the facts about all the cars, for at Boreham (and in Germany too) the staff are continually looking forward, and usually do not have time to reflect on their past glories. But Graham helped me with my own autobiography, and after that experience I can assure you that if he has not found all the statistics, then they do not exist any more!

There is no doubt in my mind that the Escorts have been the world's most successful competition machines. When Peter Browning wrote *The Works Minis* (a companion volume to this) he claimed that the Minis held that title; they did – then. Now they have been left struggling for an honourable second place.

You cannot credit a 'works' Escort to the genius of one man. Factory engineers had a lot to do with the initial structure. Keith Duckworth invented the magnificent engine. Henry Taylor himself probably invented the original Twin-Cam. Successive managers at Boreham – Taylor, Stuart Turner, and Peter Ashcroft – made sure that the pedigree was never diluted. Mechanics – in Britain and in Germany – made sure that the bright ideas were practical, and kept on working.

My last RAC Rally winner – POO 505R – was apparently the 99th 'works' rally car built at Boreham, which gives you an idea of the work centred in that modest little workshop. I also see from the statistics at the back of this book that Escorts have won 71 International rallies outright (at the time of writing – and by the time you read this that total will have risen again!), and countless races too.

They say that competition improves the breed, but after years of noisy experience I can tell you that the link between an RS1800 and the Escort 1100 is a bit tenuous. On the other hand, there is no way that an RS1800 or RS2000 could be winning without all the great joys and heartaches we suffered in earlier years.

Somebody once asked me if there was any other car I would rather have to drive than an Escort. I replied that if they could find me a car which did as much for me as an Escort, and which repaid my efforts so cheerfully and willingly, then I would drive it. I have not found one yet.

I have no doubt that there will have to be further editions of this book. If nothing else, I know that the Appendices will need to be updated. The Escort is not 'past it' yet (the mockers all say so, but then they have been saying that about me since the end of the 1960s as well!), and I have a feeling that its greatest successes are yet to come.

You see, all the drivers treat their Escorts like well-loved pets. Nothing is too good for them. Now, in my case, let me see . . . would it not be nice if we could win a Safari, then Morocco, and I would like to win the Acropolis again . . . .

Roger Clark
Christmas 1976

Last outing for a famous works team – the five Escorts ready for the 1979 Lombard-RAC rally, in which they not only finished first, second, fourth, sixth, ninth and tenth, but won the event for the eighth successive year. Hannu Mikkola's winning car was WTW 569S, second from the right, with Russell Brookes' 'Andrews' car second

Introduction

When I finalised the original edition of this book, in 1976*, I realised that the Escort's 'works' career was by no means over, but I had no idea that the best years were yet to come. The climax came in 1979, when the company won the World Rally Championship for Makes, and when the team's star drivers, Bjorn Waldegard and Hannu Mikkola, dominated the Drivers' series. Then, for two more years, Boreham contracted drivers helped the David Sutton/Rothmans cars to stay ahead, and Ari Vatanen won the Drivers' World Championship in 1981.

As in 1976, so in the 1980s, this is a book about thoroughbred cars. It celebrates the most formidable and versatile competition cars Britain has ever produced. For fourteen years the cars were always competitive, and sometimes the best in the world. But the story *is* now complete, and this completely revised edition attempts to tell the whole story of how the 'works' Escorts were conceived, developed, and refined over the years.

There have been works cars from Boreham and from Cologne, and 'replicas' built all over the world. Thousands of Escorts have been used in competition – racing, rallying, rallycross, anything where wheels are needed – but the most highly developed have usually come from Boreham. Over the years there have been engine, gearbox, axle and even bodyshell transplants, but the pedigree has remained. I know of no other car, not even the British Minis or the French Alpine-Renault, which has been so competitive for so long.

So many people have helped me to get the story straight that I could not possibly name them here. People like Mick Jones, Bill Barnett and Bill Meade gave generously from their memories, while Stuart Turner and Peter Ashcroft recalled many critical policy decisions for me. Steve Clark's photographic files were incredibly detailed, while Boreham's records were a mass (and a maze!) of information. Tony Mason, Martin Holmes and Hugh Bishop wrung out my statistical appendices, which could not have been completed without the archival help of *Autocar, Motor, Autosport* and *Motoring News*. To them, and to dozens of other people, my grateful thanks.

When Peter Browning wrote the companion volume to this book *(The Works Minis)*, he said " . . . it is doubtful whether any other manufacturer will ever equal the achievements of the works Minis." Ford did – and have handsomely surpassed them.

Graham Robson
1984

Some sections of this book were written in the mid-seventies and, as we did not wish to change the feeling of 'being there' when the works Escort story was at its climax, these sections have been left in the present tense.

1

Build-up
to the Escorts

The Ford Escort's first event was a rallycross at Croft on 3 February 1968, and its first rally win was the Circuit of Ireland in April 1968. That was just the start of a fantastically successful fourteen year record – and the proof of Ford's great efforts to develop an outright winner from their production cars. For Ford, the Twin-Cam Escort certainly signalled a beginning – and an end.

People with short memories might think that Ford's factory successes began with the Cortinas, but the competition pedigree goes back much further than that. Indeed, in the United States, Henry Ford himself drove a car at 91.37mph to take the World Land Speed Record in 1904. Surely, that's as good a way as possible to begin?

Ford cars have been winning races and rallies for decades – after all, their first Monte Carlo Rally win came along in 1936 – but there were no official British 'works' entries until the late 1940s. What started as a casual, hilarious, but very successful operation with Anglias and V8 Pilots, soon developed more serious aims in the 1950s, and really began to mature in the 1960s.

The two events which finally assured Ford's place at the top of the competition tree were these – that in 1961 Walter Hayes joined the company from *The Sunday Dispatch,* and that in 1963 the Competition Centre was established at Boreham. Two cars provided the basis for future campaigns – the first was the Lotus-Cortina, and the second was the Escort. In Britain, Ford's production cars of the 1930s and 1940s could hardly have been less suitable for competitions. The little '£100 Ford Eight' had a side-valve engine and precious little performance, while the big 30hp V8 had performance but no roadholding or brakes. Only people like Sydney Allard, who built a few very effective pre-war 'specials', could see the advantages of a big torquey V8 engine.

After the Second World War, there were dozens of cars thought more suitable for rallying and other competitions than the Fords. It was only when such stalwarts as Ken Wharton and Jack Reece were hired to drive in European events that this opinion altered. Wharton it was who took an unexpected

Ford's first four in a row in the RAC International Rally wins. These interesting photographs show the development of the cars and the change in sponsors

11

victory in the 1949 Tulip Rally in an Anglia, repeated the dose in 1950 with a massive Pilot, and rubbed it all in by winning with a Consul in 1952; only one driving test slip in 1951 stopped him making it four-out-of-four!

This, almost by default, meant that Ford of Britain had a competitions department. Right from the start, its operations had been managed by 'Edgy' Fabris at the Lincoln Cars depot, out on the Great West Road opposite the Firestone factory. Far from being an important, self-contained, unit, the department was really an off-shoot of the fleet of 'press/demonstrator cars', and Fabris also ran Ford's Publications division.

The man who made it all possible, literally made it all happen, was a kindly, chubby little man, whose pipe seemed to be as permanent a part of him as hands and feet. That man was Bill Barnett. Bell never became Competitions Manager himself, and before leaving the department in 1973 he served six bosses. Even so, it would be true to say that without Bill the administration of the rallying programme would often have ground to a halt.

As Walter Hayes once told me:

"When I came to Ford, I found this small department, with quite a distinguished history, though it certainly struck me as strange that Fabris was both Publications Manager and Competitions Manager!"

When first introduced, Hayes apparently asked Fabris what he did, and the conversation went something like this:

"I do Publications and Competitions."

"What do competitions consist of?"

"Rallying. At the end of the year we finish off Publications early, and go off on the Monte Carlo Rally."

"And who organises it all? Surely it takes a lot of planning?"

"Oh, Bill Barnett does it. He does everything."

Times have indeed changed!

Throughout the 1950s the factory relied on Zephyrs, Anglias, and later the notch-window Anglias. Names like the Harrisons (father and sons), Gatsonides, Gerry Burgess, Ann Hall, Peter Riley and even Graham Hill were prominent, but with very ordinary cars the successes were rare.

Maurice Gatsonides astounded everyone *including* Ford by winning the 1953 Monte Carlo Rally, and Gerry Burgess won a strongly-disputed RAC Rally in 1959, but that was all. Only two outright wins in ten years was nothing to get excited about. Not until 1964 would a British Ford again win a major rally or race.

Bill Barnett says that for a short time the competition department was really 'an unwanted baby' which the engineering department had shunned, and which the marketing people didn't really understand. But soon after Walter Hayes arrived to take charge of public affairs, Managing Director Alan Barke handed him responsibility for competition affairs. It was a momentous command, and came far enough ahead of the release of the Cortina for Hayes to make sense of both.

"I told Pat Hennessy and Alan Barke that we should go properly into motor sport," says Hayes, "and I recommended that the company should build a proper performance centre, not too dramatic, and to work up the Cortina. They agreed, we spent £60,000 and got Boreham going."

At about the same time corporate policy in Detroit decreed a return to 'Total Performance', and in a climate of high enthusiasm the programme which started with the Monte Falcons, evolved through the GT40 sports cars,

The **Anglia** of the 1940s was a very effective little car. Ken Wharton won several rallies in his works car. This is Geoff Holt on the 1949 Monte

The **Zephyr** of Maurice Gatsonides and Peter Worledge which won the 1953 Monte outright. Underneath that canopy are all the spot lamps. This car reappeared in the Lombard-RAC Golden 50 rally of 1982

Boreham's first rally cars — the Cortina GTs. Vic Elford and David Stone on their way to winning the 1964 Alpine Rally outright

Roger Clark — who else? — was the first to win rough events in his Cortinas. 2 ANR had already won one Scottish in 1964; here it is on the way to winning the 1965 event

and came to full flowering with the Cosworth F1 engine project, was born.

Between 1963 and 1967, Ford's standing in motor sport was transformed. The days when a team of automatic-transmission Zephyrs could be entered for a Silverstone touring car race, purely for publicity (this actually happened in 1958), were over. In future the approach would be increasingly professional. Stage One was to hire the best drivers and support the best teams, and Stage Two would be to develop the best possible versions of existing cars. Stage Three – and this was still some time away – would be to develop a car specifically for competitions.

Walter Hayes' first move was to hire a professional team manager, and he chose Sid Henson. In the event, Henson, who had moved over to Ford from the Ferodo brake linings concern, only stayed with the company for a year, presiding over a free-spending budget of £43,000 which seemed astronomical at the time, and attracted several new drivers to the team. David Seigle-Morris, Peter Riley and Pat Moss all moved over from the then BMC, attracted by £2,000 annual retaining fees, and the prospect of the Lotus-Cortina for use in 1963. Henson also courted, but failed to sign, the volatile Frenchman René Trautmann, then achieving the most remarkable deeds in the front-wheel-drive Citroens.

Henson and Hayes had very different working philosophies, and were probably never truly happy working together; in the spring of 1963 Ford's new manager, recruited from within the company, was Alan Platt. Unknown then, and little known even today, Platt was a talented administrator who brought system and control to the bustling activities of Boreham. It was under him that the sale of performance parts (necessary to back up homologation requirements) mushroomed.

Platt and Bill Barnett made a good team. In this short period they also had Brian Melia with them as Ford's first full-time professional co-driver, enticed the brilliant young Vic Elford away from Triumph, and finally signed the immensely talented Roger Clark from Rover. They also made sure that Henry Taylor continued as team captain, even if they could not, in the end, induce Eric Carlsson to join his new wife in the Ford team.

Barnett recalls that at one stage Carlsson was actually in his office at Boreham, pen in hand and contract ready to sign, but that a final chat with Pat, and a much longer talk with his existing employers (Saab) turned him away from the company. "If Eric had joined us then," said Bill, "perhaps we would have been even *more* successful?"

Lotus were to assemble the very specialised Lotus-Cortina themselves, and Keith Duckworth's Cosworth concern took on the engine development work, but the car was not truly race-worthy until 1964. To bridge the gap, Boreham developed the push-rod ohv Cortina GT into a formidable machine, especially for rough-road rallying. The Willment team showed how fast one might be on the race tracks, but it was Boreham which built the team to conquer the East African Safari in 1964.

By 1965 the Lotus-Cortina was performing miracles on the race tracks, with flamboyant-driving heroes like Jim Clark and Sir John Whitmore thoroughly enjoying their three-wheeling antics. Once the car had reverted to a more practical type of rear suspension the rally team also took it to their hearts.

With the basic organisation job completed, Alan Platt prepared to leave competitions in the autumn of 1965. One of his last jobs was to consult with Walter Hayes about his successor. They had little difficulty in agreeing that

Henry Taylor was their man.

Outwardly, it was a strange choice. Taylor was an ex-Grand Prix driver, a successful farmer and businessman, captain of the rally team, and a lover of the good life, but he was also an inventive and enthusiastic team member. When approached, he took to the suggestion at once, and promptly exchanged his bucket seat for an office chair.

Bill Barnett told me, with some amusement, that the change was rather awkward to accept at first: "After all, for five years I had been ordering him around as a team member, and now here he was as my new boss! But, in fact, we got on together very well right from the start."

Henry Taylor is important to my story, not just because he was in command at Boreham when the first Escort came along, but because he was partly responsible for its birth. As Walter Hayes told me, it was only one of many such ideas: "Henry was always full of ideas. He might call me at dawn and he'd just *have* to see me because there were a dozen things on his mind. He invented Formula Ford for me, and there was much more besides."

When Taylor stopped driving, and David Seigle-Morris left the team, they were replaced by Roger Clark and Bengt Soderstrom. At the same time the Cortina GTs were finally abandoned, and every effort was concentrated on the Lotus-Cortinas. This move was even more significant than it seemed at the time. Although the Mark I car of 1966 was replaced by the Ford-assembled Mark II Lotus-Cortina for 1967, the main mechanical assemblies were retained. An aggressive and logical development programme was concentrated on the twin-cam engine, and on the Ford-sourced transmissions which it drove.

1966 started badly in the rallying business, when Roger Clark's perfectly standard Lotus-Cortina lost a fine fourth place in the Monte Carlo Rally – due to the ludicrous lighting disqualification fiasco. It was also a year in which Vic Elford's works cars were robbed of outright victory time and time again – once due to an homologation technicality, when (after the Rally dei Fiore) it was found that the number of teeth on one gearbox wheel did not agree with the homologation form, and *nothing* could convince the organisers that this was due to a simple misprint!

Even so, the Boreham-prepared cars notched up outright wins in the Acropolis, Geneva and RAC International Rallies, with second places on the Tulip, Acropolis, Czech and Alpine Rallies. On rough roads the latest Cortinas were very fast and durable, even if they were not outstandingly fast for the latest tarmac European 'road races'.

On the race track, works-encouraged (if not actually works-prepared) cars performed their usual miracles. Even if it was a works-backed Anglia which lifted the British saloon car championship (John Fitzpatrick's Broadspeed car), Lotus-Cortinas driven by Jim Clark and Peter Arundell usually won their races outright.

The original Mark I Lotus-Cortina dropped out of production in the summer of 1966, and was not due to be replaced by a Dagenham-assembled Mark II car until the spring of 1967. Company policy meant that rallying and racing obsolete models was discouraged, and since the new car could not be homologated until May it looked as if 1967 would be a quiet year for Boreham. This gave the effervescent Henry Taylor time to think about the future. It was a very opportune moment.

Ford's problem, after only a few serious years in motor sport, was that we

Bengt Soderstrom and Gunnar Palm (Lotus-Cortina) running away with the 1966 RAC Rally. "What, no spectators?"

all now *expected* them to produce outright winners – on the road, on the tracks, and especially in rough-road rallying. Class wins and team prizes, though creditable, were no longer good enough. The problem, though, at the end of 1966, was that technical progress was beginning to overhaul them quite rapidly.

In the four years since the Lotus-Cortina had been announced, the opposition had intensified. At first the car had been good enough to tackle Jaguars in touring car races, but since then the special Falcons, Mustangs, and BMWs had arrived. Worse, there was every likelihood that the splendidly-engineered Porsche 911 would be approved as a 'touring car' for 1967!

In rallying, the Lotus-Cortinas had the measure of most cars in rough-road conditions (particularly now that Roger Clark and Bengt Soderstrom were in the team), but on surfaced roads they were beginning to struggle against the rapid little Lancias, Porsches, Alfa-Romeos and even the phenomenal Mini-Coopers.

For 1967, certainly, Ford were stuck with the new, bigger, and rather heavier Mark II Cortinas. But not after that – not, that is, if Henry Taylor could help it. He knew that Boreham and the production cars would take a back seat in 1967 as Walter Hayes' attentions were firmly focussed on Keith Duckworth and his still-secret vee-8 DFV Formula One engine. For 1968 Taylor was determined, somehow, to bring Boreham and its team back into the limelight. **17**

The answer, happily enough, was inspired by events on the Competition Centre's own doorstep. A solution appeared, almost literally, when Taylor and Bill Meade peered over the fence at what was going on inside the proving ground. For Boreham, in case you didn't know, was at the time Ford's principal secret testing ground, where cars and trucks were sent to have all their oddities wrung out. The competition staff often saw what was going on, and in 1966 some very interesting new shapes had been seen around the grounds.

It was probably Bill Meade who first commented: "Blimey, one of those things would go like hell with a Twin-Cam engine in it" – but his boss wasn't far behind. With no company involvement in the 1967 Monte Carlo Rally, Henry Taylor found himself with a bit of spare time in which to develop his latest bright idea.

While the rest of us were thundering up and down ice-bound hills in the Maritime Alps of France (and while, incidentally, a Mini-Cooper S was proving yet again how supreme it was on that sort of going), Henry Taylor was at home with his thoughts. If he got his way, and at Ford he often did, Boreham would be slack in 1967, but might never have a dull moment ever again!

2

A star is born

The cars which Henry Taylor and Bill Meade had seen on test were prototypes, rather smaller than the Cortinas which Boreham knew so well. They were, of course, first-off examples of the new Escort which – from the beginning of 1968 – was due to replace the long-running Anglias.

Taylor's problem, at that stage, was that officially he was not supposed to know much about the new car. Unofficially, of course, he already knew a good deal, because Ford's rumour machine was operating as efficiently as ever, but he could still only guess at the detailed layout.

No matter. If this thing, very important to Taylor's way of thinking, could not be tackled through the normal channels, he would have to find another way. Taylor rang up Bob Howe, from Product Planning at Dunton, mentioned his ideas, and suggested a meeting. In Bob Howe's words:

"The Escort programme was fixed, and we were all committed to other things. There was no way anybody could tackle the job in normal working hours, so Henry asked me if I would go out to his big house at Wickham Bishops during the weekend. We began to thrash out our ideas for a new rally car on a Sunday morning in January 1967."

It wasn't a long meeting. It didn't need to be. Although somebody would have to build up a car before the theories could be proved, they both agreed that the quickest, and most ideal, project would be for all the Lotus-Cortina's mechanical components to be squeezed into the new car's body shell.

The Twin-Cam Escort, then, as an idea, was conceived around a paper-strewn coffee table at Wickham Bishops. If Taylor and Howe were the car's parents, Peggy Taylor was certainly a very understanding midwife!

But one meeting would not be enough, not by any means. It might be easy for Taylor and Howe to convince themselves they had thought up a world-beating new model, but it was quite another persuading Ford management to back them.

I can sum up the next few months' events very succinctly: without Henry Taylor the Twin-Cam *might* not have happened, without Walter Hayes the Twin-Cam *might* not have happened, but without both of them it *would not* have happened.

There was every good reason why it should never happen, but the most

The men who played mid-wives to the new Twin-Cam. *(Right to left)* **Henry Taylor, Bill Barnett and Bill Meade.** There are other well-known faces in the background – Peter Ashcroft and Mick Jones near the Lotus-Cortina in the background; Ken Wiltshire, Terry Samuell, Don Partington and others in the group

compelling was the problems of scale. Machines like the Twin-Cam could not be sold in large numbers, and in small numbers Ford would not be happy to take on the job.

The Escort, after all, was to be built at Halewood, near Liverpool, and in West Germany – thousands of them every week if sales were up to forecast – while a competition car's sales could be one or two thousand *a year*.

There was also a rather chilling precedent. The original Lotus-Cortinas, between 1963 and 1966, had been assembled by Lotus at Cheshunt. No one needs reminding of the quality and service back-up problems which Lotus suffered in this project. The result was that, with a Mk II Lotus-Cortina necessary to Ford's plans, Ford decided to build the cars themselves at Dagenham. For better or worse, they decided to feed the cars down the normal Cortina lines, with no attempt to segregate them from more bread-and-butter machinery.

At about the time the Wickham Bishops meeting took place, Dagenham's production engineers were getting the Mk II Lotus-Cortina into pilot production. It was a process they would all remember for months, and it did not make prospects for a hot Escort any easier.

Henry Taylor was not deterred. Immediately after his talks at home he contacted Walter Hayes ("Nothing could ever wait until tomorrow as far as Henry was concerned") and poured out his heart on the new idea. But even miracles of improvisation take a little time, and it was not until 25 January that the proposal was finalised.

That date, incidentally, gives the clue to the Twin-Cam's project code. J25 sounded mysterious when we first heard of it (was there a J24, or a J26, we wondered?) but the truth is more mundane. The idea was finalised on 25 January, so the J25 car it became.

So far, so good, but as a project the J25 still only existed on paper. Prototype cars were scarce, Dunton were not interested in building a special car, and in any case, they said, surely Boreham realised that engineering such big changes took months and months?

Henry Taylor was appalled. He didn't have months – or so he thought. The Mk II Lotus-Cortina might be good enough for the 1967 season, but he wasn't at all sure it could survive in 1968. He wanted a new car in 1968, and he wanted it homologated early in the year. That meant building and proving prototypes very quickly indeed, getting approval rapidly, and completing the tooling for some kind of production all in a matter of months.

Only one workshop staff, he knew, could work to that sort of timetable – his own, at Boreham. They were always working to yesterday's deadline, they didn't worry over much about normal working hours, and they were second to none at the black art of cost-effective improvisation.

But did they have the time? Henry Taylor thought so, but to him all things were possible. Bill Meade, on the other hand, was more cautious. He was supplying help to Bengt Soderstrom in Sweden, to Ford of Canada for the Shell 4000 Rally, there was a host of Safari cars to be finished off, and after that there was the Calypso Racing programme, cars for the Scottish, the Gulf London . . . no, his mechanics had very little spare time.

Of course they could try to build up a car, and develop it, during voluntary evenings, in a corner, or at odd moments, but that might mean that a car might not run before the end of 1967. The big problem, of course, was that they didn't have an Escort to play with – pilot production was not due to begin for months, and prototypes were rare and precious.

Henry Taylor, with Walter Hayes' powerful support, then took the bull by the horns. He begged, cajoled, and nagged, until Dunton's engineers promised him a car. But not a runner. Oh no. And not for Boreham to keep. No way. They would lend him a plastic body-chassis unit, and they wanted it back. He could have it on a Friday, but they would collect it again on a Tuesday.

Bill Meade now takes up the story:

"We stopped all normal work on a Friday afternoon in March when the 'car' arrived in a truck. We shut the workshop doors, started there and then, and spent all weekend, just mocking up a new car."

All day and all night?

"No, it wasn't as bad as that. But we worked to midnight on the Friday and probably 12-hour shifts on Saturday and Sunday. Everybody was in on the job – Henry, Mick Jones, Ken Wiltshire, Johnnie Rule, Norman Masters and the others. Bob Howe and John Hines (of Styling) called in on the Saturday and Sunday, I'm sure. But none of the drivers at that stage. I'm sure they were not told until we'd actually done the job."

But what did 'the job' entail?

"We pulled the engine, transmission and suspensions out of it, then started to offer-up the twin-cam engine, the three-rail gearbox, the big axle, and a set of prototype Capri struts that we had also scrounged.

"Then we had a look around, a look-see really, to see how much room there was in the wheel-arches, in the engine bay, and in the gearbox tunnel.

"But it was all very rushed. We took a few measurements, but there were no drawings and not even any photographs for the record. It was just a look-see at this stage. It would be three months before we could actually have a body to keep, and we could get the drawings done before then."

Naturally, there were problems, some of which looked serious. Although Boreham had never actually built Twin-Cam Anglias for their own use, they had seen privately-converted examples. The Escort was a new animal, for sure, but built around the same engines and transmissions as the Anglia. They thought they knew, therefore, where the problems would lie.

It was not so much the problem of inadequate clearances, as of actually having clearances at all. The Twin-Cam's engine, of course, was very bulky, especially around the big Weber carbs, while the Lotus-Cortina bell housing and gearbox were both larger than those of the Escort 1100/1300.

The first mating attempt was a disaster. To be more specific, the engine simply wouldn't slide into the engine bay. It seemed to rub or jam on all sides, and the Webers were the culprits.

In an ideal world, of course, the Escort's body shell would have been modified to make conventional fitting easy. But at Ford in 1967 the production engineers were not given any brief to be helpful; Boreham would have to find their own solution.

Try again. What were the fouling points? Basically, the rearmost carburettor, the brake master cylinder, and the clutch cable were all fighting for the same space. That weekend's instant-solution was to throw away cable clutch operation (the Lotus-Cortina clutch was hydraulically-operated anyway), and to move the cylinders inside the cockpit. The fluid reservoir itself stayed on the engine side of the bulkhead, near the heater plenum chamber.

But that was not enough. If an air-cleaner and the trunking from the Lotus-Cortina were to be fitted, they would certainly foul the inner wheel arch panel on the right side of the compartment. The solution to that was startlingly simple, but disarmingly radical. The rear gearbox mounting position was retained 'in space' and the front of the engine was pushed across towards the nearside until enough space had been gained. But once that was done the battery came into contact with the camcovers . . . .

It was that sort of weekend. Moving the battery to the boot was something with a precedent – the Lotus-Cortina already had it – but the asymmetric engine positioning was new. In fact, it was a palliative which worked extraordinarily well (the drive line angles, if anything, were theoretically improved, as the line from crankshaft nose to axle pinion was more nearly straight than usual), and one which was kept on RS1800s with the new Mk II Escort body shell.

Slotting a Lotus-Cortina axle under an Escort body was not difficult; the two big problem areas were in the front wheel arches, and in the gearbox tunnel. The one had only been designed for 12in wheels with relatively small-section tyres, while the tunnel was carefully arranged to wrap closely around a compact all-new single-rail-selector design considerably smaller than the existing Cortina/Corsair gearbox which the Lotus-Cortina used.

A solution to the wheelarch problem – mainly caused by fat 13in tyres rubbing on the arches and the wing cut-outs on bump and lock – was squeezed reluctantly out of the production planners at Halewood. Specially modified panels, with flared arches, would be made available.

In regard to the gearbox tunnel, Halewood men would not budge. They were *not* prepared to modify an already-tooled pressing for a few hundred 'specials'. Any extra clearance needed would have to be found by more traditional methods – with a big hammer!

There were two rear suspension features – both, as it happens, not suuccessful. Meade decided to leave the damper positions alone, but he did offer up the layout of a Panhard Rod.

"We put a Panhard Rod under the back, because we were quite convinced we needed one. The Lotus-Cortina never had one in any form, and we were sure we needed one to get the handling and the traction right."

And that, for a few weeks at least, was that. Like Cinderella, whose carriage turned into a pumpkin at midnight, the mock-up Twin-Cam turned back into an ordinary machine at the close of the weekend. Meade and Taylor now knew that it was possible, but not easy, to turn the very ordinary Escort into a passable imitation of a sports saloon. But that was not enough. First they had to persuade Ford's volume-orientated engineers to build the cars in small quantities, then they had to build an actual car for development purposes.

Their list of required changes to production Escorts was presented to the plant engineers, so that some sort of 'aggravation-factor' could be assessed. It caused consternation, heated arguments, outright condemnation – and great interest. Nobody could accuse Halewood of not being interested in competition cars – they merely thought it wasn't their baby.

There was discussion, argument, and finally compromise. In a matter of weeks, Boreham knew what sort of a Twin-Cam Escort was possible without major dislocation. All that now remained was for the project to get the go-ahead.

To get approval, Walter Hayes, now completely convinced of its worth, needed hardware to back him up. Accordingly, he asked Henry Taylor to have a proper running prototype built at Boreham, as quickly as possible.

A 'training build' 1300GT Escort was purloined from Halewood, where the first off-tools examples were just beginning to take shape among the last flood of Anglias. All twelve mechanics at Boreham fell on it, and a repeat of the March weekend's exercise got under way.

Bill Meade recalls: "It didn't even come down to us as a complete 1300GT, it wasn't even painted, but still in undercoat. But that was all very well, and we got it running quite quickly. Then when Johnnie Rule was running it in, he rolled the car and wrote it off!"

But it wasn't Rule's fault, not by any means. The car had been circulating Boreham's test track, going quite slowly, when a bracket securing the steering rack to the front cross-member came adrift. That meant steering which did not respond, oversteer instead of low-speed cornering, and the almost inevitable accident.

In a way, this crash was a relief, because it was almost the end of the bad news. A replacement body shell was hastily whistled up from Halewood, the rebuilt car passed its management approval assessments with flying colours, and Henry Taylor and Walter Hayes were assured of their 1968 competition car.

That was all well and good, but Ford still had to decide how and where to build the production cars. Boreham, for their part, still had to produce a durable machine that any private owner might use as the basis of his race or rally car.

Time was short – it was already mid-summer in 1967 – and the Escort was due for announcement on 18 January 1968. At the same time, Hayes was

A well-publicised 'yump' in Twin-Cam testing. They didn't try any more after that! The car was later used in rallycross by Barry Lee with great success

25

determined to let the world know about Boreham's new competition car. At least one road car would have to go on the Escort launch expedition to Morocco at the beginning of the year.

From Boreham, Mick Jones and Ken Wiltshire ('the terrible twins' – and ask any maiden from Bombay to Mexico City if that isn't so?) did most of the development and durability driving on the prototypes. There were three cars in all – the re-shelled original plus another two – of which one was to be systematically battered to destruction at Bagshot's rough road test track, and another thrashed round and round MIRA or Ford's own proving grounds at Lommel.

"Our only important problems were with the Panhard Rod," says Mick Jones, "which kept breaking its mounting brackets. Really we didn't have time enough to make the mountings strong enough, that was all, but in the end it was decided to abandon the idea altogether. That was probably a damned good thing, because there would have been all sorts of drama and complication in getting Halewood to fix the extra bits and pieces on the bodies anyway."

All production Twin-Cams, and the RS1600s and RS1800s which succeeded them, reverted to the Escort GT's system of short twin radius arms, with their forward pivots under the back seats, and their rear pivots picking up lugs on the axle tube proper (and already there for use in the Lotus-Cortinas).

A lot of the driving work was high-speed endurance, and the weather was not allowed to get in the way. Mick Jones told me that a lot of the 5,000 mile MIRA run, supposed to be flat out, could not be so because part of the time there was snow on the track. And when there wasn't any snow, the tyres then available tended to overheat at the 115mph maximum speed . . . .

Lommel's facilities were very useful for validating the chassis. The structure itself proved to be entirely satisfactory, and – incidentally – very much more rigid, both against bending, and torsional stresses than the Lotus-Cortina it was due to supplant. Not for nothing had the Mk II Lotus-Cortinas in rallying been called 'bananas' – after the shape they tended to affect once thrashed hard and long over rough roads.

Various minor stiffening panels standardised already for heavy-duty 'export' Escorts would be in every Twin-Cam shell, and had already been proved by the production-car engineers in their own exhaustive and exacting ways.

Nevertheless, the Twin-Cam's body would be a special assembly, and in Halewood's terse 'number-speak' language would need to be labelled accordingly. The flared wheel arches, if nothing else, would render the two-door saloon shell non-standard for their purposes.

It is here that another bit of historical Ford 'whimsy' creeps in. Halewood-built vehicle numbers had gone in strict sequence. All the Classics were in the '10s', all the Anglias in the '20s', and all the Corsairs were '30s'. It followed that Escort numbers would be in the 40s. A base car would be a 40G..., a de Luxe saloon a 42G, and a Super saloon a 44G. The Twin-Cam would need one from this sequence. But which one?

Nobody now remembers quite who invented this, but it seems that some genius allocated 'Type 49' to the Twin-Cam. This was apparently done because of the recent appearance of the all-new and very glamorous Type 49 Lotus – also a competition car, and with a Ford (actually the 3-litre Cosworth DFV) engine!

Not only this, but the interesting little Escort GT, a much tamer relative version of the Twin-Cam, was allocated Type 48. And wasn't it interesting that Lotus' new Formula Two car was a Type 48? Someone, it seemed, had a heart after all.

Roger Clark, probably the first of Ford's drivers to be told about the hush-hush new car, was given the job of trying to destroy it at Bagshot:

"I knew something of what was going on, even in the spring of 1967, but it wasn't until I got back from winning the Shell 4000 in Canada in a Lotus-Cortina that Henry really took me into his confidence.

"But I didn't drive a car at all until the autumn, until a production spec. was ready for proving."

Bill Meade had also devised a new cast-magnesium sump guard for the rally cars, which was novel, technically brave, and very light. After all, if you were accustomed to landing anything repeatedly on rocky roads at high speeds, you would hardly expect a brittle casting to stand up to this sort of thing, surely? Tech-Del, who already supplied Ford with their splendidly resilient Minilite road wheels, thought otherwise. They produced the new guards, and defied Clark to break them.

Clark enjoyed the challenge, and in one day at Bagshot he set out to prove something. There was one section where a car could be jumped *very* high indeed. How high depended only on the driver's bravery, and on that day Clark was feeling both brave and aggressive . . .

Some of the pictures taken by Ford's Ken Shipton show Escorts at really remarkable angles, and Clark recently told me that he only packed in after one particularly lurid attempt nearly resulted in an end-over-end shunt, photographed by Shipton for posterity.

That car, in fact, deserves its own individual epitaph. XTW 368F was the car based on the re-shelled Boreham crash car, it did all the rough testing, went to Morocco for the press launch, and immediately returned to begin a very successful competition career. But that achievement and its story, belongs to the next chapter.

Before this, however, Henry Taylor and Walter Hayes were faced with a very big problem. They knew that for homologation purposes more than a 1,000 would have to be built as speedily as possible in the spring of 1968. They also knew that Halewood were very reluctant indeed to get closely involved. Their production experts were perfectly willing to have the body shells made up, because differences from standard were few, but when it came to assembling the cars on the lines they were horrified.

In the event, of course, they had little option. Taylor wanted his thousand cars – quickly – and Hayes was powerful enough to give him influential backing. Boreham, with their small workshops and tiny workforce, could not even entertain the prospect of producing cars for sale. Neither could the company yet consider building the cars in a special factory, so for better or worse Halewood were given the job.

Dick Boxall, then an executive at Halewood, told me that his initial brief was to find painless ways of building a first batch of 200 Twin-Cams. Although this would not guarantee Group 2 'Improved Touring' homologation, it would allow the car to get Group 3 'Grand Touring' approval very quickly.

His time schedule was almost impossible to meet. 'Job One' for the Escort was during November 1967, and the instruction to add Twin-Cams to the operation came even after that. Even allowing for the fact that all normal

First public appearance, and first competition, was the Croft Rallycross meeting, which was televised. The number plate is false (it should be XTW 368F) and the driver is Tony Chappell

designing and purchasing systems could be side-stepped did not help. Before February 1968 there was just no way that Halewood production could begin.

The blunt and forceful Boxall talked long and hard, to anyone who would listen, about ways and means. His solution was that Twin-Cams should take shape in and among more normal Escorts as far as possible. The J25s would go right through the production process of body assembly, paint, and trimming, but at a certain point they would be diverted.

Before the track reached the point at which a part-completed car meets its engine and transmission, the Twin-Cam shell would be whisked away. It would be lifted to a small and exclusive area, close to the trim shops, where the special engines, gearboxes and axles were waiting. Only a dozen fitters – all volunteers (and there was never a shortage of them for this job) – were involved.

Of course, the 'special' parts were not all mechanical. There was the little matter of a special black-painted radiator grille, the quarter bumpers instead of a full-width blade (as fitted to Escort vans), the badging, and other details. Taylor and Hayes made it all a bit easier by making sure that every new Twin-Cam was painted white, with black trim. They had had to compromise on instruments, which were those of the Escort GT.

28

Another procedure special to Halewood was that each and every one of the Twin-Cams had an individual road test – between 10 and 20 miles – whereas run-of-the-mill Escorts had to be content with a rolling road check after they dropped off the assembly track.

There was one particular battle which Boreham lost – and the heroes who had to drive the cars fast were the first to complain. Boreham had wanted to specify circular headlamps, whereas the production car appeared with the less-efficient rectangular variety. The reason was very simple – Ford's Product Planning department pointed out that round headlamps were reserved for cheaper Escorts, and rectangular ones for the GTs and Supers. The Twin-Cam, therefore, in spite of strident protests from its sponsors, had to fall into line. It took well over a year to get this decision reversed.

However, before Halewood production could begin, Boreham was desperate for an original batch of Twin-Cam cars to be delivered. There were racing teams, both works-favoured and private, who would be demanding cars for the start of the season, and the technical press would soon be clamouring for standard cars to test.

For better or worse, therefore, it was decided to build the first 25 cars in the Boreham workshops. It would mean no serious competition activity for several weeks during this time. Boreham's assembly area, after all, could only accommodate about ten cars at once, and all these spaces, for a time, would be occupied by embryo Twin-Cams.

Helping to build, while at the same time learning how to put the cars together, was a team of fitters from Halewood, shipped down to Essex by a resourceful Dick Boxall. Boreham, even in its pre-1970 World Cup Rally period, has never been as crowded.

The waiting, now, was over. The favoured few had been let in to the secrets several weeks early, but many members of the press were astonished to learn about Boreham's secret weapon when they were introduced to the new Escort range in the first days of 1968.

To anyone who asked him the obvious questions, Henry Taylor was quite clear. In racing or in rallying, as far as he was concerned, the reign of the Lotus-Cortina was over. The reign of the Escort was about to begin.

3

Winning ways~
the Twin-Cam years

At the end of 1967, the atmosphere at Boreham was electric. More than ever, there appeared to be uncontrolled bedlam – on the workshop floor *and* in the offices.

The shop floor certainly looked rather like an expensive shambles. There seemed to be new-fangled Escort body shells *everywhere*, there were mechanics and unfamiliar faces falling over one another, but almost no evidence of competitions activity.

There was no sensible way that Twin-Cam production could be sustained indefinitely, or even logically, but in this way it could, at least, be started. Dick Boxall knew full well that his small team's initial experience would be quite invaluable when they had to build cars at Halewood.

Team manager Bill Barnett, with an extensive 1968 season still to plan, kept well out of it all, and the team's drivers came in more for interest and a look at the strange goings-on than to progress their new cars.

Henry Taylor, however, had a new assistant – Barry Gill – who had been saddled with a really thorny job. Just a few days after arriving at Boreham for the first time, and once the enthusiasm of Ford's sales force had become clear, Gill had been told to look after allocation of Twin-Cams. It was Gill, in other words, who would have to fend off the customers until their names reached the head of the list.

Every one of the original Boreham-assembled Twin-Cams – all 25 of them – was spoken for before announcement. Ford's sponsored racing teams – Alan Mann, Broadspeed, the Boreham rally team, and a few favoured individuals with a good competition record all saw to that.

To give the Twin-Cam a flying start on the race tracks, Henry Taylor had encouraged the Alan Mann racing team to take over no less than four cars – two to be used in Europe, and two to contest the British Saloon Car Championship. Interestingly enough (and it was a portent for the future, though nobody realised it then) the British championship rules allowed the 16-valve Cosworth FVA Formula Two engine to be installed.

Dagenham Motors would get a Twin-Cam for Roger Taylor to race (Taylor's father, incidentally, was one of Ford's directors), while Ford Belgium were demanding one right away for Gilbert Staepelaere's rallying programme.

First international event – the 1968 San Remo Rally in March 1968 – was rewarded by third place, for Ove Andersson and John Davenport *(on the left of the picture)*. **Bill Meade** is testing the roof stiffness, and **Bill Barnett** the front wing!

On top of this, of course, were Henry Taylor's own commitments to a very full rallying season, and the provision of a couple of cars for the new-fangled sport of rallycross. Another car, in spite of the presence of Halewood fitters at Boreham, would have to go up to Halewood as a 'pattern' when their production got under way.

Halewood's over-worked chiefs already had big problems anyway. The Escort, right from the start, was a huge success, with sales much higher than those of the superseded Anglia. Not only that, but while all this was going on, arrangements were in hand to tear up the Corsair lines and send them to Dagenham, and to make sure that production of the still-secret Capri sports saloon could begin in November.

For the Escort's competition debut, Henry Taylor sent a couple of his prototypes to an ITV *World of Sport* meeting, a rallycross at the Croft Autodrome near Darlington. This was held on Saturday, 3 February 1968, and is a date worth noting. It signalled the definitive point at which the whole pace of British production car sport changed.

One car had a 160bhp engine, and the other a mere 140bhp. Roger Clark, Barry Lee and Welshman Tony Chappell drove the cars – one of which was the incredibly hard-working XTW 368F. In good and dry conditions, the cars were clearly astonishingly fast, as commentator John Sprinzel made quite clear.

31

Between them, they won four races in front of a TV audience of millions. At one stroke this performance made the Lotus-Cortinas and the other conventional front-engined cars obsolete.

It was an immediate proof. Proof that Henry Taylor's original concept had been sound, proof that the smaller Escort body could deal satisfactorily with Twin-Cam engine and transmission stresses, and proof that Boreham's instant design and development programmes had missed out nothing.

Now the remaining problem was to get the Twin-Cam speedily into production, on sale, and out into the serious racing and rallying business. Taylor and Walter Hayes were quite happy to leave their racing endeavour in the hands of Alan Mann and his star driver Frank Gardner, and with John Fitzpatrick and Chris Craft in the Broadspeed 1300GTs; Boreham's first rallying target was the San Remo Rally, in Italy, in March.

As soon as the Twin-Cam had been announced, orders from famous, established and frankly unknown drivers began to flood in. Barry Gill had an unenviable job in these months. Already he had had to bluff his way through an unhelpful meeting of Ford managers (who were inclined to treat the Twin-Cam as a time-consuming joke) by telling them that if he could not guarantee deliveries at once then Ford would not have a competition programme in 1968. Now he had to sort out the deserving from the merely hopeful, and the potential winners from the rich no-hopers. It would not be until the end of the year that the waiting lists began to abate.

Homologation was treated with some care. After the well-publicised fiasco involving the sports-racing 250LM Ferrari, the deep suspicion surrounding 'volume' production of HF Lancias, and the storm which followed the news that a Porsche could qualify for use as a 'Touring' car, there was no question of the Twin-Cam's approval being requested prematurely.

Even so, by a tremendous effort from all concerned, homologation into the Group 3 category (which in 1968 meant that only 100 identical cars needed to be built), was achieved on March 1. It was not enough, and it was only a start. For the time being, at least, a Twin-Cam would have to compete against the Alpine-Renaults and the hottest Porsches. No matter. The team's rally drivers were not too worried about that – they were looking for outright victories anyway!

Racing and rallying Escorts made their official debut in March 1968. A Boreham-prepared rally car made the world premiere – in the Italian San Remo as planned – but Ralph Broad's 1300GT race cars were only a matter of days behind. Neither, for what it is worth, made perfect debuts.

The Twin-Cam's first rallying performance was not like a good fairy story. According to the best *Boys' Own Paper* precedents, the new car should have won. Perhaps Walter Hayes even half-expected this – after all, his Duckworth-designed Grand Prix engine had achieved such a miracle only ten months earlier.

But things were having to be done in such a rush at Boreham that the drivers – Ove Andersson and John Davenport – were even forced to do their recce in a pensioned-off Lotus-Cortina. Apart from a few shake-down miles, their rally car was nearly brand-new when it started the event.

As it happened, XOO 355F (which therefore has the honour of being the first 'works' rally car) finished third overall. The studious-looking Swede Ove Andersson, was beaten by Pauli Toivonen's Porsche 911, and by Pat Moss-Carlsson's Lancia Fulvia HF.

32

Probably the most successful of all Boreham-built Twin-Cams – Gilbert Staepelaere's Ford Belgium car which he used from 1968 to 1970. The number plate is Gilbert's own, and this win was the 1969 Tulip Rally

Timo Makinen was introduced to the Escort by David Sutton of Clarke and Simpson, though Boreham built the car. He led the 1968 RAC Rally, then the engine blew . . . *(photo Foster and Skeffington)*

Third place was good, but not good enough by Boreham's demanding standards and, if nothing else, it proved two things – that the rectangular headlamps were lousy, and the traction and rear damping completely inadequate. How inadequate was proved vividly to Bill Meade after the event.

"Ove told me that something very strange was happening to the back end," said Meade, "so he put me in the back seat, told me to hang on, and charged off up and down the hills behind San Remo. The dampers, as originally positioned, were fairly steeply inclined, so that the further up the axle was displaced the lower the rate of movement (and effect) they had. What was happening was that on quite rough roads the dampers were fading out, and the axle was jumping up and down. The car was nearly out of control, it was leaping about in all directions. Ove convinced me that we had better do something – quick – or we wouldn't live very long!"

Back at Boreham, then, the first major development programme was to sort out what is now familiarly known as the 'turret kit'. This involved positioning the dampers almost vertically, while at the same time a change was made to the gas-filled Bilstein dampers and front struts. The only suitable Bilsteins were considerably longer than Ford's preferred length, which explains why the turret modification is rather a complex and expensive business.

On the tracks, the first Escort performance was a greater disappointment. Only one Broadspeed 1300GT was ready for the Race of the Champions meeting at Brands Hatch on 17 March. This, driven by John Fitzpatrick, soon retired with an overheating engine – but this was hardly surprising when one considers that its pushrod engine was already producing 145bhp; even Ralph Broad was looking impressed.

The breakthrough, and the first Escort victory, came at Easter. Under slightly more lenient restrictions, Boreham built up the second rallying Twin-Cam, in Group 6 'prototype' form, for Roger Clark and Jim Porter to use in the Circuit of Ireland. Against a couple of 1275S Mini-Coopers (Paddy Hopkirk and Adrian Boyd), and two hot Hillman Imps (Andrew Cowan and Rosemary Smith), it was a massacre. Clark's 152bhp machine won from Boyd's Cooper S by an enormous margin, once Paddy Hopkirk's car had blown its transmission, and it all looked very easy.

Roger was ecstatic, as well he might have been. Not only was it the Escort's first win, but it was his own first win since the 1967 Scottish Rally, when he had 'banana'd' a Lotus-Cortina.

His comments to the press were that 'it drove quicker than I could think', which makes a good story even if it wasn't strictly true. He also said, with absolute honesty, that the Twin-Cam was much more precise and responsive than a Lotus-Cortina, and – where it mattered – rather smaller when tweaked up and sideways.

The next few months unfolded like the hoped-for fairy tale. At exactly the time when BMC's Minis were finding the going too tough, British Twin-Cams came along to dominate World Championship rallying in their place.

In May and June, works-prepared cars won another four major rallies – and three of them went to Roger Clark.

There were three Twin-Cams in the Tulip (Clark, Andersson, and Staepelaere's new Ford-Belgium car), which walked over once Andruet's Alpine-Renault had disappeared. Staepelaere rolled his car, but the two works cars cruised serenely in to Noordwijk, a mere 5.1 seconds apart.

Two weeks later, Bengt Soderstrom and Gunnar Palm lifted first prize in the

Left hand down a bit, but with different results . . . Roger Clark in the 1968 Circuit of Ireland – the Escort's first big win

Austrian Alpine from under the nose of a brawny blond Finn called Hannu Mikkola (Lancia mounted), and shortly afterwards the team trio dominated the Acropolis Rally in spite of the efforts of Pauli Toivonen in a ferociously fast Porsche 911. Hard work, though, took its toll.

Andersson's car signalled its disgust at three rallies in as many months by

35

Gilbert Staepelaere in the 1968 Tulip Rally. Some stupid restriction about advertising accounts for the black patch

shedding a wheel on one section, while Soderstrom's car refused to fire up for the Tatoi airfield test at the close of the event. Since Bengt's car had been driven down from winning the Austrian Alpine to start the Acropolis with no time for a rebuild, there was some excuse. Even so, at one stage the works cars were in first, second and third positions.

Back at home, Roger Clark took the Circuit-winning car out on the Scottish rally, broke up a team of works Saabs, and won, easing up, by more than ten minutes.

Quite suddenly, too, it was obvious that Halewood-built Twin-Cams were getting out and about; Jack Tordoff's car finished sixth and Alan Allard's car ninth, in this event.

In July, two important things happened. In the Gulf London Rally, Ove Andersson's hard-working Twin-Cam was beaten, narrowly, by Ake Andersson's Scania-Vabis Porsche 911, while Hannu Mikkola was finally captured by Bill Barnett to drive for Ford.

The fact that an Escort might be beaten by a Porsche was something Henry

Roger Clark proving that a well-built Escort was faster than a works Porsche in 1968. The three-wheeling stance was normal in those days

Taylor had feared ever since Vic Elford's performances in Stuttgart-built examples during 1967. It meant that the engines of his Twin-Cams would have to be enlarged, and super-tuned, while the transmissions would have to be beefed up. It was the start of a process of evolution which is still going on.

Barnett's capture of the young Mikkola was a stroke of genius, nothing less. Even though it was every British team manager's ambition to have a Swede or a Finn in his team, Mikkola was still available. Stuart Turner, at BMC, had started the trend. Now, with three Scandinavians available to him, Barnett's team possibilities were tremendous.

Even so, the local trio did not mop up all the prizes in the Finnish 1000 Lakes event. Mikkola, in a brilliant first event for Boreham, won outright, while Soderstrom's car took third prize, behind Simo Lampinen's Saab.

On the French Alpine Rally, not one in which Ford have often shone, all three works cars retired. Development was proceeding apace. One practice car was tried with a five-speed ZF gearbox, while Roger Clark's training mount had been kitted out with the 16-valve Cosworth FVA Formula Two engine.

37

A rare picture – Jim Porter drives while Roger Clark rests! On the 1968 Alpine Roger drove a Group 6 'prototype' which explains the lack of bumpers and the vast non-standard headlamps

The FVA, intended for use when the Escorts were running as 'prototypes', was not used on the rally. Quite simply, it was very 'peaky' and revved so highly that a much lower axle ratio would have been needed to make it effective.

Neither was it very tractable. However, John Davenport, writing in his regular *Autosport* column, said " . . . that when the engine was induced to stay above 7,000rpm my conception of what is a 100 yard straight was entirely altered". Also: "The FVA has been returned to Mr. Duckworth to have a little metal removed from the pointed bits on the cams."

Innovations which did reach the start line – all on Clark's 'prototype' Group 6 Twin-Cam – were a dry-sump kit, fat wheel arch extensions, rear wheel disc brakes, ultra-wide Minilite wheels, and a coil spring rear suspension. All except the coil spring rear suspension would subsequently become 'standard' fittings on the very fastest racing and rallying Escorts.

On that rather unhappy note, Boreham's 1968 rallying season came to a close. Priority, until the end of the year, would go to the building of a fleet of Lotus-Cortinas in which to attack the London – Sydney marathon. One car, lease-lent to Clarke and Simpson, was used by Timo Makinen in the RAC

Hannu Mikkola's dynamic entry into the Ford team – winning the 1968 Thousand Lakes. The car is going left-to-right, theoretically in a straight line – no wonder co-driver Jarvi looks a bit worried!

Rally, led it for many hours, but eventually had to retire with a blown cylinder head gasket.

For the rallying team, 1969 was a year when things seemed to go wrong. A lesser team than Ford might easily have become demoralised, but the setbacks of this difficult year merely spurred the Boreham boys on to greater efforts of preparation and development.

Although the record books show up several important wins – Mikkola in the Austrian Alpine and in the Finnish 1000 Lakes, Roger Clark in the Circuit of Ireland, Ove Andersson in the Welsh, with Gilbert Staepelaere taking four of the less-important European internationals – it also shows where the Escorts could be and often were, beaten.

Piot's tremendous drive in the Monte rewarded Ford with fourth place (and a win in the Touring category) – but two Porsches and an Alpine-Renault were well ahead of him. Neither works car figured in the San Remo, while Clark struggled to get second in the Acropolis behind Toivonen's Porsche.

All four cars retired from the Alpine, while Andersson's fourth place on a very snowy RAC Rally was behind three front-wheel drive cars (two Lancias and a Saab).

39

Rare bird and World Cup Rally prototype. This was the V6-engined car, with ZF gearbox and Taunus axle, which Roger Clark used in the 1969 Alpine Rally *(photo Autocar)*

Early on in the year, two new cars (BEV 781G and 782G) were worked extremely hard in several events; it was 782G which won first, for Roger Clark in the Circuit of Ireland, equipped in Group 6 'prototype' form with an enlarged 1,850cc engine, all-round disc brakes, and coil spring rear suspension.

The fact that the cars were having to struggle for outright wins against the very special and very expensive sports cars meant that development was intensified. A look at the Twin-Cam's homologation papers shows that a great number of options were already approved by November 1968 – including five-speed Hewland and Jack Knight gearboxes which were only trustworthy on the race tracks.

However, from 1 January perspex side and rear windows, a 'heavy duty' exhaust manifold (surprise, surprise – it was also more efficient than the original, and liberated more power!), and a 5.3 axle ratio were all approved. From 1 April they were joined by alternative axle ratios and alternative internal ratios for the five-speed gearbox, from 1 May by glass-fibre boot and bonnet panels, while from 1 July the Atlas (or 'Taunus' as it was called at the time) axle, limited slip differential to suit it, many alternative ratios, high-output oil pump, compression-strut front suspension, and knock-off Minilite wheels were all added.

TV Rallycross in the winter of 1969/70, Ove Andersson leading, in this ex-RAC Rally car battle

However, as long as the Twin-Cam was to be used as a Group 2 'Touring' car, there was no way that its engine, homologated at 1,558cc, could ever be enlarged to more than 1,600cc; the regulations forbade that. In the beginning, too, it looked as if 1,600cc was about the practical limit from that existing cylinder block.

Where regulations did not limit enterprise, or in the events where there were classes for prototype cars, the more adventurous tuning shops soon found ways of enlarging the engines even further, though with existing cast cylinder wall thicknesses this was always a very chancy business. Even so, as the pressure of competition bore down more and more heavily on the works Escorts, Henry Taylor and Bill Meade tried desperately hard to do the same.

The tuners in their little workshops resorted to the boring bar, and to the welding in of steel liners with a much bigger cylinder bore. This was all well and good, and worked well on the race track, but for long-distance rugged reliability Bill Meade knew that it would not be good enough for Boreham. Peter Ashcroft, by then in charge of engine development, was commanded to find a more permanent solution.

With the engine's deep breathing, and high-revving ability in mind, there was no point in looking for further increases in the stroke. Since 1959 and the Anglia 105E engine's birth, the stroke had been pushed up from 48.4 to **41**

Splendid debut for Frank Gardner's racing Twin-Cam at Crystal Palace in 1968. Note: Every one of the cars is a Ford!

72.7mm anyway; there simply wasn't room (or technical compromise on con-rod angularity) for more.

The bore, on the other hand, had changed only slightly. The pushrod Fords all used an 80.97mm bore, and the Twin-Cam production engine was enlarged to 82.55mm. In 1,594cc 'Group 2' guise, that bore became 83.55mm, and the cylinder walls were becoming a bit thin. Ford, in fact, were being defeated by their foundry's own expertise. When the bare bones of the engine had been laid out in the 1950s, the walls were capable of being cast quite thin, while

retaining cooling water all around them. That extra 2.6mm wasn't much, but it was enough to worry Ashcroft and his bosses.

By selective machining (and quite a lot of waste) it was possible to get a rather precariously reliable 1,650cc, but this was merely playing with the problem. Boreham wanted to see lots more than that, and the only way they could get it was by altering the block casting. Dunton, the bread-and-butter car engineering centre, were horrified. To cater for larger cylinder bores would mean thicker casting in the cylinder bore area. That in its turn, would mean 'siamesing' the bores, and that – they were convinced – would lead to bore distortion and possible piston problems. In any case, as they made it clear, the

43

Immaculate Broadspeed preparation of their 1300GT race car. Chris Craft won dozens of classes with XOO 341F. That is Lucas fuel injection, and the engine is installed vertically. Broad's GTs had inclined engines and vertical inlet ports at one time

Twin-Cam block was obsolete as far as they were concerned, being based on the pre-cross-flow engines which had already been superseded on the latest production Cortinas.

Even though Keith Duckworth, of Cosworth, gave it as his opinion that Dunton might be right, Peter Ashcroft decided to have a go. It was, in all truth, the only thing left to try anyway. It took time, and it took a lot of development work, but in the end the siamesed (or 'thick wall') block was proven. Ford's Thames Foundry division agreed to make a few from time to time, and gave it the ultimate accolade by christening it the 'Ashcroft block', a name that has stuck to this day.

For rally use, Ashcroft then chose an 85.6mm bore (or, more mundanely, a 3 3/8in dimension), which gave 1,791cc. Perhaps there was a little more to come, as he was to find for the 1970 World Cup Rally, but the practical limit for long-life was around 1,850cc.

The reason for choosing that particular dimension was also that it had been the 16-valve Cosworth FVA formula 2 cylinder bore since 1966, and although Cosworth's own piston had a rather different crown it could readily be adapted for Boreham's use.

Although the power could be pushed up by perhaps 15bhp only, the increase in torque was *very* noticeable, and the cars were immediately that much easier and more flexible to drive.

The question of the 1,600cc class limit still rankled, though, and when Stuart Turner came to homologate the RS1600 in 1970 he made sure that the problem was erased, in a most ingenious manner.

From the middle of 1969, thoughts, preparations and development in connection with the 1970 World Cup Rally began to intrude (see Chapter 8). It explains why Roger Clark, a not-very-willing 'guinea-pig', was given a V6-engined car to drive in the Alpine, and – of all things – a Mk IV 3-litre Zodiac for the Three Cities.

The 2.3-litre V6 car – ETW 882G was the first – was the very first Escort to bring together a ZF gearbox and 'Atlas' axle in an event. Though it was all meant as a World Cup Rally trial (and the engine was the most significant item) it proved very little.

A very unhappy Clark suffered all manner of problems. Engine and transmission overheating were things he could not control, while peculiar understeery handling was almost as bad. The big German engine developed so much heat in the confined space of the Escort's engine bay that it cooked the transmission very effectively. This prevented Clark even from changing gear after a time, when certain clearances tightened up. The cause remained a mystery for some time – every time the mechanics took time to work on the car, then tried it out themselves up the road, the machinery had cooled down enough for the part-seizures to free themselves!

It was all very strange and very unsatisfactory as a debut, but nowadays, of course, a ZF gearbox and an Atlas axle are indispensable fittings to properly-prepared and competitive Escorts.

The axle itself is originally a German Ford design, and found its way variously into Taunus saloons and Transit vans, even before it was adopted by Ford of Britain for the 3-litre Capri. It was Ford Cologne, with interests in racing high-powered Escorts, who suggested that this unit might be suitable for Escort use.

In 1968 and 1969, rear axle failures were not nearly as prevalent as they had become in the Lotus-Cortinas. This was mainly because the Escorts were lighter, and could break traction a bit easier in shock-loading conditions, but there had also been some development in halfshafts and gear production in general.

However, with the 180bhp Twin-Cam engines – in 1.8-litre form – ready for use in 1969 (and the 16-valve BDA a twinkle in Walter Hayes' eyes for 1970), breakages looked like becoming a problem soon. Now that the big flared wheelarches had been adopted by Boreham, a wider track was no problem – though the Atlas is not all *that* much wider than the Lotus-Cortina type used at first.

An Atlas is heavier than the original, but this was controlled fairly comfortably by the big and reliable gas-filled Bilstein dampers. Adapting it to an Escort's leaf-spring position was no problem, nor to the coil spring rear suspension also used for a time (until the Group 3 regulations were tightened up).

From Germany, also, came the ZF limited-slip differentials, already matched to the new axles, while there was also a fair selection of ratios. After all, if the axle had to deal with the 120mph capabilities of a big-engined Capri *and* with the load-carrying stresses of a Transit van, there had to be a big spread. The 5.1 ratio now normal to present-day high-revving Escort rally cars was available right from the start.

The story regarding gearboxes is quite a bit more complex. The Twin-Cam Escort, let us not forget, had picked up the Lotus-Cortina box in 1968. This,

If you corner on three wheels there is less rolling resistance. Gardner at Brands Hatch in 1969 in the Championship-winning XOO 349 F

Daily Express meeting, Silverstone, 1969. When it was wet nothing could touch the Escort's getaway, not even Nick Faure's Porsche 911

to go back a few more years, had been a close-ratio version of the 1962 Cortina all-synchromesh gearbox. In its turn that box had been developed frm the 1-litre 105E Anglia's gearbox, announced in 1959. That box had to deal with less than 40bhp, so it is really rather remarkable that even a 'Bullet' or 'Rocket' gearbox could still deal with the power and torque of a fully-tuned Twin-Cam.

First of all, the racing drivers, and next the more deep-thinking rally drivers, began to clamour for stronger gearboxes with more ratios. Five speeds instead of four were inevitable once the engines started to rev much higher than 7,500rpm *and* still had to keep some sort of low-speed flexibility.

None of the unsynchronised five-speeders tried on the race tracks were at all satisfactory for road use, nor – in any case – did they have the reserves of torque capacity which Henry Taylor and Bill Meade wanted to have for the future.

There was no way in which time and investment could be spared at Ford for a special five-speed gearbox to be designed and developed. One of the very rare breed of proprietary units would have to be adapted for Escort use. Both Boreham and Cologne cast around for an alternative; it was Ford-Cologne through their German connections who approached the notable ZF concern for their help.

Space inside the area of the Escort's floorpan and tunnel was a serious problem. ZF's offer, though it was a very tight fit in all directions, could – with a bit of pushing and shoving (and the use of a big hammer in judicious places on the sheet metal) – be assembled into an Escort.

Certainly there was going to be no torque-limitation problem with the ZF box – it was newly-designed, specifically for use in Fiat's 180bhp Dino. The model was not, incidentally, the first version of the car (which had its own Fiat-designed transmission) but the much-improved 2.4-litre Ferrari-engined car announced in 1969.

Right away the Boreham mechanics nicknamed the new gearbox, affectionately, the 'noddy' – because its ratios were really not suited to a racing or rallying Escort. In the original 'noddy' ZF box, there was a bottom gear internal ratio of 2.99 – much lower than that of Ford's own 'Rocket' box – the fifth gear of which was an overdrive, with 0.874 internal ratio.

Yet it was better than not having a strong enough gearbox at all, and for a time Ford would have to live with the ratios. The mechanically-minded will have realised that with such ratios a very low (numerically high) axle ratio was needed. Such ratios – above 5-to-1 – could be supplied in the original Twin-Cam axle, but were certainly not suited to the blast of torque a 1.8-litre engine could now deliver. The Atlas (or Taunus) axle was doubly valuable on that score.

People at Boreham still talk with some amazement of the way ZF buckled down to modifying these unsuitable ratios for Ford's special use. Even so, the World Cup cars – used in the spring of 1970 – retained the 'noddy' ratios, coupled with rather high (numerically low) axle ratios; this was not so that an enormous top speed could be used, but because the Holbay-based 1850GT engines were to be kept at no more than 6,000rpm in non-emergency situations.

Other customers following Ford to ZF's doorstep have not been so particular about ratios. In the late 1970s, several competitions customers including Vauxhall and Opel (says ZF-rebuilding specialist Terry Samuell) have all stayed faithful to 'noddy'.

For 1970 Stuart Turner's preferences became more and more obvious. More than one mechanic or tuning specialist previously linked to BMC products had been persuaded to work with Ford. Turner's well-known predilection for cars with memorable numbers also showed through – the World Cup cars were to have FEV 1H to 4H, while the stay-at-home European cars were to have 5H to 8H inclusive.

More exciting, though, was the specification of the cars being built up for the year's first serious event – the Monte Carlo Rally. It would be Ford's most formidable attack on the event that Henry Taylor always disliked. The 'lighting fiasco' of 1966 had left a scar, right enough. Turner was not keen on the event, or its organisers, but recognised that a win was possible, and the publicity worthwhile.

The new cars were the nearest thing to 'ice-racers' that Boreham could build – and not at all like their previous machines. There was no question of compromise, or rough-road preparation. It helped, of course, that January homologation changes included rear-wheel disc brakes, the ZF gearbox in 'noddy' form, a dry sump system with a big reservoir in the boot (already proven on race cars), and a whole variety of engine tuning parts.

Rear suspension was by coil springs and radius arms – also a race-tested layout, designed originally by Len Bailey for Alan Mann's Twin-Cams. The latest tweak, thought to be potentially very valuable at hasty wheel and tyre change points, was that knock-off Minilite wheels were to be used.

The cars were magnificently prepared, splendidly supported and serviced, bravely driven (Makinen, Mikkola, Clark and Jean-Francois Piot making up the team) – but they did not win. Worse, they were outclassed. It was this, as much as any other occasion, which persuaded Turner that the Twin-Cams were already reaching the end of their short careers. The weather was most un-Monte-like, with virtually no snow and ice. This should have made the Escorts even more competitive than usual – but the best that Roger Clark could

Left One of Roger Clark's rare track appearances, with Chris Craft, resulting in his Nurburgring class win ...

... and *above* John Fitzpatrick finished close behind

Jackie Stewart raced an Escort only once (Ralph Broad's Twin-Cam in the 1970 Tourist Trophy race) and thoroughly enjoyed himself. Fourth overall after one session, the car blew its engine later

achieve in a faultless run was fifth overall, with Makinen seventh. Four engine-over-driven-wheels cars (three Porsches and an Alpine-Renault) were ahead of the Escorts.

One year before Piot's car had been fourth, so even with almost race-standard cars the Escorts were not improving their position. It wasn't enough for Turner that the Touring Category was his – outright victory was all that would have satisfied him.

That was the bad news. The worse news was that Mikkola's car had been eliminated at an early stage when the gearlever of the ZF box jammed in reverse as he accelerated out of a service halt. It was a troublesome portent of one of the ZF's failings that took many months to be sorted out.

As in 1969, so in 1970, it was the Finns in Finland, and Gilbert Staepelaere all round Europe, who saved Boreham's bacon. Mikkola made it a personal *and* a Ford hat-trick in the 1000 Lakes, while he and Makinen won one each of the Finnish winter events. This year, though, there were no home successes. Roger Clark won the Circuit of Ireland, and did it in FEV 5H, but they were blooding a 16-valve BDA engine in prototype guise.

While the seven-car team were flogging round the world in the World Cup Rally, the stay-at-homes competed in the Austrian Alpine and the Acropolis, but Ove Andersson's third in Greece was the best they could achieve.

Makinen and Mikkola both retired their brand new 'KHK' cars from the RAC Rally in November after Makinen had led a snowy event for some time – both for the very sinister reason that their Atlas axles had suffered repeated drive-shaft failures. Both Stuart Turner and Mick Jones have since told me that the words 'drive shaft' will be found engraved on their hearts when they die . . . .

The RS1600 – the Twin-Cam's successor – had been homologated from 1 October 1970, so it was no surprise to see Roger Clark entrusted with a car on the TAP in October (where he retired with engine failure – a valve stem snapped), and in the RAC Rally (where his car succumbed to the epidemic of transmission failures). A gearbox jammed in second (shades of Mikkola's Monte Carlo Rally problem?) was but one of his many troubles.

The end of 1970 saw the end of the Twin-Cam as a serious Boreham-built rally car. New cars were built to tackle the 1971 East African Safari (see Chapter 8), but only because Peter Ashcroft, by now Ford's engine specialist, would not trust the new-fangled BDA units in hot and dusty endurance conditions.

Throughout the Twin-Cam years, Boreham's racing banner was hoisted most capably by Alan Mann Racing, and by Broadspeed – both being prominent in British events, but only Mann's cars appearing regularly in Europe.

Ralph Broad's Escorts were 1300GTs at first, and soon settled down with their customary reliability and success. Broad's Anglias had already set new standards in saloon car power production, and in preparation. Nobody was unduly surprised when the 1300cc engines were advertised as giving 145bhp, with Cosworth bits and TJ fuel injection.

It was Alan Mann's Twin-Cams which were expected to produce the fireworks, and this they duly did. Mann took delivery of four cars very early in the life of the Twin-Cam – all from the original batch of 25 built at Boreham in the winter of 1967/68.

The master stroke was in making sure that FAVO designer Len Bailey should be in charge of racing development, and that Alan Mann should operate the team. Bailey, his work on the F3L Cosworth-engined project complete for the moment, could bring all his circuit-design expertise to the Escorts, while Alan Mann with his driver Frank Gardner would attack both the British and European saloon car championships.

Regulations, at that time, were fairly slack – Group 5 'prototype' rules would apply in 1968 and 1969 – so Bailey had no hesitation in throwing away the Twin-Cam's leaf-spring rear suspension, and installing a radius arm and coil spring layout, along with a Watts linkage for sideways location. This, incidentally, was the basis of rear suspension still used in many Escorts, private or works-backed, where appropriate. On the latest cars, only the length of the radius arm has been altered.

The engines for British championship races in 1968 would be nothing less than 1.6-litre Cosworth FVA units. Producing more than 210bhp, they were eligible under British rules because the same basic Twin-Cam cylinder block was retained – though even that was heavily modified. In Europe, where interpretation of regulations was rather more strict, Bailey and Mann were limited to race-tuned 1,594cc Twin-Cam engines, and rather less than 180bhp.

Hewland and Jack Knight five-speed gearbox clusters were tried, but transmission would remain a weakness until the newly-homologated ZF box became available for the 1970 season.

The other big, and obvious change (apart from turret dampers, adopted in the spring of 1968) was the bulbous wheel arch extensions. Like several writers, I long held to the legend that these were merely surplus Ford Transit van pressings, 'found' to be so useful in making space for an extra-wide tyre on racing Escorts.

It makes a good story, but unfortunately it simply isn't true. The more mundane truth is that Len Bailey 'designed' them straight on to the Escort in

Building the 1970 Monte 'Ice Racers' at Boreham

Jean-Francois Piot and Jean Todt, sliding their way to the top of the Turini in the 1970 Monte. The car later completed a season in French events in BP colours

a freehand manner. With homologation in mind, Ford then took fibreglass moulds, shipped them off to Abbey Panels in Coventry, and ordered press tools.

Bill Meade told me that they thought they might eventually sell several hundred sets – and that he personally can recall re-ordering tools on three occasions to bring up total sales to more than 7,000 sets. So much for the people who talked about fiddled homologation . . . .

The first car, well ahead of homologation, was ready for testing in March 1968 – the only hold-up to the programme being that Jackie Oliver promptly wrote it off at Goodwood when a tyre deflated and pulled off the rim!

The cars could not race before they were homologated (this matured on 1 May) so in the meantime Mann's leading driver Frank Gardner amused himself in a Lotus-Cortina. The two British championship cars appeared at Crystal Palace early in June, where Gardner easily won his class in the FVA-powered car. The rest of the year was splendidly successful – Gardner won his class in all eight remaining events, and in two (both at Brands Hatch) he also won the races outright. Drivers of Porsches and 4.7-litre Ford Falcons were not amused!

The other car was used by a variety of drivers – Graham Hill, Peter Arundell, Jackie Oliver and Roger Clark – and used a simple, and quite ineffective, electric heater motor to 'blow' air into the fuel injection trumpets. This allowed it to qualify as 'supercharged', and put it into the Falcon/Mustang class where it took valuable class positions away from the bigger cars.

Ford were so proud of XOO 349F for winning the British championship that they gave it a place of honour on their Earls Court motor show stand. It was all a bit of a trick, for the 'same' car raced at Brands Hatch during the show, and the one on display didn't even have an engine installed, as the injudiciously placed flood lighting revealed.

The team was so busy winning the British series that the European championship had to be neglected. This car, used on occasion in Britain, normally had a Vegantune Twin-Cam engine and around 170bhp. Gardner won his debut race outright – at Zolder – but otherwise had to settle for class wins.

Ralph Broad's immaculate maroon 1300GTs won six classes in the RAC series, but even this was not enough to defeat a works Cooper S in the end. Only once did Broad take these cars into Europe – to the Nurburgring six-hour race, where Chris Craft and Roger Clark easily won their class. Incidentally, their best lap time was 10 min. 17 seconds, which compares rather well with Fangio's Mercedes W196 Grand Prix record of 9 min. 50 sec. in 1954.

There were to be no Ford-of-Britain forays into Europe in 1969, but both Alan Mann racing and Broadspeed were to be very active in the British 'Group 5' series. In 1969, however, their fortunes were reversed. The Broadspeed cars dominated their class, and Gardner was pipped into third place in his.

For Gardner, however, there was an excuse. His usual car – XOO 349F – was always fitted with the 'supercharged' engine, and competed against the Falcons for outright wins. It managed this three times, even though its Boreham-built engine had no more than 185bhp from a Twin-Cam engine (the FVA engine had been banned for 1969), and it was therefore less powerful than in the previous year.

53

Alan Mann practised a turbocharged car (with 260bhp) on several occasions, but this was never actually raced.

Ralph Broad's cars were never beaten on performance, but both retired on two occasions. Their tally, therefore, was 'Won 9, Tied 1, Lost 2' in the class – the tie being with another Escort. Chris Craft made the best start to the season, and was thereafter 'team-managed' to several wins that John Fitzpatrick might otherwise have had; he won six times and Fitz three times. Their season's performance was such that the team also won the Lombank Entrants' Championship.

For 1970 – the last of the 'Twin-Cam years' for the racing as well as the rallying fraternity – Ford's works-supported racing efforts were re-shuffled. Alan Mann packed in his racing team of Escorts (Frank Gardner actually went off to drive a Boss Mustang with great dash and success), while Broadspeeds were asked to run one 1300GT and one Twin-Cam.

British racing was under Group 2 regulations (rather less forgiving of modifications than the obsolete Group 5), but this did not stop Broad producing, on Ford's behalf, some fiercely-competitive cars. His Escort 1300GT, driven through the year by John Fitzpatrick, now boasted nearly 150bhp, and the usual Broad type of modified 'downdraught' cylinder head was used, along with TJ fuel injection.

The Twin-Cam, if anything, was even more exquisitely modified than an Alan Mann car ever had been. Rear suspension of both cars, incidentally, had to include leaf springs according to the new Group 2 regulations, but the radius arm/Watts linkage location was a further refinement of the original Len Bailey system. The Twin-Cam engine, with many special Boreham/Broadspeed features, boasted more than 180bhp at 8,000rpm – and during the season this was to be squeezed even higher. The fuel was metered through a Lucas fuel injection system and camshaft drive was by chain (whereas the Alan Mann cars had used a much-modified gear drive layout).

Significant to this work, and the obvious carry-over of Twin-Cam racing experience from the Alan Mann team, was that Keith Greene had joined Broadspeed as team manager; in 1968 and 1969 he had managed the Alan Mann Escorts.

The cars operated entirely in Britain, in the RAC's saloon car racing championship. Broadspeed's usual immaculate preparation and development can be summed up simply by quoting the results – in the 1300GT John Fitzpatrick won seven classes, while Chris Craft won his class six times in the team's Twin-Cam. Fitzpatrick also managed to confuse the historians by running his 'GT' with Twin-Cam power at the Motor Show 200 meeting – and winning the race outright. That, also, was Broadspeed's only outright win of the year. Though both drivers won their categories, the Mustang/Camaro 'big car' opposition was too strong for them to win the championship overall – Fitzpatrick, in fact, was third overall.

For the International Tourist Trophy – held in two two-hour sessions at Silverstone – Ford persuaded none other than World Champion Jackie Stewart to share the driving of the Broadspeed Twin-Cam with Chris Craft. Stewart was to drive the first session, and Craft the second. Stewart had not driven a 'tin top' car since 1966 – when he had hurled an Alan Mann Lotus-Cortina around Snetterton in the TT – but appeared to be thoroughly enjoying himself in the beautifully prepared and presented Twin-Cam.

Stewart's performance, even to those of us who knew all about an Escort's

Getting rid of the empties – ETW 882G lay down and died in the Ethiopian Mountain Rally, so Ford sold it to the Ford importers

giant-killing potential, was astonishing. From the rolling start JYS tucked the maroon car into fourth place, behind Frank Gardner's 5-litre Mustang, Brian Muir's 5-litre Camaro, and Rolf Stommelen's works' Ford-Cologne Capri with a 2.4-litre fuel-injected engine.

After two hours, Jackie's Escort was still in fourth place, behind the Camaro, the Capri and Hezeman's 2-litre Alfa GTAm, with several larger cars including the other German 'works' Capri behind him.

The second session, unfortunately, was an anti-climax, for Craft discovered that a valve-spring was broken in the delicately-tuned engine, and had to retire the car. It was one of the few Broadspeed 'failures' of the year – but what a stirring and gallant one it had been.

John Fitzpatrick's Twin-Cam win at Brands Hatch in October was a fitting climax to that model's racing career. What depressed the opposition, beaten by what was already known to be an obsolete motor car, was that Ralph Broad was determined to go one better in 1971. His entire effort would be in an RS1600 – and he was only interested in outright wins.

This was the message filtering out from Boreham as well – for with the potential of Keith Duckworth's 16-valve engine under the bonnet, they were also convinced that the Ford Escort had been completely reborn. They could have had no idea, in 1970, just how much longer the car would remain a winner!

4
Men and machines

BDA debut — Clark and Porter winning their third consecutive Circuit of Ireland in 1970. The car had been a Twin-Cam for Mikkola on the Monte

There is this romantic fiction, this legend, that a factory competition department is the most pampered of all, that nothing is too much for them, and that their every whim is satisfied. It's a good story, but often it *is* fiction. Life isn't always like that – certainly not at Ford.

I have seen press reviews of other firms' racing and rallying facilities. Pictures show buildings which house rows and rows of cars, banks of spare bodies and engines, and seemingly limitless quantities of spares and equipment.

If the competition centre at Boreham complied with the blueprints, it would be a luxurious, clinically-clean, self-contained plant. Its staff would all be dedicated fanatics. It would be unapproachable without security clearance, and there would be guard dogs roaming freely to back up patrols.

Take heart. It might be glamorous, but it certainly isn't Boreham. Boreham isn't like that. And if you suggested it should be, to Peter Ashcroft, Mike Kranefuss or Stuart Turner, you might get a pained response. Mention the thought to a 'Comps' mechanic and he would laugh in your face.

The breeding ground for fast Escorts is in the country, and it couldn't be further away from Ford's normal image. World-wide, they are an immense company. In Britain, Ford sell more cars than any other single make. In general the staff tend to think in terms of millions of pounds, and in thousands of cars.

But at Boreham, thank goodness, things are different. Boreham *is* different, and Boreham *is* Ford of Britain in competitions. In fact, when you consider that well over a hundred of the finest competition cars in the world have been born at Boreham since 1968, the surroundings are rather a let-down.

I apologise to the civic dignitaries of Essex, but I have to say that Boreham airfield is not in one of Britain's most beautiful places. There are more factory buildings than green fields in the foreground, not a hill in sight, and a rather unprepossessing approach from the main road past gravel workings.

I have already mentioned why the competition centre is here at all. First there was Boreham airfield, built during the Second World War, used as a motor racing track in the 1950s, but more recently taken over by Ford for a development and proving ground.

The location is ideal. The building itself, modest, small – too small almost from the day the department moved in – and simply laid out, is far enough away from the mainstream of the factory to get some peace, but near enough to the Dunton engineering centre if help is needed. 'Comps' were always told to 'get on with it'. They do.

Mike Kranefuss' other department at Cologne is more modern, and perhaps better equipped, but I must ignore it for the present. He would agree, I'm sure, that Boreham is *the* home of the works Escorts.

There are no dramatic company signs pointing the way to the Centre – and no wonder. At one stage, let's not forget, publicity for a secret proving ground was the last thing Ford wanted, and the team cars were being built on the very door step.

Things aren't as bad today, nor security quite as tight, now that Ford's big proving ground in Belgium has taken over much of the secret work. But still there isn't a sign. "Take the left turn in Boreham village, over the A12 and the railway," said Bill Barnett when first I had to ask the way, "then turn left at the telegraph pole with three white hoops painted on it. Then go SLOWLY. It's a narrow road and you might just meet a truck coming the other way!"

I called at Boreham one day in 1976, and found workmen busily giving the offices a fresh coat of paint. Peter Ashcroft and secretary Pam Goater had chosen the colour schemes. They soon roped me in to comment on their taste. And did I know, they asked, that this was the first re-decorating session since 1963?

That typifies Ford's approach. One thing you most certainly wouldn't find at Boreham is any 'bull'. Peter Ashcroft has rude words to decry all such pretence, and Rally Engineer Mick Jones uses *much* ruder ones still. They don't need elegant surroundings to do a good job, and they all know what their business is about. Boreham's job is to make the fastest, the strongest, and the most effective Escorts in the world. This is done superbly, and with speedy precision.

The drivers might be super stars, even if Mick Jones and his mates don't treat them like that. They may be brave, and brilliant, and necessary, but without their cars they could achieve nothing. In this tight little world the cars have strong personalities too.

When Roger Clark rolled his Cossack RS1800 on a 1976 British event (through no fault of his own), its body shell had to be scrapped. Mechanic Norman Masters led me gently out to the back of the building, almost wiped a tear from his experienced old eyes, and showed me where the cut-up wreckage had been piled. But in the next move I was steered into the paint shop, where that familiar shade of red was already being sprayed on to a new shell. His eyes gleamed, and suddenly he looked much more cheerful. It was like a hospital patient which had suddenly taken a turn for the better. One car might have been badly hurt, but re-birth would not long be delayed.

Walter Hayes still thinks that one of the best decisions he ever made was to set up the specialised competitions centre at Boreham. Before then, race and rally cars had been prepared in a vast hall at Lincoln Cars in Brentford. The press fleet and other demonstrator cars were usually alongside, and more than one car found itself doing both jobs during its life. A mechanic might have been working on a Liège-Rome-Liège car one week, and on a road test Anglia for the Robert Glenton *Sunday Express* column the next.

The position at Boreham, alongside the company's test track, was ideal. The new building, even though purpose-built, would be no palace. The whole thing – workshop, test beds, offices and facilities, would cost £43,000 – not a fortune, even then, but it bought a good deal more in 1962/63 than it would today.

In those days the stores looked after works team parts *and* the homologation stocks. It was always over-crowded, and always intensely personalised. It was a modest little building that might easily be mistaken for a warehouse. The penalty area of a football field would have swallowed it.

Somehow, too, Boreham doesn't operate as you might expect a small but very sophisticated business to do. True, you usually tell a mechanic from a staff man, because the mechanic is wearing overalls, but even that is not a foolproof definition.

The legs poking out from underneath a new car might not be encased in working togs, and if the language floating out from the area is hot enough to boil the office kettle, you can be sure they belong to Mick Jones. Peter Ashcroft, Boreham's manager, decides what should happen: Mick Jones and his mechanics make it happen.

Nobody quite *looks* the part. The studious and very civilised-looking young

59

Roger Clark making suggestions (but to whom?) – also in this testing group are Anita Taylor, Chris Sclater, George Hill, Mike Wood, Stuart Turner, Tony Fall, Hannu Mikkola and Alec Poole

man floating around with a sheaf of papers in his hand ought to be a school teacher or a dedicated researcher – after introductions you find you are talking to Charles Reynolds, once of the Ford Rallye Sport Club and Peter Ashcroft's right-hand-man on event organisation.

John Griffiths, on the other hand, looks his part. With a shock of greying hair, and a perpetually incredulous expression (which often breaks into a grin) he ought to have responsibility for development and homologation – and does.

Boreham, of course, has already known four managers. Stuart Turner, arguably the most famous, later ran Public Relations at Ford. Peter Ashcroft, his successor, is the present manager. Before Turner was Henry Taylor – but Alan Platt was both first and almost unknown.

It was Platt who, in Walter Hayes' own words "knew very little about competitions at first", but who welded Boreham together into an efficient, functional little department. Hayes plucked him from a humdrum exporting job at Ford International to set up the operation, and once he had successfully achieved it, he was promoted back into the main stream of Ford's activities.

Alan Platt, according to his staff, learned the wrinkles of the game very quickly, and well. In his two-year stay at Boreham, the Cortina was honed into

The godfather and one of his pupils . . . Hannu Mikkola about to do *exactly* what he is told in tyre testing. Mike Wood *(left)* is impressed

a formidable rallying and racing tool, drivers like Vic Elford, Bengt Soderstrom and Roger Clark were all introduced to the team, and sales of competition parts rocketed.

Platt's team captain was Henry Taylor, a retired Grand Prix driver, whose introduction to the crazy world of rallying had been the 1961 Monte (with journalist Dick Bensted-Smith as his co-driver) in an Anglia. As a team driver he had nothing but bad luck, several shunts, and not a single outright win – there is many a team captain with that sort of record; it seems to go with the responsibilities of the job!

Even though Taylor was both a successful businessman, and ran a large farm near Clophill in Bedfordshire, he was always attracted by the idea of full-time involvement in motor sport. He had a persistent bubbling-over enthusiasm for cars, the team, and the programme, which Walter Hayes admired. When the time came, in 1965, for Alan Platt to move on, Taylor was offered the competition manager's job – on the condition that he immediately stopped driving.

He took the chance, moved into the manager's chair, and rather hilariously provided a worrying few minutes for his deputy, Bill Barnett. Bill, who had effectively been running the rallying programme since the 1950s, had already

Terrible twins, both sets. Roger and Jim, Ken Wiltshire and Mick Jones, before a 1970 Monte practice trip

Well deserved champagne for Hannu Mikkola, Bill Barnett and Gunnar Palm after Ford's 1972 Safari win

Bill Barnett can't believe his eyes, and Peter Ashcroft *(left)* thinks he ought to buy another stop watch ...

Pit-lane conference between Henry Taylor, Frank Gardner, Peter Arundell and team manager Keith Greene, before the Alan Mann Escorts go out to race

'Ginger' Devlin, who always thought rallying was for 'high-speed cross country tinkers' directing roadside service operations

served under 'Edgy' Fabris, Sid Henson and Alan Platt. But, as Rally Manager under Platt, Barnett says: "On more than one occasion, at the end of a season, I threatened not to sign up Henry Taylor again. So here we had a situation where a driver I might have sacked once or twice, now had the power to sack me!"

Henry Taylor's big service to Ford was that he was not only keenly involved in Boreham's team, but thoroughly enthralled by the whole motor racing scene, and everything Ford could achieve in it. He was, after all, as well-known for his racing exploits. Taylor, in a Lotus-Cortina, had raced with success in the Alan Mann team, and was as fast as anyone except the supreme Jim Clark or the ebullient Sir John Whitmore.

His appointment caused a considerable stir. Drivers, after all, are not supposed to make good managers. Taylor triumphantly disproved the theory, and Walter Hayes later repeated his ploy by enticing Jochen Neerpasch out of a Porsche driving seat into the equivalent job at Ford Cologne.

I have already detailed how Henry Taylor was one of the founding fathers behing the Escort Twin-Cam project, and there is no doubt that he should be remembered, above all, for this. Allied to this was his resolve to take initial build and development of the competition Escorts by the scruff, get the first 25 cars out to hand-picked users, and encourage them to start racing right away.

It was Taylor, admittedly following the Turner/Abingdon doctrine, who introduced Scandinavian drivers to his team. The excesses of the Sid Henson era had been swept away by Alan Platt, whose regular rallying team was Vic Elford, David Seigle-Morris and Henry Taylor himself. By 1967 a big re-shuffle (and Elford's advance to higher things) saw Roger Clark join the team, backed by Bengt Soderstrom and Ove Andersson from Sweden. A year later Hannu Mikkola from Finland had also joined the team, and the transition was complete.

For a pressman, or an outsider, Henry Taylor was a difficult man to know. He had a healthy distrust of the breed, probably not without reason, and found it difficult even to respond to intelligent interviewing. By the late 1960s the whole of the motor sporting business was becoming more and more cynical. The miracles Taylor achieved with what we had better call 'imaginative' homologation did much for Ford's Escort performances, but he found them difficult to justify in public.

His successor, Stuart Turner, was never in any trouble. Even before leaving BMC after six phenomenally successful years he had this splendid reputation for outgoing bonhomie, and could show off a fine line in balloon-pricking cynicism. Walter Hayes knew exactly what he was doing in appointing this deep-thinking and very complex man. Turner's impact at Ford was so important that I bracket him with Hayes and Keith Duckworth as a main architect of the Escort's persisting success. Nothing less than a complete chapter (the next one) will suffice to analyse these men.

Turner's reputation, and standing, at Ford took off like a rocket. When appointed Director of Motor Sport he could still manage Boreham fairly comfortably, but once Hayes asked him to take on the responsibility for the AVO operation at South Ockendon he had to move out. His problem, then, was to find a new manager for Boreham, and find him fast. "Whoever it was", chuckled Turner "would have to step in at exactly the wrong moment. After all, we'd just managed to win the 1972 Safari, the first time with a non-African driver *and* the first time with an Escort. He'd have to match that, and probably beat it the year afterwards!".

Turner and Walter Hayes agonised over the appointment, which most of the press were sure would go to Bill Barnett. Bill's biggest problem seemed to be that he was quite indispensable as an administrator – he had, after all, been doing that job since the 1950s – and the new competition manager would have very little time for that.

Even so, when the announcement came, it was a great surprise – plucked out from running Boreham's engine shop to be the new (and still current) manager was Peter Ashcroft. Turner's reasoning was, as usual, ruthlessly sound: "We knew Peter was a first-class engineer from way back, but what really impressed me was the work he did on Cologne's racing V6. He went out to Cologne, and to Weslake's own workshops in Sussex, for only a matter of months, but he turned that German engine, which was in a bit of a development muddle, into a real race winner".

It was, in fact, Ashcroft's first office job ever. He, like Mick Jones and Norman Masters, had worked at Boreham since the day it opened in 1963, but before then he was Gilby Engineering's racing mechanic, and before that a tiny garage proprietor of his own.

Mike Kranefuss, Ford's
European Director of Motor
Sport during the 1970s, and
now at Ford USA, in Detroit

66

Peter Ashcroft, present
incumbent of the manager's
chair at Boreham

Left to right : Henry Liddon, Hannu Mikkola, John Davenport, Bill Barnett, Andrew Cowan, Timo Makinen, Roger Clark and Tony Mason. Somewhere underneath is Timo's 'Milk Marketing Board' car which has just won the 1973 RAC Rally

The famous meeting of November 1969 where Ford's London-Mexico assault was finalised. Jean-Francois Piot (to Gunnar Palm's *left*) was the only driver present who did not do the rally

There was an 18-month gap in his Boreham experience when he went off to work for Peter Sellers Racing, and incidentally this is where he met Brian Hart, who raced a Lotus 41 for that team. By 1966, however, Ashcroft was back at Boreham, soon in charge of engine development, and building up a very close relationship with Brian Hart Ltd at Harlow.

"That was in the good old days of generous budgets," recalled Ashcroft recently, "we built up to five men, working on anything from Twin-Cams with Tecalemit-Jackson petrol injection to British and German V6s".

Ashcroft, then, had been in the driving seat at Boreham for more than four years, and had had a really difficult time. When he took over, the department numbered 40 people, and within 18 months he had to get it down to no more than 20. The budgets were slashed to ribbons ("I lost 2/3 of my allocation in two seasons, and still had to keep some sort of programme going") and he had the very difficult job of paying off some of the most experienced fettlers and developers in the business.

Not that Ashcroft, the blunt and forthright Lancastrian, was ever totally depressed. He now runs a very tight little shop, and is probably closer to all his staff than ever before.

But it wasn't easy for everybody to accept the sudden rise of this engine builder to become a manager: "Dirty hands and overalls to collar and tie, just like that, was a big step." And Turner was right about the 1972 Safari success being difficult to follow: "But he went out and won the RAC Rally with Roger, and I'm sure that helped a lot!"

When Bill Barnett, Peter Ashcroft's deputy in the same way as he had helped Stuart Turner, Henry Taylor, Alan Platt, Sid Henson and 'Edgy' Fabris in earlier years, left Boreham in 1973 it came as a rigid shock to almost everybody – Barnett included. "Stuart reckoned I needed a change, and he may have been right. I wasn't happy after he moved on," says the cheerful and kindly Chelmsford man, "and there were those people who were beginning to treat me like a fixture. Graham Hill once said he left BRM because he thought they were about to paint him green and stand him in a corner between races – I know now what he meant!"

But Barnett was the strongest link of continuity that a competition centre could ever have. Walter Hayes has already pointed out how much the Lincoln Cars operation depended on him – and the dependence didn't wear off as the years rolled by.

I have known Bill Barnett for a good few years, and I cannot remember a time when he was not unfailingly helpful, organised, and *ready*. When it came to being prepared for a rally, Bill had no peers. Throughout his tenure in the department the 'Barnett Bibles' for any important event became more and more legendary.

It was typical of the man. Before the event, everybody connected with the team – drivers, management, mechanics, publicists and sponsors – would all be given a detailed dossier. Emblazoned across the cover would be the words 'Strictly Confidential', and inside would be page after essential page of facts. Crew pairings – cars – chassis numbers – hotels – 'phone numbers – travel arrangements – Ford agencies and locations – airline contacts – service schedules – emergency procedures – medical needs – customs requirements – it was all written down.

There were hours of good reading in a 'Bible' – if you ever had time to digest it all. Usually one voluminous folder was good enough, but on the *Daily Mirror*

World Cup Rally the 'Bible' was so fat that it had to be issued in sections.

Naturally, Bill Barnett was a hive of information. I once mentioned casually to him that I was about to go to some God-forsaken part of Europe on business. Bill paused, took out the ever-present pipe, wrinkled up his eyes, and quietly suggested a good restaurant and hotel that I might try. I was astonished. Had he been there in recent weeks? No, but he had been there with – pause – a named driver in – pause – quoting the year, and it had been excellent then. And would I please tell him when I got back if the standard had gone down?

If his competition manager was the deep planner, the policy-setter, and the negotiator, it was Bill Barnett who was the organiser. Under him things happened, and if they didn't he used to blow his top in short, spectacular and entirely justified bursts.

In 1973 I once saw a list of priorities for the workshop which Bill had produced – not just three or four – but no less than a list of 25 projects! The mechanics didn't laugh when they saw the list. They knew it meant sense, and worked to it.

In himself he was, and is, a neat and tidy man. It shows through in all his planning. The wall behind his desk would be covered with charts (and others would be covered by maps). One chart, usually, referred to cars, and it was nothing to see an Escort's usage planned for six months ahead. "New car – Unreg." in November would already have pencilled in beside it the magic words: "Monte (Timo), then rebuild for Safari (Junior?), and back for Scottish (Hannu)." If a car was badly crashed in the middle of it all, and ruined Bill's planning, he almost took it as a personal affront.

Every team needs a man like this, and even though the times were a-changing, when Bill Barnett moved on, he could never properly have been replaced by the young and effervescent Tony Mason. Tony's job was different, and yet the same, but he was much more addicted to the glamorous world of sponsorship and publicity than the daily grind of administration. Life with Bill Barnett was all method, all preparation, and all three-dimensional chess. With Mason it was lively, and either fun or deep gloom. Not even the annual traumas of an RAC Rally ride with Roger Clark could alter that.

Among people like this, the shop floor could live with a spot of anarchy, and thrive on it. With Mick Jones around this was absolutely assured. A long-time Boreham mechanic, he must be the only spanner-welder ever to have a complete BBC *Wheelbase* programme devoted to him, and in a business needing 'characters' he must surely have been the prototype.

Today he is the Rally Engineer, and in charge of all the mechanics, but he doesn't believe in the white coat approach. He has that certain reputation among his equals, one shared with predecessors 'Ginger' Devlin and Bill Meade, that when the chips are down, and there is no time left for protocol to be around, he can turn his hand expertly to any job on the cars.

But it doesn't do to bandy words with him – for a start, he probably knows more picturesque ones than most people, and he doesn't hesitate to use them. The story goes that he spoke his mind to a new President of Ford of Europe on a Boreham visit not long ago – who went away with some choice new phrases to try on board room colleagues!

As Stuart Turner still remembers: "The first time I met Mick Jones – and he still owes me for it – I was working for BMC. I was trying to fry up some steaks in a pan on the back of an A110 service car one day, he stabbed my steak with a screw-driver, and ran off up Mont Ventoux with it – and I never saw it again!"

The steak-stealing incident is now forgiven, if not forgotten, for Jones is the sort of man Boreham needs to rely on in a crisis. At the height of the clutch-change dramas which so-nearly cost Ford its RAC Rally victory of 1974, Jones was the first service-car driver to hear the call for mechanics over his two-way radio. As foreman-mechanic that year he wasn't even supposed to be mobile that day, but was moving before the message was off the air, hollered through his own transmitter when he realised that the message wasn't getting through, and was down in Pickering at the chosen garage before rally cars had even arrived.

His partnership with Ken Wiltshire (now with Ford of South Africa) became legendary. To see the two of them working away at a stricken car, in the dark against time, was to see artistry of a rare kind. It was not a place for the local vicar or an impressionable young maiden to stand – unless they wanted to add to their vocabulary in a most unorthodox manner – but it was where the latest mechanical miracles would be wrought.

His description of the chaos caused by Timo Makinen and his many crazy ideas could never be printed here without breaking the obscenity laws, but his admiration for the winners (as opposed to the unprintable other kind) is as whole-hearted. Mick Jones will do anything for a driver as long as he will produce the impossible performance for him.

But you should never expect him to look serious. Involved, perhaps, and often quite absorbed, but never serious. In any case it would be quite inappropriate. This lanky Brummy-turned-cockney, all hands, legs and a wicked expression, could never be treated solemnly. But never under-estimate the man for all that.

It was Mick Jones who shook the prototype Twin-Cams into shape, who worked out the practical use of a bulky ZF gearbox, and who kept nagging away at his drivers to get the rally cars lowered, and therefore better handling.

It was also Mick Jones who celebrated a Safari win by lifting a tray of drinks, complete with its African waiter still attached, and walked into a hotel swimming pool with it . . .

Mick Jones' precedessors also made their names, but not in the same extrovert way. But, after all, there have to be times when the laughing has to stop. Under Henry Taylor, the open-faced and self-confident Bill Meade had been in charge of the workshops. Along with Bill Barnett, Meade was bright enough to be asked for advice on drivers, cars, homologation – anything. Henry Taylor relied very much on both of them. Meade, in particular, was the ace car-developer, and had many firm and often-stated views about 'his' drivers.

That, perhaps, was a problem after Stuart Turner arrived. Turner was quite determined to make every decision at Boreham his very own for a time, and backed this up by importing new people – mechanics and drivers – from Abingdon. It could be no coincidence that Bill Meade moved across to the newly-formed AVO (and Henry Taylor) within months.

Meade's successor was 'Ginger' Devlin, not an ex-Abingdon spanner man, but fresh from a notable job at Cooper running the 'works' Cooper S racing cars for some years. 'Ginger' was that because of his hair, and if you had called him by his real name of Michael he would probably not have answered. Ginger was about as different from Bill Meade – or from Mick Jones, for that matter

– as was possible. Before arriving at Boreham he had never been involved with rally cars, apart from an occasional RAC Rally foray as Stuart Turner's chauffeur, and perhaps he never truly got used to the different atmosphere. Racing and racing cars, to him, was all about precision development. "Rallying", as he often said "is for highspeed cross-country tinkers." We never really knew if he was serious.

Perhaps he meant it, after all. After only three years in the hurly-burly of Boreham, Ginger disappeared to work in the calmer, more sane, atmosphere of a West Country motor trade workshop.

If we hadn't seen his pictures so often in the past, we might easily have decided that it was this collection of anarchists who had sent Motor Sport Director Mike Kranefuss quite bald! For although he only had responsibility for Boreham's big decisions from 1975, he has had links, from the Niehl, Cologne, competitions department since 1968.

Don't be misled by the bald head, for Kranefuss lost his hair before his fortieth birthday. His link with Ford came about through friendship with Jochen Neerpasch, who stopped Porsche racing to become the first Cologne team manager. "We both started on August 1st 1968, when there was *no* competition organisation . . . ."

Now of course, Neerpasch is a deadly business rival, having moved across from Ford to BMW in 1972.

Kranefuss himself is a one-time racing driver, who never reached the heights, but it does mean that he understands that side of motor sport very well. On the other hand, he has never competed in any sort of rallying. Zakspeed's links with Cologne, apart from the fact that they chose to run Escorts as being the best available, are helped because Kranefuss drove for Erich Zakowsky on a few occasions.

The big re-shuffle came in the late spring of 1972. Neerpasch suddenly, and quite without warning, left Cologne to go to BMW. Kranefuss, his four-year deputy, was pitched straight into the Cologne job at the time when the racing 2.9-litre Capris were still struggling for pace and reliability. Neerpasch's new job, he knew, would be to develop the BMW 3-litre cars to beat his old charges at their own game . . . .

From then on, Stuart Turner, at Boreham, was Mike's boss, though he was encouraged to be his own master and make his own decisions as much as possible. Turner's move to AVO, and South Ockendon, made the self-sufficiency aspect even more important.

Mike's final elevation, to running Ford's competition programme throughout Europe, came in November 1975, when Stuart Turner moved up, yet again, to take over the Public Relations chair in Britain. But, following another reshuffle, Stuart came back to competitions early in 1983.

What peace and quiet Kranefuss had kept since 1972, therefore, suddenly disappeared. Not one, but more than a dozen, countries now came under his scrutiny, and in the aftermath of the energy crises and manpower shedding which Ford had been forced to carry out, he had to look ahead to a restricted but still coherent policy.

The boss has every functional advantage, but one other Kranefuss holds is the ability to speak perfect and colloquial English. There is never any communications problem between Cologne and Boreham. Somehow, and I am sure he will be delighted to admit it, Mike Kranefuss does not look German. The bald head is joined by a neatly trimmed moustache – and what

The engine which rejuvenated the Escort – Keith Duckworth's brilliantly conceived BDA – here seen on test at Brian Hart's Harlow New Town workshops

I am sure we could call a cosmopolitan outlook.

Such, too, was his attitude to Ford's future in competitions. He had no doubt that the Escort would be their spearhead for some time to come, but wasn't at all convinced that rallying should be the dominant factor, Nearly all

Without mechanics the drivers would either be lost, or just lonely! Roger Clark talking to Norman Masters, with Ford-recruit Andy Dawson and Don Partington finding it all very amusing *(photo Martin Holmes)*

the RS2000's homologated improvements originated in Germany – including the controversial twin Solex carburettor installation which surprised, and conquered the opposition in the 1974 Tour of Britain for its debut. Racing, after all, is much more important in Germany than rallying.

5

The three
wise men

Designing, developing, and winning with any competition car is a team game. Let us never forget that. The 14 year success story of the Escort is a perfect example. Even so, since 1968 there have been three outstanding personalities in the Escort's life – they are Walter Hayes, Keith Duckworth and Stuart Turner.

Their contributions have been obvious, and persistent. Walter Hayes encouraged the Escort's competition programme, and has always seen that it continued. Keith Duckworth's design genius made the Twin-Cam engine work properly, then inspired the 16-valve BDA unit and its derivatives. Stuart Turner became Boreham's competition manager in June 1969, and effectively directed operations for six years.

With a flair for publicity which perhaps even exceeds that of Walter Hayes, Stuart Turner came to Ford when the Escort was already established, but soon found his name irrevocably linked to it. He is the first to insist that the Escort was not his idea, but the last to say that he has not influenced matters since. The only blot on his six year record is one that he cheerfully admits; that the Boreham-inspired mid-engined GT70 prototype turned out to be a bit of a lemon.

There are, of course, many other personalities who should not be forgotten, but have not had quite the same influence on events. Henry Taylor, as we have already seen, was really the father of the Twin-Cam, and it was *Autocar's* Harry Mundy who designed the engine for Lotus. Mike Kranefuss and Peter Ashcroft both had much to do with the Escort's continuing development under Turner's direction, while the unsung heros like Ray Horrocks (AVO's first chief) have had much responsibility for supply of cars and parts to customers all over the world.

Even so, not many people would argue with my choice of 'The Three Wise Men', where the Escort is concerned. It is quite without surprise that I learned that all three became, and remain, good friends. Affection for the same sort of business approach goes further in their case. Turner and Duckworth, in particular, show a healthy disrespect for any established attitude – that is, until their own ruthlessly applied logic proves it to them.

In 1969, just before Stuart Turner joined Ford, I once made the mistake of inviting him and Keith Duckworth to meet each other at my house in the Midlands. You might say the meeting worked; after a few minutes they were so deeply into conversation that I might just as well have been a fly on the wall; for all I know they are still talking!

We have already seen that the competition Escort's story began with Henry Taylor and Walter Hayes. It was Taylor's enthusiasm and Hayes' vision which turned a good idea into a world-beating project. But, more than this, the Escort's competition programme was Walter Hayes' responsibility. If the Twin-Cam failed, Boreham would be vastly disappointed, but determined to sort out the problems; Hayes, for his part, would have to justify the waste of money to his directors.

Not that this sort of gamble had ever deterred him previously. As an editor in the notoriously volatile atmosphere of Fleet Street, he was quite used to that. In 1961 Hayes was editing the *Sunday Dispatch,* but moved across to Ford to direct operations in the Public Affairs department.

Ford, even then, were very half-hearted in their commitment to motor sport. Hayes controlled the publication department, which employed Edgy Fabris and Bill Barnett. This, automatically, meant that he was running the competition programme as well.

However, it was not Hayes who decided that Ford's involvement in sport would increase; that privilege belonged to Detroit. It was in 1962 that the company decided to break away from cosy North American agreements, to begin to emphasise the performance of their products once again, and to encourage the addition of higher-performance cars to their new ranges. Hayes remembers quite clearly that there was no Cortina GT in the original range, that it was added at the last minute, and that he immediately thought it might make a good competition car.

His early interest in motor sport had centred on Colin Chapman, who wrote a regular *Sunday Dispatch* motoring column, so it is not surprising that he hatched the idea of a really high performance Cortina with Colin Chapman. The Lotus-Cortina, of course, arrived in January 1963, and was the real mechanical ancestor of the Escort Twin-Cam.

A diversion here to tell the true story of the Lotus twin-cam engine . . . Its origins lie in the fact that Colin Chapman thought he was paying far too much money for the Coventry-Climax FWE units fitted as standard to his Lotus Elite. He conceived the idea of having a twin-cam conversion of a Ford engine then fitted to Anglias and Classics, and approached Harry Mundy, Technical Editor of *Autocar,* to design the conversion.

Mundy, of course, already had a fine reputation for engine design, being ex-ERA, ex-BRM and ex-Coventry-Climax. He, along with Richard Ansdale, designed the head for Chapman, on the basis that it was for a production car, that the standard cylinder bore would be retained, and that flat-topped production pistons also would be used. "Otherwise", says Mundy, "there was no way I would have designed a competition engine like that. In any case, converting someone else's designs was never the right way to go motor racing seriously!"

The Elite then dropped out of production, the Twin-Cam engine was first fitted into a Lotus 23 racing sports car, and was then earmarked for the new Lotus Elan sports car. When the subject of a designer's fee was mentioned, Mundy was offered a generous £1 for every engine built; not too trusting of the

75

appeal of the new car, he turned this down, and settled for a lump sum payment instead.

"I regretted this several times in later years, but especially a few years ago", says Mundy, "when Colin invited me to a reception to greet the arrival of the 25,000th twin-cam Lotus engine! Colin thought it was all very amusing."

Walter Hayes, along with Chapman, was the sponsor of the original concept of the Lotus-Cortina, and championed its Dagenham-built successor at a time when the reliability and production engineers wanted nothing to do with it. His encouragement of Chapman in his search for better and even better Grand Prix cars is well known.

It is also not secret that Colin Chapman persuaded Hayes that Ford ought to sponsor the design of a new Grand Prix engine, nor that Hayes and Engineering Vice-President Harley Copp proposed this at Stanley Gillen's first board meeting, six days after he arrived from the United States. The meeting was at the end of 1965, and the work began at once.

Neither Hayes nor Colin Chapman ever considered more than one man – Keith Duckworth. Chapman, of course, was consulted because the new 'Ford' Grand Prix engine would primarily be for his Lotus car, but only exclusively for the first season.

Ford's agreement with Keith Duckworth and Cosworth went further than a Grand Prix design – it would also embrace, first of all, a 1.6-litre Formula Two engine (the FVA), which should prove satisfactory before work on the vee-8 DFV unit went ahead.

That agreement, effective from 1 March 1966, but not signed by Duckworth until 23 June, secured one of the most cost-effective projects in engineering and publicity which Ford have ever known. For an often-quoted £100,000, the company found itself a splendid and competitive Grand Prix engine, a ubiquitous Formula Two engine, and developments from them that only Walter Hayes could have foreseen at the time.

The magic letters 'BDA' are not mentioned anywhere in the agreements with Cosworth, because at the time such a road-going engine was only a twinkle in Walter Hayes' eyes; Duckworth himself had not thought of it.

In 1965, Hayes had already been looking askance at the Lotus Twin-Cam engine, knowing from what it had already achieved that an end to its development was in sight. In 1967, when committed to approving the J25 project powered by the engine, he was already thinking about its successor.

Not, by any means, that Hayes is a great engineer. He admits that himself. But he is an enthusiastic thinker and planner – and he was repeatedly being bombarded with Henry Taylor's bright ideas.

Taylor, of course, was always nagging away for more power for his competition cars, so when the original Ford-Cosworth agreement came about, Hayes' fertile imagination was already ticking over. Given time, he was sure, the four-cylinder engine could become a road engine too. There was a precedent, after all, with the Lotus twin-cam. There was another – precedent also suggested that if Hayes wanted it, he would surely get his way in the end.

It was Hayes, too, who went out and captured Stuart Turner from the obscurity of Castrol, to run his competition programme after Henry Taylor was promoted. That, as he has told me, was not easy: "I first approached Stuart when he was still with BMC, but he felt it was not the loyal thing to do to leave them and join the competition; that was one of the things I instantly liked about him, because I think loyalty is very important in motor sport.

Then rivals – Stuart Turner (then at BMC) and Alan Platt of Boreham – enjoying the pre-Alpine sun of 1964

"Eventually, of course, he joined Castrol, saying he'd done his last rally, and that he never wanted to stand on top of another mountain waiting for his cars to come through.

"I didn't believe that then, and I don't believe it still. But it was difficult knowing exactly when to approach him again. There's a moment in every man's life – and every woman's, for that matter – when the answer will be 'Yes' – the trick is to know the moment, and that's what makes it hard.

"It was obvious how much he was enjoying the London-Sydney Marathon, so after the Burmah takeover I rang him again, asked him if he knew where his destiny lay, and he joined us in June 1969."

Walter Hayes, too, made the final decision to support the unsuccessful F3L racing sports cars (built and raced by Alan Mann), and agreed to the development of the mid-engined GT70s without any guarantee of success. His was also the responsibility of 'finding' a lot of extra money to back Turner's conviction that Ford could win the London-Mexico World Cup Rally in 1970.

The thinking behind the original formation of the Advanced Vehicle Operation (see Chapter 6) came from his office, as does the way in which the competition programme has progressively developed under Stuart Turner and Mike Kranefuss. He has also provided backing for a continuing commitment

Walter Hayes, without whom there would have been no Works Escorts

to motor sport, even when Ford's economic fortunes have been at a low ebb.

His most glamorous link with motor sport must surely be the DFV Formula One engine (and what might follow it), but his support for an exotic Escort programme will surely have benefited more people. When I talked to him about the book, he insisted most strongly that what he had wanted first of all for the Escort was a 1600 option:

"I wanted to go in at first with something like a 1600GT, and I didn't altogether want to go for a TC. It all sounded a bit exotic – rather like putting a Grand Prix engine into an Anglia.

But I was told very firmly that I couldn't have both because the Halewood manufacturing people wouldn't do both – and in this company the plant manufacturing men are supreme."

Now, in the 1980s, Walter Hayes is several stages removed from the shop floor of Ford motor sport, at Ford's European headquarters, but it does not mean he is out of touch with developments.

It was Hayes, not Stuart Turner, for instance, who first discussed Ford's thought on a replacement for the DFV Grand Prix engine with the press in 1976. Hayes, as closely as anyone, was involved in the decision to close down AVO's production lines at the end of 1974, *and* behind the pressure to get the more-specialised Mexicos, RS1800s and RS2000s built in among bread-and-butter cars at Saarlouis.

Though Hayes and Stuart Turner get on well together, they are very different people. I could never visualise Walter Hayes standing out in the middle of the night, half-way up a windswept mountain, with the rain and sleet coming at him horizontally, just to watch for a few rally cars. Turner does it, still.

On the other hand, the thought of Stuart Turner in a chauffeur-driven car,

The genius behind Ford's 16-valve power – Keith Duckworth. His hair is grey nowadays, but the ideas are as fresh as ever

in the gilt and chandeliers of a London club, staying overnight in a company flat instead of getting home very late, or jet-setting all over the world, does not ring true.

The basic difference is that, though in similar jobs, Hayes is the arch-publicist, while Turner is the enthusiastic competitor. That Turner later controlled the Public Relations division of Ford of Britain might sound incongruous, but it is not so. 'Competitions' was still in his 'parish', and his involvement as committed as ever. As Peter Ashcroft recently said:

"When John Waddell was in that chair, he let Stuart and I get on with it. I probably heard from him once a month. All that has changed. Stuart, Mike Kranefuss and I see each other very often."

Or, as an affectionate but un-named colleague said: "What, Stuart give up competitions – never! He'd *always* develop the job so that it was his responsibility."

When Stuart Turner arrived at Ford in 1969, he already had a distinguished competition record.

The Staffordshire lad who first wanted to be a doctor ("It was great cutting up worms, but then I cut up something that bled, and that was the end of the Doctor Kildare kick . . ."), started learning to be an accountant, learned to speak Russian on RAF National Service, and did his first rally in the back seat of a 1937 Rover 14, has come a long way since then.

'Doc' MacIntosh's VW Beetle gave him his first RAC rally ride in 1956 ("but there *are* older rally people than me – Mike Wood was a star navigator, even then!"), and he did his first factory event with Ron Gouldbourn in a Standard Pennant. Winning the *Autosport* Navigator's Trophy in 1957, 1958 and 1959 helped to consolidate the co-driving legend, but his RAC Rally win of 1960 with Eric Carlsson clinched it.

Pure chance led to his becoming the first 'Verglas' at *Motoring News* in 1960, but his rallying reputation was enough for Marcus Chambers to recommend him for his job at Abingdon in 1961.

Peter Browning's book, *The Works Minis,* reveals in splendid detail the great achievement of Abingdon in the 1960s, most of which involved Turner and his developing organisation. But he makes no bones about the real reason behind those successes – the right cars (Minis and big Healeys), the right staff, and finding the right drivers. Cars and staff would have been there, no matter who was in charge. The driving team, the planning, and the motivation, was special to Turner himself.

Between 1961 and 1967, when he left BMC, Turner changed BMC's outlook on competitions. The nice people, the pleasant good triers, disappeared, while the professionals and – most important – the Finns, came in. For that, more than anything else, Turner's BMC years are a legend. The Finns, and their professionalism, altered the face of British works teams. Triumph, incidentally, were next to join the fashion, and Ford followed them.

But what caused him to join Ford?: "I got over the staleness of the hectic Mini days, and certainly the London-Sydney Marathon re-kindled my enthusiasm. The prospect at Ford was so exciting – it was a bit of an awesome place to an outsider, but then I knew most of the people already . . . ."

He could not have arrived at Boreham at a worse time. The Twin-Cam was being beaten, more or less regularly, by Porsche and Alpine-Renault. Even in the 1970 Monte Carlo Rally, when the new batch of 'FEV' cars were the nearest possible thing to 'ice racers' that Boreham could build, Roger Clark and Timo Makinen were comprehensively outpaced by the opposition.

"Roger and I flew back from Nice together, and were so depressed it was pitiful to see. Roger said 'Well, I just couldn't have driven *any* faster,' and I said 'Well, we couldn't built the cars to be *any* quicker', and that was when we started thinking about the GT70.

"If any car was conceived on the back of an envelope, the GT70 was. Between Nice and London we decided that we wanted to beat Porsche and Alpine. We couldn't beat 'em, so we decided to join 'em. After that it was my job to get approval."

History tells us that the GT70, for all the design expertise poured into it was a failure. It is interesting to speculate about its fate if the 16-valve BDA engine had not come along, and completely rejuvenated the Escort as a competition car.

However, not only was it the RS1600 which quickly followed Turner's arrival at Ford, but the cohorts of new drivers. Ove Andersson was quickly released (branded as an 'unlucky driver', he then embarrassed the company by having a splendid period with Alpine-Renault and – later – Toyota), while Timo Makinen was signed. Two more of Turner's BMC protégés – Rauno Aaltonen and Tony Fall – were given drives on the World Cup Rally.

At a very gloomy point in the RAC Rally, Turner's team of Escorts was floundering in ice and snow. Roger Clark, in particular, was having a very unhappy rally, which no doubt prompted his team manager to give that now-infamous TV interview ("British drivers are just not good enough for me. Before long the Ford team will have Scandinavians in every car").

He now admits that he was wrong. More specifically, he admits that he and Roger Clark did not 'hit it off' for a time. But we can thank this misunderstanding for the competitive state of British rallying today. Clark was offered so little work for the 1971 and 1972 seasons that he branched out on his own in British events. His exploits with Esso and later with Cossack, his domination of the British forests, and the way in which British driving standards have improved from his example, were the result.

Even so, since Clark there has never been another regular British team driver. Next along came Markku Alen – a Finn. Ari Vatanen, another Finn, followed him. But it was very significant that when Turner had to trim his team at the end of 1974 he retained two drivers – and one of them was Roger Clark.

It was Clark, too, who jerked Boreham out of successful lethargy about three years ago. As Turner admits: "I now reckon that there is still a lot more, curiously enough, to come out of Escorts. But we had two years when not much happened, and Roger pulled us up when he sent me a copy of *Motor*. They had fixed a fifth wheel to Timo's RAC-winning car, and blow me if it wasn't really any quicker than Roger's 1969 Twin Cam. Now look at them – they're a hell of a lot quicker than the 1974 cars."

But apart from being the enthusiast, and the strategist, Turner is the thinker. It was his idea, and his alone, that the company should go in for a series of well-promoted 'forums' in 1973/74, when the aftermath of the Yom Kippur war had brought motor sport to a grinding halt. His was the inspiration beyond the Ford 'Rallyman of the Month' award. His has been the inspiration behind some of the more noteworthy sponsorship deals – who else would have visualised works Escorts running in Milk Marketing Board colours, or advertising Colibri lighters on their sides? And who else would have linked the previously unkempt Roger Clark with advertising for Cossack hairspray . . . .?

There are people in Ford (and wild horses wouldn't drag their names from me for this book) who dread the thought of what inspired scheme will come from his office next – not because it might not work, but because it will most certainly be right outside of their normal experience.

The press, of course, have no complaints. Turner the public figure is impressive, amiable, outgoing, and always quotable. He has worked on motoring magazines, on radio and television. He understands the importance of the media to motor sport. Ford's annual motor sport conference, usually held at the beginning of January, was a model of goodwill and enthusiasm, tempered with the sheen of good PR and a dash of self-congratulation. Only Ferrari have the wit to do the same. The opposition should learn.

Stuart Turner was Competition Manager at Boreham for only 14 months before Walter Hayes created the post of Director of Motor Sport, Ford of Europe for him to fill. This meant that although he stayed in overall control at Boreham, he also had to oversee the activities of Jochen Neerpasch's racing department in Cologne.

Immediately after that memorable Safari win, the whole management team changed. Jochen Neerpasch 'defected' from Cologne to take up a similar job at BMW, Mike Kranefuss was appointed in his place (he had been at Cologne from the start), and Turner was asked to become Manager of the AVO factory. This meant that his day-to-day responsibilities at Boreham had to be handed over. The man chosen, after much deliberation, was Peter Ashcroft: "He called me to his house near Danbury one evening, asked me straight out if I could think of any good reason why I should not become Competition Manager, but then said that I was to start the following morning in any case!"

Stuart Turner's time at South Ockendon was both happy and sad, It saw the continued success of a very professional assembly operation, the launch of the RS2000 – now much the most popular RS model – and the forced run-downs at the end of the Mark I Escort series in 1974. This was a corporate decision, incidentally, which almost everybody now regrets.

His move, theoretically if not practically, away from motor sport, came suddenly in the autumn of 1975, when he moved across to head up Public Relations. His predecessor, John Waddell, had gone to Ford of Canada.

In 1969, when they met, it was no surprise to anybody who knew them both, to find that Turner and Keith Duckworth got on very well. Both, within the meaning of my definition, are Northerners, and both have the same characteristic and sometimes blunt approach to life and business.

Keith Duckworth's initial contact with Ford had been through Henry Taylor and Walter Hayes, and his very first involvement with the product was when he started tuning the new Anglia engines for Formula Junior racing in 1959 and 1960. The former London University student got involved in motor sport by the time-honoured method of first building an Austin Seven special, and followed it up by assembling one of the earliest Lotus Six sports cars.

A bit of part-time and evening work for Lotus at Hornsey (where his first 'boss' was Graham Hill) led to his joining Lotus after obtaining an engineering degree in 1957. It was his disgust for the current Lotus gearbox transaxle, which, perforce, he was asked to develop, which prompted him to leave to set up Cosworth Engineering Ltd with Mike Costin, also of Lotus.

Cosworth's success early in the 1960s in persuading more and yet more reliable power out of a Ford 105E engine made him an instant legend in the motor racing business. His were certainly the first pushrod ohv engines to achieve 100bhp/litre, and for years Ford-powered Formula Junior cars were world-beaters.

Walter Hayes (who else?) picked Duckworth as a future world-beater at an early stage, and when the production-block 1-litre Formula Two rules came into force in 1964 he soon agreed to support Duckworth's design. This was important. Up until then, Duckworth had been the arch-modifier; now, with a new cylinder head and all the auxiliary drives to be considered, he would have to be the designer as well.

The result, like most Duckworth designs, was an instant success. The 1-litre SCA unit (SCA = Single Cam, Series 'A'), based on the five-bearing Cortina/Classic cylinder block, produced 125bhp/litre at once, and before the end of 1966 this had risen to a very peaky 143bhp/litre.

It was, incidentally, Ford's first direct financial grant to an independent engine designer in Europe. It was a dramatic precedent for Walter Hayes, and – as it transpired – of historic significance.

Duckworth, by now, was well established at Edmonton, in buildings once rented by Lotus to assemble the prototype Elite in great secrecy. However, the events which really led up to the Escort's splendid BDA engine can originally be credited to Colin Chapman and to Coventry-Climax. Right at the centre of the whole complex series of events was the announcement at the end of 1963 that a new 3-litre Formula One series would be introduced in 1966.

Coventry-Climax, under Walter Hassan, as ubiquitous on the British racing scene then as Ford would become later, supplied every Grand Prix team except Ferrari and BRM with engines. When they announced, at the beginning of 1965, that they would not be building engines for the new formula, it threw motor racing into turmoil.

Colin Chapman first tried to persuade the SMMT to sponsor a new 'national' Grand Prix engine, but when this move failed he then pleaded with Walter Hayes for Ford to do it alone. As is now well known, Ford agreed to do this, chose Keith Duckworth for the job, and have certainly never regretted it.

Walter Hayes never doubted that Keith Duckworth should do the design work for the new generation of 4-cylinder and 8-cylinder engines. Happily for all concerned, Colin Chapman, who would be the first recipient of the DFV vee-8, never really thought of anyone else but Duckworth in this project.

Duckworth has said that he was always determined to design and build a four-cylinder 1,600cc Formula Two engine in any case – whether or not Ford had decided to back him with £25,000 of the joint contract. He had, after all, gained a splendid reputation with the original SCA unit, and customers all over Europe were queueing up to buy a new engine for the start of the new formula in 1966.

With Ford's substantial backing, however, he could settle down to design the engine, then – as soon as he was sure that the four-valves-per-cylinder layout was working properly – he could carry the principles, if not the components, to an entirely special Formula One vee-8. So it was that in 1965 the FVA (Four Valve, Series 'A') came into being, and the vee-8 DFV (Double Four Valve) unit followed it.

Between 1965 and 1967 Duckworth the designer was almost completely bound up in these two projects. There was just no way that he could have found the time to tackle yet another design. However, it is worth recalling that although the original Lotus Twin-Cam engine had been designed by Harry Mundy for Colin Chapman, and produced initially by J.A.P., it had been Cosworth who undertook all the competition development. Right through the 1960s, indeed, Cosworth, either for themselves or for their several engine-modifying friends in the business, were much involved in designing and producing special parts.

In 1967, then, after the DFV had notched up its first Grand Prix successes, and after the secret J25 Escort project had got off the ground, Walter Hayes felt that he could approach Duckworth again. Even before the J25 Twin-Cam was ready for release, he had been thinking of the future, and one part of this, he hoped, would be a J25 with a road-modified FVA 16-valve engine.

Incidentally, Keith is at pains to make it clear that there is virtually nothing in common between the vee-8 racing DFV and the road-going BDA – nothing, that is, except the philosophy of a narrow-angle four-valve engine. As Keith said: "The only things common to FVA and DFV were valves, valve springs, the cotter set-up and the actual valve train length. The cylinder centres were different, the valve angles were different, the bore and stroke were different – everything else, in fact, was different."

Predictably enought, when Keith Duckworth was asked to make a proper road-going 16-valve engine, he did not merely de-tune the FVA for his purpose. Too many people, in fact, describe the Escort's BDA engine as a 'de-tuned Formula Two engine'. It is not. Nothing could be further from the truth. The man who went into purdah for nine months to produce the Grand Prix engine (incidentally living largely on steak and cabbage, and losing 40lb in weight) was not about to take the quick way out.

Ford's basic 'building blocks' tend to confuse even the experts, so the fundamental difference between the FVA and the BDA can be stated at once. The FVA Formula Two engine, designed in 1965, was based around the five-bearing 1,500cc 116E cylinder block. The BDA engine for the Escort RS1600, designed in 1967/68, was based on the rather taller, five-bearing, cross-flow-type, 1,600cc cylinder block. In every basic dimension except bore size and cylinder spacings the engines were different.

Henry Taylor and Walter Hayes jointly talked to Duckworth about their new requirement, asked for something around 120bhp from the 1600 version, and all the built-in capability of tuning it up for FVA levels which, in 1968, meant around 240bhp. Duckworth himself was still far too busy with other racing projects to do all the pencil work himself, but: "I made suggestions as to how it should be done, and what should be changed from the FVA . . . Mike Hall did most of the actual drawings."

Publicly, of course, the BDA engine was first shown in a Capri, when that car was announced in January 1969, and at the time Ford publicity had it that 100 BDA-Capris would be built, sold and possibly raced. Cosworth were actually instructed to make provision for the engine going into Capris or Escorts, but even Keith Duckworth was confused about their true intentions:

"You see, we had the problem of two sumps − one with a well at the back, one with a well at the front, and an oil pump problem. In fact the engine inclination came as a late surprise − the engine was inclined backwards − which was a bit of a blow as most of the oil from our cam carrier was supposed to be draining over the front . . . so we had to make a hole and do all kinds of things around the back end . . . ."

A recent interview with Keith Duckworth elicited all the basic changes he suggested for the BDA, as compared with the FVA:

"The FVA, based on the five-bearing 1500 block was bored out as far as we *thought* we could go, and the dimensions were 85.7 x 69.3mm, 1,599cc. When we came to do the BDA, we had to keep to standard 1600 dimensions − 80.97 x 77.6mm, 1,598cc. By a strange and lucky coincidence, we found that top tolerance engines slipped over the class limit to 1601cc, so that was how the engine was homologated.

"We simplified the valve gear of the BDA. The FVA had had normal bucket tappets, but very long extended valve stems above the cotter grooves . . . we redesigned this with a conventional biscuit and bucket tappet arrangement . . . .

"Cylinder head detail was very different. To fit into a car more easily, the exhaust ports were basically the same profile as an FVA, but curled over, so that the port face of a BDA was 30 degrees away from vertical . . . .

"The FVA had a cylinder head water flow system across it, with water taken out by separate manifolds immediately above each exhaust port. In the BDA the block and the system generally encouraged a front to rear flow then up through the head, we kept to that. The distribution and collection system was therefore entirely different; we also had a thermostat housing cast in to the side of the head to make car installation easier . . . .

"We had very complicated cam carriers, individually cast, located in a fairly difficult manner on the FVA. This was not thought to be productionable, so we changed to having cam carriers with large diameter journals, so that cams could be slipped in from one end, and the cam carrier formed the side of the casting . . . .

"About that stage there seemed to be fair evidence that belts were a fairly reliable way of driving camshafts. In the FVA there was difficulty in maintaining drive gear centres – it was very expensive – and controlling the gasket head/block joint was extraordinarily difficult. The whole practicality of gears in production engines was just not on – anyway at odd periods you get gear crash occurring, and it makes a noise enough to waken the dead . . . .

"Why did we choose a belt? Well, if the cylinder block has not got a cast projection to support chains it is very much easier to decide on belts. Also you don't have to enclose the belt, which can be hung on externally . . . .

"We made slight changes in valve centre dimensions for convenience, but otherwise the valve gear and the breathing arrangements were made the same as the FVA . . . .

It was, in other words, a logical rethink of the way a 16-valve engine should be designed to enable it to be manufactured in thousands rather than in dozens, even though all the basic precepts of the full-house racing engine were retained. Incidentally, while the FVA had a 40 degree included valve angle, and the Formula One DFV had a 32 degree included angle, the production BDA stayed with 40 degrees.

The BDA unit, in prototype form, immediately produced the 120bhp demanded of it, and showed signs of being able to run on very low octane fuel. It therefore met Ford's requirements for a road-going engine, but would it be as tunable as an FVA?

Keith Duckworth told me that almost as soon as the engine was running Cosworth had built what he calls an FVA/BDA – in other words an FVA block and moving parts allied to a race-prepared BDA head, with the FVA fuel injection system grafted on.

"I think it gave 238bhp from the start, and it was certainly immediately competitive with the FVA as we knew it . . . Then of course there was the possibility of enlargement. Very early on we made a 1700, then tried out an FVC and took it out to around 1790. Later, of course, we heard of people cutting everything out and welding in new liners, so we had a go at that.

Ford, of course, went to an alloy block to get the full 2-litre out of the engine, which wasn't possible with the existing block. With our racing BDFs and BDGs the iron block had all the liners bored out and different liners vacuum brazed in. And that, now, is a very reliable and long-lived engine."

But this is running ahead of events. In 1968 Cosworth had completed the design of a 16-valve production conversion for Ford – I nearly said it was *the* first 16-valve production unit, but that would be to ignore the claims of Bentley and Sunbeam, in the 1920s.

In 1969 Ford showed the engine publicly, and in January of 1970 they were ready to make it available to the customers. There was no way for Cosworth to machine the thousands of sets of parts Ford would need, so after a careful search around the industry for a 'contract builder', Harpers of Letchworth were chosen for the job. They were starting something which would completely revive Ford's competition hopes.

The BDA engine, of course, was by no means the last important job which Keith Duckworth completed for Ford. Far from it. Apart from the race-tuned version already mentioned, and continuing work on development of the DFV Formula One engine, he also undertook the development of a four-cam 24-

valve conversion of the Essex vee-6 engine for Capri and – later – Formula 5000 use.

The last project was, financially for Ford at least, rather a disaster. No sooner had the engine been made race-worthy in Capris than a change in regulations and a change in policy rendered it obsolete. A stack of beautifully machined, part-assembled, but dust-gathering engines in a storeroom at Boreham bears witness to the completion of 100 engines as required by regulation.

The last few pages have stumbled over many different sets of initials – DFV, FVA, BDA and the like. But the result of Duckworth's efforts in 1969 would soon give rise to yet another set – AVO and RS. For Walter Hayes had, at last, got his way on a very important project – competition cars, at least those intended for competition tuning, ought to be built in a separate factory. It had taken him nearly three years to bring this one to maturity – but the Advanced Vehicle Operation, and the Rallye Sport cars coming from it, were about to appear.

6

The Rallye Sport revolution

When Graham Hill drove the first AVO-built RS1600 off the production line at South Ockendon on 2 November 1970, he confirmed a unique achievement. It was another Ford 'first'. No other firm, before or since, has ever set up special production lines to build customer competition cars.

The reasoning was simple, and logical. Ford's philosophy was this – that if a competition programme was to be supported, and private owners to be supplied, enough cars to secure honest homologation would have to be made properly. A production line away from Halewood's hustle and bustle could do the job, and specially-trained staff would build the cars.

However, I must make one thing quite clear. There was no way that the new plant could supply ready-to-race, or ready-to-rally cars; time and expense would rule that out. But the intention was that certain very popular extras – roll-cages and flared wings are obvious examples – *could* be built in to a new car.

No other car firm has done this. Of course, Fiat encouraged their Abarth subsidiary to develop special cars, then adopted them for their own 'works' use (the Fiat-Abarth 131 is a perfect example) while you might argue that every Alpine-Renault or Lancia Stratos is really a competition car; but that doesn't really count.

Not even BMC, in the great days of Mini-Coopers, found a way to take production away from Longbridge. And, make no mistake, that was a nuisance. When Stuart Turner had demanded standardisation of twin petrol tanks for homologation purposes, the trauma among production planners had been considerable. Group One approval of the Cooper S by the end of 1965 was only achieved by the skin of everybody's teeth.

Not that Turner's arrival at Boreham was critical to the setting-up of a special production line. Thoughts about this sort of project had been circulating for some time. Almost as soon as the competition department had been established at Boreham, the sale of parts and accessories began. By 1967 Boreham's profits from sales exceeded £30,000, and for 1968 a hoist to £50,000 was expected. In terms of sheer volume, total sales were expected to beat £250,000 before 1970.

Two things, then, turned Walter Hayes' thoughts away from Boreham. The first was that the parts sales business was threatening to take over. The second was that he was already considering the merits of a Performance/Customising centre. One factor that made him jealous of lost profits was Jeff Uren's Cortina Savage – the Mark II Cortinas into which the 3-litre Zodiac vee-6 engine was shoehorned so successfully. If Uren could do it well, reasoned Hayes, then Ford might do it even better.

In 1967 the Mark II Lotus-Cortina was being made at Dagenham, to the noticeable inconvenience of the production lines, while development of the 'J25 Anglia' – the Escort Twin-Cam as it was still coded – was under way. In spite of their helpfulness to Taylor's and Hayes' plans, Halewood planners made no secret of their dismay at the thought of building ultra-special Escorts 'down the lines'.

Hayes then asked Bob Howe, of Product Planning, to work up a proposal for a new performance centre – *and* to look around for a place to site it. Planning the theoretical department was fairly easy, but finding a home for it was not. If for no other reason, Hayes wanted to establish it without spending much money.

The favourite site, the front-runner, in the winter of 1967/68, was a redundant factory at Romford, only five miles from Dagenham, though part of an ex-Beautility factory in Brentwood was also considered. Not only that, but premises all over the district, including Ford's own buildings in South Ockendon, were also considered.

In the meantime, Ford's own Rallye Sport Club had come into being. Launched in a blaze of publicity, it was a club intended to bring all Ford enthusiasts together, and would promote motor sporting occasions, special trips far and near, and would market many accessories, items of clothing, and the like, along with a magazine which would keep its members up to date with the very latest news in competition developments, and the doings of the works-contracted teams.

With the Rallye Sport Club, at first administered from Ford's Regent Street offices in London's West End, came the now familar 'RS' insignia. From here, and with the Escorts becoming more and more specialised as time passed, it was but a short step to consider the setting up of a special sales network for the Twin-Cams and what might follow them.

What followed was very logical. With production of the Escort Twin-Cam never much more than the basic minimum of 1,000 cars a year needed to ensure homologation in Appendix J Group Two, and these cars having to be distributed both at home and overseas, it meant that their dealer presence was spread very thinly indeed.

More than this, there were hundreds of otherwise very worthy Ford agents who wanted nothing to do with this sort of motor car, and had neither the staff nor the inclination to support their sale.

The answer was for Ford to create a dealership chain within the main chain. By comparison with the entire network, only a handful of Ford dealers (who would *volunteer* for the job) would also become RS or Rallye Sport dealers.

Release of this information came at the Brussels Motor Show in January 1970, but it was linked with even more exciting news for Escort enthusiasts. Not only would there be specially set-up and specially equipped Rallye Sport dealers, but Ford intended to build – for them to sell – a 16-valve engined Escort in a new factory reserved entirely for performance cars.

It was the news every Escort enthusiast had been waiting for. We had all read about the new Cosworth-developed BDA engine in January 1969, been discouraged by the lack of news ever since, and now found to our delight that it would be fitted to the Escort after all.

Almost overnight, as it were, the Twin-Cam engine – and car – would be obsolete. Everyone from the most humble private owner to the factory itself could see what was in prospect – the limits in power output would be pushed up from around 190bhp to perhaps 260bhp in race-tune, *and* the new lump would rev much faster.

The factory, and Boreham in particular, were at pains to stress that sales would not begin until April. Deliveries would be very restricted at first, and – where international competition was concerned – FIA homologation was not expected before the end of the year.

To show that they were not going to corner the first supplies for themselves, and so make it even harder for the private owners to keep up with them, Boreham registered a quartet of new rallying Twin-Cams for 1970 (FEV 5H, 6H, 7H and 8H), whilst Ralph Broad took over a brand-new Twin-Cam for his works-backed 1970 saloon racing season.

The factory also confirmed more good news – *very* good news for the private owners – that, when available, BDA engines could be slotted into existing Twin-Cams without too much trouble. Chassis number sequences would be unaffected (very handy for homologation purposes), and installation would present no problems. This again, was not idle talk. Several Boreham cars – the 1970 'FEVs' and the 1971 'LVX' Safari Twin-Cams, would eventually benefit. LVX 942J, originally a 1971 Safari Twin-Cam, was to become arguably the most famous RS1600 of all time for Roger Clark.

In the meantime, in January 1970, there was still a great deal to do. The new factory would not be ready until the autumn, and with production BDA engines promised from Harpers in April the first RS1600s would have to come from Halewood.

Halewood, and its enthusiastic little Twin-Cam assembly shop, was not perturbed. In that resourceful Merseyside way, they merely treated the BDA engine as a different shaped 'black box' from the Twin-Cam, and slotted them in with due aplomb. For several months, the two models were made side-by-side in the same department.

Plans for the AVO factory, however, were well advanced. As Walter Hayes told me:

"I sold the idea of AVO to a meeting in London on 13 October 1969, just two days before the Motor Show opened. I still keep a copy of my presentation – here it is – which requests and recommends the setting-up of a self-contained organisation. It would need an investment of $790,000, which was not a lot of money on a long-term basis.

"The idea of AVO, initially, was mine. It came about in rather a complex way. Basically the first company, the one which built GT40s, was called Ford Advanced Vehicles Ltd, whose directors were John Wyer, Leonard Crossland, and myself. I was very sad when that operation had to be folded up, I liked the *idea* behind it, and when it became clear that we weren't going to get all the derivatives we needed through the big plants I knew that we needed a new operation like it."

AVO, the Advanced Vehicle Operation, was already a long way from Hayes' original thoughts on the subject. At one stage it was thought that transplants

Graham Hill driving the first AVO-built RS1600 off the production line in November 1970

might have been carried out – that Cortinas might have had V6 engines grafted in, or that Detroit V8s might go into Zodiacs. Overdrive and automatic transmission conversions would also be offered.

What is also interesting to see is that as early as the autumn of 1967, in the initial documents referring to such a factory, there were references to the installation of 'productionised FVA' engines for Escorts and Lotus-Cortinas which could be assembled there.

In 1969, of course, Stuart Turner arrived at Boreham, while Henry Taylor moved across to become Performance Operations Manager, with a long list of additional responsibilities that – had we known it – also included further development of the AVO dream.

At the beginning of 1970, with wraps off the RS1600, but nothing as yet to sell, the Advanced Vehicles factory was founded. At that stage the staff consisted, quite literally, of Ray Horrocks, who would manage the operation, Dick Boxall, whose Twin-Cam experience at Halewood made him an ideal candidate for the planning job – and a spacious factory floor area in the South Ockendon building. Among its many previous jobs, this area had once hosted Ford's design and development team, before they moved into a new and ultra-modern complex further out on the Southend Road.

A general view of the AVO lines, Aveley 1971. Every car in sight is a Mexico

Boxall's brief was to establish a moving production line, operating on the merry-go-round basis, which should first accept Escorts but should later be able to accept other 'specials' – for instance, Capris.

It would not, for obvious reasons, have to build the body shells from scratch. These, as in normal Twin-Cam fashion, would be assembled alongside and among other Escorts at Halewood, would be painted and partly trimmed, and then would be sent to South Ockendon by lorry.

Neither would Twin-Cam production be shifted to South Ockendon. It was intended that the RS1600 would replace it altogether – though production overlapped for nearly a full year, with the last Twin-Cams being made at Halewood early in 1971.

By autumn, South Ockendon's facilities were ready, and a small team of all-volunteer assembly workmen had been moved the few miles from Dagenham to the AVO facility. Even while working only a single shift, AVO could turn out 100 carefully-built special Escorts every week, and though Ford might have liked to sell that many RS1600s, there was no way that they could.

The factory, therefore, looked likely to be seriously under-used, and in a rare botched-up launch Ford did not explain otherwise. Within a couple of weeks, however, the mystery was revealed – the gap-filler, and the *real* seller from AVO would be the new Mexico!

Walter Hayes' 1967 dream had come true at last, and it was really Boreham's big win in the *Daily Mirror* World Cup Rally which finally assured it. If a modified pushrod engine could take an Escort half way round the world *and* win, it would surely be a seller.

The rally finished in May 1970, the Mexico was announced in November, **91**

1971 Safari cars in build at Boreham. The odd men out are a Capri near the far end, and two Mexicos (ramp and driveway), with the Sony racing RS1600 paying a flying visit

and deliveries began towards the end of the year. It was a creditable and speedy achievement, not really as dramatic as all that because the Mexico was effectively a Twin-Cam with the standard Cortina/Capri 1600GT engine. Only the paint-job, and that was optional, was new.

The Mexico accounted for more than 80 per cent of all South Ockendon Escort production in 1971, and nearly 90 per cent in 1972. Once the RS2000 was announced (which is jumping ahead of our story line a little) the ultra-sophisticated RS1600 really took a back seat. By then, however, it was well-and-truly established, and was only made in sufficient numbers to satisfy the sporting authorities regarding homologation.

Ray Horrocks, soon assisted by Rod Dyble as his engineering manager, found the AVO plant amply big enough for his needs. The building might have been too small both for Vehicle Engineering, and for Spares storage, but for this select little band it was ideal. It was not long before the idea of selling ready-customised cars became practicable, Not, though, that this encompassed the hot-rod Zodiacs and Cortinas once considered. The customising eventually made available included building Escorts with ready-fitted roll cages, auxiliary lamp clusters, and – on occasion – wheel arch extensions.

The statistics show that AVO was a cottage industry. The assembly floor itself covered 85,000 sq ft, with less than 200 people involved actually in building the cars. The offices, and experimental workshops, were about a quarter-mile away, further south along Arisdale Avenue.

There was always the worry about output. Considerations of line speeds, and a certain standard of quality that Horrocks and Boxall would not depress, limited production to a few cars every day. It was theoretically designed for 13 cars a shift, Rod Dyble told me, but by various underhand methods this was squeezed up to nearly double the rate. Until the RS2000 was announced, this was satisfactory; afterwards, with the RS2000 being so popular, it was embarrassing.

Limitations, incidentally, were in the re-work and rectification area, and in AVOs own paintshop. Dick Boxall was such a tartar for high quality that every car had some measure of paint rectification before he was satisfied with it (and this, remember, was done after Halewood's inspectors had cleared the bodies); even at 16 hours a day working there had to be paintshop limits.

Everything at AVO was different, even the 'systems'. Dyble and his men had to come to all manner of compromises in specifications, even though legal requirements could not be flouted: "I arrived in June 1971, when the market was expanding hard and we were selling into Europe. One of my first tasks was to look after legal validation of models in all those countries.

"You would think that was easy, but – in Italy, for instance, there was a suspension requirement for a minimum ground clearance. The Mexico had to be set up uniquely for Italy with different dampers and different springs."

There was also the problem of Ford's mainstream-engineering design standards: "There are manuals which spell out engine compartment and transmission line clearances. The fan to radiator clearance must be at least 30mm, the sump to rack clearance must be more than a certain amount. We had to resolve this in several ways. At AVO we could react to this sort of thing quickly; if it means having a guy giving the tunnel panel a welt with a hammer 20 times a day we could live with that. At Halewood or Saarlouis where they build 80 cars *an hour* it just isn't on."

Purchasing and component collection was all modelled on Ford's mass-production system, but AVO operated alone. "For instance," Rod Dyble told me, "we ran the Escorts down the line on $5\frac{1}{2}$J rims instead of 5Js like mainstream cars. So we did a 'Meccano kit' operation where we could assemble mainstream parts like the wheelcentre to a different rim, and Dagenham's River Plant did them for us."

With such quantities involved, the number of RS dealers would have to be limited. In Britain the network started with 65 dealer outlets, and has now stabilised at 70 after a brief (1973) spurt to 75. In Europe 88 outlets were started initially (all in Germany) and the chain now totals nearly 750. Count the number of dealers, and – even allowing for the fact that Cologne were building Capri RS2600s – you realise that each could only have a limited supply.

The Mexico, of course, brought Escort motor sport to a completely new class of drivers. Not many could afford the 'full-house' RS1600, which even in the early 1970s could cost around £5,000 – £6,000 depending on the engine specification. More, many more, could go rallying or racing with a Mexico.

Stuart Turner encouraged this, at once, by setting up a Mexico racing championship and a rally championship, Jody Scheckter, for instance, made

Pre-Safari preparation, Nairobi 1973, with Hannu Mikkola's RS1600 in the foreground

his name in an Escort before he started driving single-seaters. Several of today's top British RS1800 drivers – including Nigel Rockey – and others like Andy Dawson and Will Sparrow, all embraced Mexico events as (they hoped) a relatively cheap way to fame. The prime example, of course, was Russell Brookes, who never drove other than a Group One Mexico before Boreham started to loan him more powerful machinery.

Boreham rarely played the 'big fish in a small pond' game by entering their own Mexico, though they made an exception of this in the case of farmer's wife Gill Fortescue-Thomas, who went racing and rallying very decoratively, but without much success, and in the case of HRH Prince Michael of Kent, who rallied a Mexico for a couple of seasons.

In fact the Mexico, after its 'prototype' and much-modified debut in the London – Mexico Rally, was rarely of interest to Ford for 'works' use. The fact that Brand Hatch's team of performing Mexicos all had Essex registration numbers, and were allocated to Boreham's fleet, was merely a convenience for Ford publicity. There was no active factory involvement – and, indeed, at times they must have found the antics of the cars extremely embarrassing.

AVO set up the 'Special Build' department alongside the main production lines, where a tiny handful of very special, almost 'competitive replica', Escorts

Safari preparation detail – note the wing-top mounted spot lamp, the turret cross brace, and the 'roo' bar protecting lights and radiator. The windscreens, too, were bullet proof

could be built. A few RS1600s were supplied to overseas countries, usually in the 'GNO . . .' registration series, where they proved remarkably successful.

Their most important achievement, to date, was hatched in the winter of 1972/73. Realising that there were more people looking for the RS1600's performance than were prepared to pander to its complication, Stuart Turner and his AVO product planners decided on a compromise.

What was needed, they reasoned, was a fast but quiet Escort. Either it should be a refined Mexico with a lot more performance, or – put another way – a refined RS1600 without the 16-valve engine. Looking around Ford's available power units on Rod Dyble's 'meccano' principle, it was soon obvious that only one engine could fit the bill – the overhead cam unit fitted to the 2000 Cortina.

In theory, at least, the RS2000 was born easily. In fact, however, it was not that simple. There would be no question of a six-week development programme, such as had sufficed for the Mexico in 1970. This time, it soon emerged, the engine was a very tight fit indeed.

As Rod Dyble recently recalled, with a wry smile, "It seemed to foul everywhere, and everything, at first. It's taller than the 'Kent' engine, and also a lot longer. The basic problems were to clear the bonnet, the suspension crossmember, and the radiator.

95

"In the end we had to design a new cast aluminium sump and oil pick-up that allowed the engine in under the bonnet – had to live with a very tight air-cleaner/bonnet clearance, but we just couldn't sort out the fan/radiator problem.

"We finished up with a unique radiator, and an electric fan to do the cooling job."

Gerry Birrell (so tragically killed in a single-seater accident in 1973, just before this car was announced) had done a lot of work for the company, completely re-assessing the suspension settings which had been unaltered since 1967. As a result, the RS2000's springs were much firmer at the front and a mite softer at the rear; the rear ride height was also reduced.

Mechanically, the engine was standard, though the use of the electric fan increased the power output to 100bhp. The gearbox was that of the RS1600/Mexico, and the overall gearing was rather higher than before.

Rod Dyble had even found time, and experience, to carry out some NVH work (Ford's 'shorthand' for work to suppress Noise, Vibration and Harshness).

The result was a very desirable competition (or competition-intended) Escort, with a 110mph top speed, flashing acceleration, and overall fuel consumption possibilities of around 30mpg. The RS seats, standard on this car, and the extra sound-deadening, made it a very desirable car.

Demand from Germany was so high (and that in Britain for the Mexico holding up as well) that all the initial production – more than 700 cars – was reserved for that country.

As with the Mexico, so with the RS2000 – it was another special Escort that was of little interest to Boreham or Cologne. Boreham, in fact, had one or two cars for special events (detailed in the next few chapters), but a plan to make Roger Clark use one in most of his British events fortunately came to nothing. His one outing in an RS2000, in the Mintex Dales rally of 1974, resulted in him winning the event by a mere two seconds, and being heard to complain that 'he didn't mind driving hard, but this was . . . ridiculous!"

In 1974, with the RS2000 available all over Europe, the South Ockendon factory had never been busier. This, incidentally, was in spite of the fact that the 1973 Yom Kippur War, and the oil price increases which followed it, knocked the mainstream factories sideways.

Whereas Halewood and Saarlouis both suddenly found themselves with a lot of spare production capacity (even for building the economy-car Escorts), the AVO lines were choc-a-bloc with orders. Stuart Turner also found, to his surprise, that quite a number of potential Mexico customers switched their preference to RS2000s, which consequently out-sold the cheapest AVO product by a large margin.

Even so, in spite of this production hiatus at Halewood, AVO were asked to do an important rush job early in 1974 – the completion, with special fittings, of no fewer than 5,000 special Escorts – the 1300E saloons. Mechanically the cars were complete when delivered to South Ockendon, but AVO workmen looked after the fitting, and the pre-delivery checking on the entire batch.

In 1974, AVO were becoming increasingly professional, and accomplished, in everything they tackled, and were looking forward to the next year with some relish. It was by now, in the industry, a very open secret that Ford would be introducing a completely re-styled Escort for 1975. AVO planners had looked at the car in its development stages, had appraised the possibilities, and were well on the way to developing new models.

Towards the end of the year, suddenly, the blow fell. AVO's production lines at South Ockendon were to close. When the last Mk 1-shape RS2000 rolled off the lines before Christmas 1974, there would be nothing to follow it. After just four successful, famous *and* profitable years, Ford's special factory would close down.

Motor sport enthusiasts were shattered. Where had AVO gone wrong? What sort of dreadful punishment was this? Did it mean the end of hot Escorts?

Company spokesmen were apologetic, persuasive, but somehow not very convincing. Five years earlier they said, all production lines had been flat out. They could not build special performance Escorts, even if they had wanted to – and in fact they didn't want to. Nowadays, so it was said, things had changed.

There was plenty of production capacity in Britain and Germany. New, improved Mk 2 shape RS Escorts would certainly be available – but only from the mainstream factories. AVO development would continue, and all their experience would be in the new models, when they appeared.

They took ages to appear, as is well known. Only a handful of the RS1800 (now, in standard form, fitted with a single carburettor 16-valve engine) were built at Halewood, before production transferred to Saarlouis. The new shape Mexico (with 1,593cc overhead-cam engine) and the wedge-nose RS2000, did not appear until January 1976. For almost a whole year, there was an absolute blank in AVO products.

I headed this chapter the 'Rallye Sport Revolution'. Unfortunately, this probably means that the wheel has turned full circle – at least, for the moment. In 1967, when the J25 project was conceived, there was nowhere suitable to build it. Later, AVO was founded, and proved to be an ideal breeding ground for fast Escorts. The AVO production line is closed down, and – worse – the AVO engineering team has been disbanded.

Both Walter Hayes and Stuart Turner are unmoved in the face of enthusiasts' protests. They say, quite firmly, that the RS Escorts will be built, developed, and sold, as long as there are Escorts on the market. Times, they say, change. But it will take a lot to convince me that Ford's very capable mainstream engineers in Britain *care* enough about competition cars. They may know enough to ensure the succession, but will they be committed enough to make sure it actually happens.

Have we, then, already seen the best of the Rallye Sport saga? I hope not.

7

The nut behind
the wheel

It must have been some wise-cracking American who coined the phrase. His colleagues were discussing, with great passion, the most important parts of a car. It was an enormous argument.

One man thought the engine was critical, another chose the seats and fittings, and a third plumped for suspension and steering. Our anonymous friend waited patiently for a lull in the battle, leaned gently forward, and spoke his piece: "You're all wrong," he murmured, "the really vital part is the nut behind the wheel!"

Not, you understand, a nut holding down a wheel, but the nut behind the wheel – the steering wheel. The driver. Without him any car could, at one and the same time, be a dead lump *and* a safe lump. No matter how clever a designer or mechanic you employ, a competition car is quite useless without him. An outstanding driver can certainly win events in rather ordinary cars; in a good car he ought to be unbeatable.

Ford, with their works Escorts, have rarely had to worry. The cars have usually been fast and competitive, and inevitably they have attracted the best drivers. Walter Hayes and Stuart Turner have always been able to pick and choose. Boreham's reputation is such that almost every driver in the business – and that includes three-times World Champion Jackie Stewart – has been happy to drive for the company.

Boreham's preference has always been for rallying, where – by the time the Escort Twin-Cam was announced – domination by Scandinavian heroes was complete. In January 1968, when the Escort was born, the only British team driver was Roger Clark, already a bit of a British folk hero. He had two Swedes – Ove Andersson and Bengt Soderstrom – alongside him, and none of them was designated as team leader. One interesting point was that Henry Taylor had not, by then, joined the faction which was convinced that only Finns were world-class rally drivers.

Two Finns, in fact, were to drive Escorts for the first time in 1968, and both – Hannu Mikkola and Timo Makinen – would have lasting links with the team. The remarkable thing, in what is supposed to be a young man's sport, is that both Clark and Makinen were full-time members of the Ford team for many years.

In nearly ten years of winning Escort campaigns, very few drivers have had long-term links with Ford. It is these three men – Clark, Makinen and Mikkola – who have meant most to the cars.

Inevitably we have to start with Makinen. He is still, arguably, rallying's only true Superstar. Timo, the big burly and cheerful Finn from Helsinki, is immediately recognised wherever he goes – and that might equally be in West Africa or Stockholm, Greece or Scotland, Monte Carlo or Morocco. For years he was the 'standard' by which everyone else's performances were measured. Many were sad to see him leave the team in 1976.

Stuart Turner, who always likes to glamorise his own drivers, still insists that he has seen spectators at a rally control jostling each other so that they could touch Makinen's rally jacket, or fondle the car he was driving: "In 1971 we hadn't entered cars for the Monte," Turner told me, "but Timo and I took the prototype GT70 along to watch. We drove up the Turini to watch the fun, and parked the car. It was amazing. As we struggled out of the car, a whisper went round the crowd – 'Makinen, Makinen, Makinen' – and quite literally they made a passage so that we could stroll through to the side of the road! Unbelievable – but I saw it happen."

Makinen was a rally-winner in 1963, and still won in the later 1970s. When the Escort was ten years old, Timo was forty, and that is an anniversary when both ought logically to have been put out to grass, to graceful retirement. As Henry Liddon said at the time: "Timo is now the 'Old Fox'. He doesn't go any faster than necessary, which makes people ask if he is competitive any more. But he's still unbelievably 'easy' on his cars – and you can't knock a man with a hat-trick of RAC Rally wins, an easy success on the 1976 Total, his Peugeot drives in the Bandama – and when he needs to there is still all that old 'fire' in a crisis."

Even so, when Lord Stokes decided to run down British Leyland's Abingdon competition department, and Makinen was pitched out of a job, there were plenty of people ready to swear that he was finished. That was in 1968. They were wrong. One man – Stuart Turner – thought otherwise. One of his first moves, and a very unpopular one at the time, after arrival at Boreham, was to sign up Makinen for his team. As one Swede – Ove Andersson – was released, the Finn took his place.

Turner it was who had 'discovered' Makinen in the first place. Timo had started rallying in Finland in a TR3, but by 1962 was using a Mini-Cooper with some help from the Morris importers. His first 'works' drive was for BMC in the 1962 RAC Rally – with co-driver John Steadman – where he finished seventh overall and helped BMC to win the team prize.

That was creditable enough, but his drive with Christobel Carlisle in an Austin-Healey 3000 to take the Grand Touring category in the 1963 Monte was a remarkable show of determination in atrocious weather conditions.

After that Makinen rapidly developed from a fast and very 'hairy' clown prince into a mature and tremendously exciting-to-watch BMC team member. Timo and the Cooper S, Timo and the big Healey were soon potential winners all over Europe. But Makinen demanded a lot of his cars, and there was no doubt that the Cooper S was still too fragile for him. There were seasons when Makinen led every event he started, but in which mechanical troubles often intervened. At first he had been the 'wild man', with every corner a challenge,

"I don't believe a word of it" – footballer Jimmy Greaves *(left)* **and Tony Fall, listening to propaganda from Roger Clark before the 1970 World Cup Rally**

and accidents a possibility. He was even more outstanding in after-rally celebrations than on the roads in the events. His first big win was the Tulip Rally in 1964 (and this, incidentally, was the successful debut of the 1275S Mini-Cooper), after which he matured rapidly.

His Monte win of 1965 was another 'classic', as was his 'win' (though disqualified) the following year. His series of big Healey assaults on the RAC Rally are a living legend. The Makinen-Mikkola domination in the Finnish Thousand Lakes rally began as long ago as 1965, and it was Makinen who started it all; three of his four wins (1965/66/67) were achieved in 1275Ss.

When Abingdon wound down its programme, Makinen moved out. As a rally driver his next year was spent as a 'wandering Jew', a freelance, with drives for BMW, Lancia and Ford (through David Sutton on the 1968 RAC Rally); it was a poor year, and he had no wins. On the other hand, he drove Pascoe Watson's power boat so well that he dominated the 1969 Round Britain Power Boat Race, and won comfortably.

By then, of course, Stuart Turner had arrived at Boreham. He listened to the comments that Makinen was finished – and was not convinced. When the time came to re-shape Ford's team, Turner pounced. Makinen signed for Ford in

100

Old man 'superstar' himself – Timo Makinen – probably the most popular rally driver in the world – and winner of three RAC rallies in Escorts

October 1969 – with nothing in a recent record to suggest that he was still a world-beater.

The first win came quickly. With a local co-driver, Makinen won the Finnish Snow rally outright, leaving the young wonder-boy Hannu Mikkola behind him in third place. The fact that his next Escort victory was delayed for two years (Hong Kong in February 1972) was an irritant, but nobody lost faith in him. Apart from, on occasion, the meteoric Hannu Mikkola, Makinen was still the fastest Escort driver in the world.

More than any other achievement, his series of wins in the RAC Rally have proved the point. Experience, ability and pace, carefully mixed with a dash of cunning, an element of naked bravery, and the overriding control by long-time co-driver Henry Liddon, all contributed to a number of outstanding displays. Anybody lucky enough to own an ex-Makinen RAC Rally car should be proud of it.

Yet Makinen was not popular with everyone at Boreham. Timo's two well-known habits are his hero-worship of Stuart Turner almost to the exclusion of everyone else, and his constant search for improvement in his cars. Under the system of 'one mechanic, one driver' which Peter Ashcroft has encouraged,

101

Roger and Jim again – with champagne and RS1800 – after winning their sixth Scottish Rally in 1975 (*photo Colin Taylor*)

Timo's closest contact with the cars was Robin Vokins, but even he admits that it wasn't easy to keep up with the Finn's whims and fancies. Vokins, who is as proud of 'his' driver as the next man, had a hard time building and re-building cars; Makinen, probably more than any other modern driver except Rauno Aaltonen, is a compulsive 'improver'. The car which wins a major international for him is not necessarily good enough for the next. He is full of ideas, and only a proportion of them make sense. Indeed, there are people at Boreham, even in management, who cheerfully admit that Timo 'is a bloody nuisance, a time waster'. Another once told me: "Timo would never take 'No' from me; he would always ring up Stuart to ask him to change my decision!" and another: "There was a freak snow-storm on the Scottish rally – *in June mind you* – and Timo got very mad with us for not taking along snow tyres just in case!"

When I last talked to Stuart Turner about the difference between Roger Clark and Makinen, he paused, then commented with a wry smile:

"We need *somebody* who is a bloody nuisance, in every team, someone who keeps on ringing us up saying 'Why haven't we tried a seven-speed gearbox, or 19 inch wheels, or an engine on its side behind the seats . . .' that sort of thing. Timo is that sort of guy. It was Timo who rang me from Finland (when we were both at BMC) as soon as he saw the Monte regs one year which limited the

Gilbert Staepelaere, who won more rallies than any other works driver

number of tyres to eight per car – could we use Pirellis with the removable tread bands, could we have a one-event contract, and could he start testing next week?

"Before the 1975 RAC Rally it was Timo who took the trouble to demand an axle change to revise the handbrake fittings. He won the event, but Roger had brake trouble because he hadn't delved that far.

"I must say he's led us up some strange blind alleys from time to time. There is the classic case of the 15 inch wheel saga, which he and Hannu invented for the Escort. But he is a trier, all the time. On the last Texaco Tour of Britain, when we had very simple cars, it was Timo who spent most time at the Dunlop wagon hand-picking his buffed-down road covers the night before the start. He's just that concerned."

He is now at the stage when he ought to be too old, and kicked out of any team. But how can you match the performance of a man who goes to Africa for the Total, finds that his car will not be arriving, accepts a substitute from

Ove Andersson *(left)* **and Gunnar Palm, before the 1969 Monte Carlo Rally**

Boreham built up in just four days, and wins with all the composure of a man who has practised for weeks?

Not that his in-car performances are all that composed when he is driving in anger. Both Henry Liddon and Paul Easter (who used to partner him in Minis and Austin-Healeys) confirm that although he is very easy on his cars he works extremely hard on a stage. Always dressed up in the obligatory flameproof overalls, he sweats and grunts his way through a section, with absolute and total concentration, then relaxes instantly with a glistening grinning face after the finishing line. With victory ahead he is cheerful and at peace, but with disaster staring him in the face, and a car which is breaking up, he never panics or throws his considerable weight about. Makinen in the darkness, at the side of a streamingly-wet road, on the RAC Rally is always good for a laugh too – I once heard a solicitous mechanic lean in, ask if he wanted a drink, and get the softly spoken answer: "Yes please, just a scotch and coke!"

Roger Clark, in many ways, is Makinen's absolute opposite, though both have very similar driving methods. Clark, for all his boisterous after-rally celebration habits, is very calm and quiet about his rallying. The car might be asked to do the most extraordinary things at very high speeds, but the man's face is usually deadpan, almost switched off, while it is happening.

Clark's rallying history starts way back at the end of the 1950s, and his Ford links stem from 1964. It was Roger who gave the Escort its first big win in 1968, and in nine years he has been the only British driver in Boreham's team. He is the only driving link between the very first Twin-Cams and the latest RS1800s and RS2000s.

Clark, unlike Makinen, is not a great analyst, nor a great pusher for modifications and improvements, and puts absolute trust in mechanics (usually Norman Masters, in his case) who prepare his cars. Unlike Makinen, he rarely sees his car between events, and I can quote several occasions when he has been introduced to a new machine at scrutineering before a big event.

If Makinen is rallying's world Superstar, then Roger is the British national equivalent. When the media are putting out news bulletins about an event's progress, they usually quote the current leader, then (if that event is not being led by Clark) quote Roger's position. At any public occasion, or any rally halt, his car is immediately surrounded by fans, spectators, little boys, and hangers-on. It is often difficult for him, in this country, to open his car door without getting a microphone or camera lens thrust towards his face.

Clark has lived with the Escort through all its triumphs and troubles. Unlike Makinen, and to an even greater extent Hannu Mikkola, Clark is no rallying 'nomad'. As many of Timo's big pay days in recent years have come from Peugeot as Ford, while Clark never drove any other make before 1980. Overtures to him from a Far Eastern team panicked Ford management so much at the end of 1975 that his season's programme was sorted out and settled in double-quick time!

Yet Clark's links with Ford have often been diametrically opposed to those of Makinen. Whereas Roger has always been liked by Boreham's mechanics, there are those who do not 'get on' with Timo. On the other hand Makinen's place was always guaranteed at a time when Stuart Turner was falling out of love with British drivers. In 1971, for instance, with Boreham's activities cut right back, it was only the timely Esso-backed national programme which kept Clark regularly in a Boreham seat.

Things then took a remarkable turn. A season's triumph in Britain, followed by that majestically serene RAC Rally victory, made Clark once again a fixture in Boreham's line-up, and when the time came to cut back dramatically on drivers in 1974 it was first Roger, then Timo who survived. Hannu Mikkola and young Markku Alen were adjudged to be surplus.

Clark, controlled, even 'programmed' (if you will accept the computer analogy) by co-driver Jim Porter, never drives any faster than necessary, which makes some people sure that he is a lazy driver, and convinces others that he is lucky. You don't often see Clark winning by great margins – his reasoning is that this would be wasteful of the car and of himself.

Makinen is the professional, who eats, drinks, and sleeps rallying. For Roger Clark there is no time for that. He and his brother control a string of garages in the Leicester area, he drives powerboats for fun, and has his own private aeroplane hangared at home for business and pleasure.

If Timo retires from an event he usually repairs to the nearest bar; if Roger retires, he looks for the quickest way of getting home. Clark as a person is the busier man, and it shows.

It isn't the slightest use asking Clark to analyse his driving methods. He won't do so. There are those who suggest that he never has. Certainly, by my book he must be the most naturally talented of any British driver, and his consistency over the years proves this. His Boreham mechanic, Norman Masters, would tell you that he is also very easy on his cars.

Hannu Mikkola, on the other hand, is not. Hannu is another big burly Finn, who drives hard and expects his cars to stand up to the treatment. He was Bill Barnett's 'discovery' in 1968, and drove for Ford in six of the original-shape Escort's seven years. He was, and is, arguably the fastest of all the Finns, and has a surprising propensity for finishing the longest and toughest of events. The Escorts, as this book makes clear, have triumphed in Africa on the Safari, and round the World on the *Daily Mirror* World Cup Rally. Hannu Mikkola (and co-driver Gunnar Palm) drove both of the cars.

His rallying career started in typically impecunious manner in Finland, with a five year old 80,000 mile Volvo being bought for his debut. He first came to prominence in Finland by beating Rauno Aaltonen (already a BMC star) in a national championship qualifier, in a rather better Volvo than his first. Sponsorship from a Volvo dealer followed, in spite of his rolling their car out of the Thousand Lakes at first. By 1967, Lancia were sufficiently interested to lend him a Fulvia for the Monte, and within a year he had also been invited to drive the bulky and ugly Datsun Fairlady.

Performances on the Acropolis, and the Austrian Alpine, led Bill Barnett to offer him that legendary £250 to drive a Twin-Cam in the 1968 Thousand Lakes' ". . . and expenses," says Bill, "which turned out to be expensive, because we didn't foresee that he was going to cover 9,000 kilometres on his recce!"

He won the Thousand Lakes, as already recounted, and within weeks had been snapped up by Henry Taylor on a year's contract. Two wins in 1969 – the Austrian Alpine and the Thousand Lakes – led to the World Cup Rally success of 1970, and complete stardom for the curly-haired Finn. His hat-trick in the Thousand Lakes followed (the last big win by a Twin-Cam), but as luck would have it this was followed by Ford's very restricted 1971 season due to budget problems.

From then on he lost a one-make contract, and balanced his Boreham-blessed appearances with successful forays in Volvos (Finland only) and Peugeot.

Jim Porter, who has sat alongside almost every top-class Escort driver, once told me that he didn't consider Hannu to be consistently quicker than Clark or Makinen, but that it showed sometimes. "He's harder on his cars too – he is much more likely to go charging up to corners and stamp on the brakes, and be that little bit more sideways and scrabbly through them than the other two. But he's very quick and usually very safe too."

Mikkola had all the big wins, and very spectacular they were too. Nobody will forget his epic drive from London to Mexico City, even though it was the media-conscious Gunnar Palm who did most of the talking at press interviews. Gunnar talked very well, too, after Hannu's Safari victory in 1972 – so well, in fact, that Walter Hayes decided to use his talents more effectively. Even before the popping of champagne corks had stopped, Hayes let slip the news that Gunnar would immediately be taking on a Public Relations job with Ford of

Even Mick Jones, on the roof, looks relieved, as Rauno Aaltonen *(driving)* and Henry Liddon bring their 1850cc pushrod Escort to the football stadium in Mexico City

Sweden. It was the first the ebullient Palm had heard of it!

Somehow, later and without Palm, Mikkola was not as successful as he had been before. He gave *Motor* journalist Hamish Cardno the ride of his life to win the Scottish a few weeks after that Safari drive (and used Robin Hillyar's ex-Safari car to do the job), but didn't chalk up another win for fourteen months.

Ironically enough, the brand-new car which let him down on the 1973 Safari with broken steering when he was leading the event for the third successive year, was the instrument of that next win. After the Safari it was shipped out to New Zealand, for the Heatway Rally, and preparatory to being sold off to the local company – where it behaved impeccably and gave Hannu a long-overdue win.

Even so, it seemed that Hannu's Ford-luck had changed. His 1974 season, apart from one good win in the Thousand Lakes (which made it four Escort victories for him, and five in all for the car), was a great disappointment. It was almost as if Stuart Turner's theories about 'unlucky drivers', once applied to Ove Andersson in similar circumstances, was coming true again. At the end of that season, and in spite of the fact that he was still arguably the fastest rally driver in the world, Mikkola lost his Boreham drives.

107

For the next three years, Hannu found employment with Fiat, Peugeot and Toyota, and it was not until Ford intensified their World Championship attack for 1978 that he was invited back to Boreham. By then, even that was something of a surprise, for although his driving had obviously matured, and his brilliance was never in doubt, Hannu had not enjoyed a very successful three-year sabbatical. In all that time he had won two World Championship events (Morocco in a Peugeot, and the 1000 Lakes in a Toyota, both in 1975), and his 1977 record had been as unlucky as ever.

From 1978 to the end of 1980, however, the Mikkola-Ford links were strong, and seemed to be perfectly amicable. In 1978, after taking two second places behind a supremely in-form Bjorn Waldegard (in Sweden and Portugal) he then won the Welsh and Scottish events at something of a canter, followed up by a dead-heat finish on the Burmah in his first-ever Eaton's Yale sponsored drive, and won the Lombard-RAC Rally outright on the occasion when the team's drivers had to muddle on in a 'Dealer Team Ford' organisation.

In 1979 it was really the story as before, for Bjorn Waldegard won the Driver's World Championship even though he won fewer events, while Mikkola finished close behind him. There was now no doubt about his ability, or his 'form' – like Makinen in the 1960s, Hannu seemed to lead every rally which he started, and usually won if his cars did not let him down. The partnership with co-driver Arne Hertz was quite obviously ideal, and he seemed to have a real empathy with management and workforce at Boreham. Three outright victories during the year – in Portugal, New Zealand and in the Lombard-RAC – also lined up with two drives for Mercedes-Benz (second in Africa, and another victory in Bandama). It was no wonder that he was one of the two drivers contracted to David Sutton and his sponsors for 1980, though he also found time to drive for Mercedes-Benz in four events.

In many ways, Hannu's last year in Escorts was as unlucky as he had often been in the past. There wasn't a single win in World Championship rounds, even if this could be balanced by two wins and a second place in the British series, and by second place in the Lombard-RAC, which was the first time an Escort had *not* won in nine years!

At the end of that season, Mikkola left David Sutton, and Ford, to take up a very exciting (and lucrative!) contract with Audi, to lead the attempt to turn the four-wheel-drive Quattro into a World Championship winning machine. Even at the time of writing this definitive edition (1983), Hannu is still looked on as one of the world's best rally drivers, and at the age of 41 that has to be a real compliment to him.

The other unlucky driver to lose his place in the financial squeeze of 1975 was the other meteoric young Finn, Markku Alen. 'Discovered', like others before him, because of his high-flying Volvo antics in Finnish events, he was brought to Stuart Turner's attention by Timo Makinen during 1973.

Accordingly, he was given his first Ford chance in the 1973 RAC Rally. The car, though owned by Boreham, was prepared and entered by David Sutton's Clarke and Simpson dealership. It had already completed most of a season in Finland, and a couple of forestry events for Roger Clark. The new boy really made it fly.

It flew a bit too far in Sutton Park, where it joined dozens of other cars off the road at the same point (and this included two more of the works-prepared cars), and dropped Alen down to something like 178th place. His chase back up through the field was stirring and dramatic to watch.

Now there's an appropriate registration number! Actually that car is MEV 34J, as raced by Broadspeed in 1971, usually with great success by John Fitzpatrick

Everybody agrees that it is easy for a works-driver of that calibre to start overtaking tail-enders, and even mid-field runners, but with a handicap of around ten minutes it was surely out of the question that he should penetrate the top half dozen again?

It was quite unprecedented, but he made it. The records show that he clawed his way back up to third place behind two other works Escorts. In spite of another big, but brief, shunt, he finished up a mere seven minutes adrift of Makinen's winning car.

For 1974, even with a restricted programme in prospect, Stuart Turner signed up Alen, and was speedily rewarded when the Finn won the Welsh. A repeat performance on the Scottish was promised, but the event had to be cancelled at the last minute, and his RAC Rally showing was spoiled by car troubles.

Alen, unlike Mikkola, has found new fame in a new team – his drives in the conventionally laid out, but all-independently-suspended Fiat-Abarths and Lancias are always worth watching.

I have already mentioned the 'unlucky' Ove Andersson, who was one of the original trio of Escort drivers at Boreham, in 1968 and 1969. Ove, a Swede, had graduated to a Boreham-built car through his original successes in Cortinas provided by Ford of Sweden, and was a very hot property for a time. Out of a car he was always very quiet and unassuming, deceptively so, because his performance in a car was completely different. Even so, he was eventually quite ashamed that he had to start using spectacles for driving.

What, bored already? **Gerry Birrell** *(right)* **and Claude Bourgoignie with their RS1600, at Monza for the start of the 1972 racing season**

Good though he was, and in spite of his obvious 'feel' for the cars, he only ever won one event for Boreham — that being the relatively unimportant Welsh Rally of 1969. With Clark and Mikkola showing that they liked the feel of the winner's garlands around their necks, and with Timo Makinen already signed for 1970, poor Ove had to be released.

His 1969 season had been more 'dnf' than 'finish', and the irony was that his final Boreham-contracted appearance — in the 1969 RAC Rally — led to a very fine fourth place against all the odds of a *very* wintry event. The irony of it all, as Stuart Turner now happily admits, is that Andersson then went on to great success with Alpine-Renault — winning four events on the trot in 1971, which matched anything Boreham could achieve that year.

Ove is now, of course, the guiding light behind Toyota's competition programme in Europe, and by no coincidence his number one driver at one time, was Hannu Mikkola.

But you don't necessarily have to be glamorous, and a Scandinavian, to be important to the Escort. Roger Clark has proved it — dozens of times. When I asked Stuart Turner, not so long ago, who had probably done most to promote the Escort, he had absolutely no hesitation:

"Purely in terms of value for money — in wins for the amount of effort to back them — it has to be Gilbert Staepelaere. No doubt at all. Gilbert has never been the glamorous man swanning round the World Championship circuit, and only rarely has he been in Boreham's front-line team. But we've supplied him with a car for many years, and he must have won *dozens* of events in Europe.

110

"His car comes back to Boreham whenever it needs major attention, otherwise Ford of Belgium, in Antwerp, look after it. And Gilbert, of course, works for us full-time."

Although in his fortieth year at that time, Staepelaere was still the fastest Escort driver on 'Common Market' events, as he had proved so very many times. His RS1800 was not delivered to him until the second half of the 1975 season, but it won more events than any other, and that includes the battered old APG machine which Ari Vatanen used to dominate the British championship season in 1976.

He always seemed to rally Fords, right from the start of his motor sporting career. His first (of many) wins in the Belgian International Rally Championships was in 1964, in a Cortina GT, and things have never really looked back since then.

With Simo Lampinen, in the London – Sydney Marathon, he might have won a glittering prize (they crashed 150 miles from the finish when leading), and he has also co-driven Roger Clark (East African Safari) and Timo Makinen (*Daily Mirror* World Cup Rally).

After Staepelaere, Europe's most consistent Escort driver must surely have been Hans Heyer, of the Zakspeed team. Not that he has been a German superstar for all that long in cars – it was in karts that he became famous. It was not until 1972 that he first drove Fords on the race tracks, but in 1974 Zakspeed's phenomenal run of success with their works-backed RS1600s was spearheaded by the 31-year-old West German.

The year before he had driven the fiercely-fast 3-litre Capris which Cologne had developed, but for 1974 all his attention was taken up by the European *(and* the German Touring car championships). It was an altogether successful year which he never managed to repeat with the Mark II Escorts – mainly because there were far fewer events in 1975 and 1976 to exercise the cars.

Birmingham's John Fitzpatrick, though, was Britain's 'Mr Escort driver' for even longer. John, of course, had started his racing career with Ralph Broad in the early 1960s, when the fast-talking Broad was already known for building the fastest privately-prepared Mini-Coopers in the business. When Broad 'had words' with BMC, he was quickly snapped up by Ford for 1966. With him, to drive his smart new Anglias, was Fitzpatrick.

It was a partnership which lasted for several years, but prospered at once. In that first season, with Anglias more delicately and carefully built than anybody else had ever essayed, Fitzpatrick won the British saloon car championship. His love affair with Ford was under way.

With Escort 1300GTs in 1968/69/70, he shared an enormous run of Broadspeed successes with Chris Craft, but it was in the new RS1600 for 1971 that he really became a potential *race* winner, as opposed to merely an outstanding *class* winner. It was also the year in which Jochen Neerpasch hired him to race the Cologne-built RS1600 which started out so strongly in the European series. It was inevitable, of course, that he should graduate to greater things. Fitzpatrick is now renowned for his mastery of big fast Porsches, which must be even more exciting than the Capris he drove for Cologne towards the end of his stay with Ford.

There have, of course, been several other 'nuts' who achieved great things in Escorts. Jean-Francois Piot, the nervously-excitable Frenchman, who drove Escorts for Ford France between 1969 and 1972 (and for which team Jim Porter was team manager in 1971). Vic 'Junior' Preston of Nairobi, whose

111

local knowledge of Safari conditions was a very valuable asset to Boreham in their Safari expeditions, and Marathon-winner Andrew Cowan, whose drives in *Scotsman*-sponsored works Escorts were usually over-shadowed by Roger Clark at his brilliant best. Tony Fall, that blunt and extrovert Yorkshireman who now runs the Opel competition programme in Europe, was another who appears briefly in my record.

Piot it is, who is described by one Boreham executive as 'even more of a nagger, even more of a nuisance, than Makinen, and that isn't easy!' He was everything that you would expect of the Gallic race, and he drove an Escort accordingly. There was never a full-time place for him in the Boreham team, but his exploits in France were successful.

Later, of course, he was attracted to Alpine-Renault, and the delights of a specially-designed rear-engined 'production' car. Not even the possibilities of the then-new mid-engined GT70 could keep him loyal to Ford.

Tony Fall suffers from only one problem – that for years he was the best British rally driver bar one – and that one was Roger Clark. Fall came on the 'works' scene at BMC, in a Cooper S, when Abingdon's team was stuffed full of Finnish talent. He was still coming to his prime when the BMC department was run down.

Stuart Turner, who picked him at Abingdon, drew him into the net at Boreham, first to tackle a few odd-ball events, including the Peruvian Rally of the Incas (which he won outright with Gunnar Palm) and later to run a semi-detached factory car under the Autobars sponsorship banner.

In any other team Fall would have been an asset – especially for his ribald good humour and his almost unquenchable spirit at all times. I don't think any of us who saw it all could forget the antics of Messrs Fall and Jimmy Greaves on the 16,000 mile World Cup Rally in 1970 – especially the time when their car arrived at a control on three wheels and a brake disc, with an exhausted Greaves pushing away behind. And only Fall could, later, have hit an unfortunate donkey in full flight, smashed the windscreen, nearly been blinded by the splinters, and made a huge funny story out of it all.

Before 1975, a lanky young Finn – yes, another of that breed – was unknown outside his native country. Like others of his ilk, Vatanen was incredibly fast in a loose-surface rally car, and seemed to be quite without fear. Like the others, he had been up to the most agile and audacious tricks on the yumpy stages of Finland – but it was when he started beating Mikkola and Makinen on occasion, in his own very battered Opel Ascona, that Ford's 'scouting system' began to operate again.

Timo and Hannu had both noted this new talent, and mentioned him to Stuart Turner, but it was his drives in Britain during 1975 which finally proved the point. His Ascona was really very tired by the time Vatanen tackled the Welsh, and almost ready to die when it finished eighth on the Scottish.

As a try out, Vatanen, still only 22 years old, was offered a drive in the 1000 Lakes event in one of Timo Makinen's RS1600s. With Geraint Phillips of *Motoring News* in the other chair, Ari set up a series of fastest stages times, then a pointless accident due, as he admits, "to my memory slipping. I got the mental pace notes just a bit wrong."

His first ever RS1800 drive was in the 1975 RAC Rally, co-driven by the cockily-confident Peter Bryant. A cultured first day's drive, without fireworks, left him in fourth place. The next day saw a monumental high-speed accident in Clipstone Forest, near Nottingham. At that point the car would have been flat out in fifth gear, certainly pulling more than 110mph. Unfortunately there was this sudden dip in the road . . . .

It was no consolation to him that both Clark and Makinen nearly had big smashes at the same point. But he could, at least, look at what had been a brand new car and know that it was a really comprehensive write-off.

His talent, though, and lots of sheer youthful bravery, shone through. For 1976 Peter Ashcroft decided to bring him to Britain, base him near Boreham, and make sure he tackled all the British championship events. When announced at Ford's competitions press conference at the beginning of the year, this brought storms of protest from the magazine press. Ashcroft and Stuart Turner just sat back, smiled serenely – and waited.

His car was the APG-sponsored machine with which Timo Makinen had already won the RAC Rally. Never out of the hunt on any event, he chalked up his first win on the Welsh Rally, was dominating the Scottish when the back axle failed (by then, an 'unknown' problem on Escorts), won the Manx in a most relaxed and self-assured manner, and later clinched the RAC rally championship. All this, mark you, in his first year in a competitive car.

It was not, of course, without incident. Whereas the experienced Roger Clark does not often make driving mistakes (his last shunt on the Manx being a rare exception), Vatanen's car rarely reached the end of an event without damage of some sort. It got to the stage when we all started to feel sorry for it, and sentimentalise over its future. On one occasion at least it should have been written off after a roll, and a bent wing, nose or door was considered normal. There was so much rallying activity at Boreham during the year (too much, some critics said, pointing to the drooping reliability record), that quick repair jobs were always needed instead.

There is no doubt, though, that up to then he led a charmed life. Without exception in his victorious first full season, his 'offs' had been within range of a crowd of helpful spectators, and even his axle failure on the Scottish occurred on the downhill run to the end of a stage, with Ford service nearby. The easy availability of a replacement would have put him back on the road, probably to another easy win.

But as the pundits have often said before, the superstars who start by driving at 105 per cent, and eventually crash their way down to 99 per cent, win a lot of rallies. Those who start at 95 per cent rarely work up to the pace. Ari had already won several events, and one of them – in a 'standard' RS2000 in the Tour of Britain – was in a car quite unsuited to his normal way of driving.

Vatanen, as the fact sheet points out, used to drive road rollers and excavators for his living (which might explain his liking for the edges of tracks as well as the centre), but his long thin frame belies any strength, which was obviously needed.

He has that little-boy-lost expression which the females of several countries have already found to be misleading, and seems to be quite incapable of getting to the start of an event on time. On more than one occasion co-driver Peter Bryant had to start up the car, and even drive it up to the starting ramp, before a bashful and rather shame-faced Ari appeared. On the one occasion when he was very early, he even had an excuse: "My watch was wrong!"

Ari had won his first international rally at the amazingly young age of 23 years, and there was obviously so much boundless talent to be harnessed that Peter Ashcroft made haste to keep him under exclusive contract for the next four years. Not that this helped, for luck quite deserted the Finn in the next three seasons – after winning the Arctic at the beginning of 1977, and repeating the performance a year later, he did not actually win another rally in a 'works' car until Cyprus in September 1979.

It was not merely that Vatanen was unlucky, or that he kept on crashing cars (though, to be sure, he suffered both such traumas on several occasions), but that almost everything else seemed to happen to him. If it was not that he was laid low by severe back pains, it was that he was disqualified because his co-driver missed a passage control.

In 1979, however, the tide turned. Ari forged a new partnership with David Richards, who was already a marketing consultant to Rothmans, and the Vatanen-Richards-Rothmans-Escort combination became more and more successful in the next three years. For 1980 he was Rothmans' principal driver in the David Sutton team, though still under contract at Ford, and in 1981 (in spite of having to fit in some Finnish army service) he was even more close to Rothmans.

The results speak for themselves. In 1980 his record reads like this: 2nd, DNF, 2nd, 1st (Welsh), 1st (Acropolis), 2nd, 2nd, 2nd, 2nd, 2nd, DNF, some of those defeats being at the hands of team-mate Hannu Mikkola, and others (such as the 1000 Lakes and San Remo) being in the face of superior machinery.

It was in 1981, however that 'The Vatanen Touch' (to borrow the title of a film made about him, at the time) became so evident. Rothmans set him up as their leading driver in an attack on the World Championship, and as the season progressed they approved entries in more and more events to gain that objective. Aided by truly remarkable physical fitness, and an avowed 'lift' due to a happy home life, and newly developed religious beliefs, his gruelling season was marked with great success. Apart from winning the Welsh rally, in the British series, he competed in no fewer than ten of the twelve World Championship rallies, winning three of them, and taking second place on two others. Even though he was still famous for crashing his cars (retiring twice due to accidents, and finishing the Bandama/Ivory Coast event with a running 'write off'), he was also extremely tenacious and versatile. To win the Acropolis, in Brazil (in a hastily prepared car, replacing that crashed in Argentina), and the Finnish 1000 Lakes, plus taking second in the Swedish and Lombard-RAC events, says it all.

In the end, he chalked up 96 points during the season, compared with Talbot's Guy Frequelin, who amassed 89 – and no other driver won more than twice, this being his ex-team mate Hannu Mikkola in the new four-wheel-drive Audi Quattro.

Vatanen, therefore, became World Champion when 29 years old, and it was a sobering thought that he could remain at the top for at least another ten years. Like most rallying World Champions, he was neither as busy, nor as successful, the following year. Once again, he signed a Ford contract, though as the Rothmans sponsorship had been transferred to Opel he spent the British season driving an Escort RS for MCD Services. That season, I should say, was almost entirely without success (third on the Mintex being the best result), though we were all continually amazed by the pace of the Escorts built for him. There was a fierce commitment present which we had never previously seen, even from Vatanen, and the fact that the Escort was well and truly obsolete by this time did not deter him.

114   It was no wonder that Rothmans, and Opel, made haste to sign him up for

1983. I have no doubt that the best of Vatanen is still to come.

Between 1977 and 1979, however, there is no doubt that Ford's most successful (as opposed to the fastest) driver was Bjorn Waldegard. He came to Boreham at the end of 1976 after spending two successful, but increasingly traumatic, years with Lancia, during which time he had proved to everyone's satisfaction (except, perhaps, his team manager, Cesare Fiorio) that he was the fastest Stratos driver in the world. Life at Lancia, however, had become increasingly 'political', for Sandro Munari (an Italian) was expected to win as long as his car kept going, and this meant that Bjorn had sometimes been instructed to finish behind him to keep the peace! To move to Boreham, where there was only one front-line British driver (Roger Clark) and no team orders, must have been a real relief.

Bjorn's arrival at Boreham coincided with that of Allan Wilkinson as the team's engineer, and the start of a concerted World Championship programme. The Waldegard-Clark-Vatanen line-up was formidable by anyone's standards, but as I make clear on other pages, there was not enough luck on Boreham's side in that season for the Championship to be captured from Fiat.

1977, however, was an extremely successful year for the tall, blond, 33-year-old Swede from Ro, who invariably seemed to be partnered by Hans Thorzelius. Having started at Boreham with third in the 1976 Lombard-RAC, he improved on this with second in Portugal, then capped it all by winning the Safari outright and, a few weeks later, also winning the Acropolis. There was bad luck in the San Remo, when his car handled very badly indeed in the wet on untested tyres and suspension, but at the end of the year he won the Lombard-RAC rally very comfortably indeed. Three major World Championship victories – arguably the three most difficult ones, at that – in his first season!

Throughout that year, too, Waldegard was visibly relaxing, for there were no insane pressures at Boreham, and no chauvinistic pressman to be tolerated. By 1978, when his good friend and rival, Hannu Mikkola, had joined the team, the Swede had become positively benign.

1978 was the 'year of the strike', when Boreham's programme was so sadly cut short in September due to industrial trouble all over the Ford empire, so it was small wonder that Waldegard only won one major event – the snowy Swedish rally on his own home ground – though he also took second place on the Lombard-RAC rally for 'Dealer Team Ford' after, at one point, spinning his car into a very stout tree and choosing, by his own admission, "to go in backwards, because I knew the Escort was strong enough for that!"

It was in 1979, however, that Waldegard had 'his' year, which also coincided with the Escort's best-ever season in World Championship rallying. The cars were absolutely in their prime – fast, strong and versatile – and Peter Ashcroft used Waldegard purely for World Championship events. Like Hannu Mikkola, Waldegard tackled seven events for Ford, and also found time to enter two more (Safari and Bandama) for Mercedes-Benz. In seven events for Ford he did not once retire, his worst finishing position was ninth on, of all events, the Lombard-RAC which he likes so much, but he also notched up two outright wins, three second places, and a third.

The victories came in the Acropolis, (which was enormously fast, hot, and gruelling (his Escort was the only front-line works Ford to finish), and in Quebec, which must have been one of the wettest events on record, while he

115

Roger's greatest win – with Tony Mason in the 1972 RAC Rally. That is his second Esso car – LVX 942J – known affectionately as 'Esso Blue' after its colour scheme

finished second in Monte Carlo, Sweden and Portugal. The cliff-hanging disappointment, of course, came in the Monte, when there is no doubt that Waldegard should have won, and deserved to win.

Driving one of the very special 'tarmac-racing' Escorts (actually, the rebuild of VHK 74S), he swopped the lead at half distance with team-mate Hannu Mikkola (who later fell foul of traffic laws, and the merciless French police), but started the last night of stages driving with a 6min. 27sec. lead over Bernard Darniche's 'private' Lancia Stratos. Ford's tactical error was over tyres (it is now generally agreed that the ideal combination was studded racers, which Ford and Dunlop had not provided), but Waldegard would still have beaten Darniche by a small margin if he had not tackled the penultimate stage, first on the road, and been forced to stop for his co-driver to leap out and move boulders which had been placed by saboteurs to stop him. Nothing was ever done to annul times (this was the Monte Carlo rally, after all, and Darniche was French . . .), Waldegard was dispirited, and eventually lost the rally by a mere six seconds.

At the end of the 1979 season, of course, Boreham officially withdrew from international rallying, having given all their team drivers several months' notice, and a great organisation was effectively broken up. Hannu Mikkola and Ari Vatanen continued to drive arms-length 'works' Escorts for David Sutton; Bjorn Waldegard went off to drive for Fiat, Mercedes-Benz and

Have a drink, you nice car! Timo Makinen and Henry Liddon after Timo's fourth 1000 Lakes win of 1973. Colt? That is a Finnish cigarette, and one of Timo's personal sponsors

Toyota; Roger Clark changed his allegiance for the very first time, to try a Triumph TR8 for BL; Russell Brookes exchanged his Andrews-sponsored Escort RS for an Andrews-sponsored Talbot Sunbeam-Lotus.

If, and when, Ford come back into big-time rallying, they will want to assemble a similar galaxy of stars. My own judgement is that they will find it a very difficult task.

8
Rallying
round
the world

Jumping for joy
after the finish of
the World Cup
Rally is Timo
Makinen's Escort

World Cup Rally start, 1970, for Hannu Mikkola, with Sir Alf Ramsey waving the flag, and John Sprinzel *(second right)* **looking on**

Any follower of athletics will tell you that it isn't easy to train one man to be a sprinter and a marathon runner, not at one and the same time. The same applies to cars. A rally car can usually be developed into a sprint car – a special stage winner – or into a long distance runner. To be excellent at both is not easy.

This is where the Escort flouted all the conventions. Not only have the works cars won just about every important International, but they have also won the East African Safari *and* the London-Mexico World Cup Rally. No other famous rally car can boast about this – and Boreham is very proud of the achievement.

That famous victory in the *Daily Mirror* World Cup Rally came only just in time. In time, that is, to restore Ford's faith in their Escorts. It might seem strange now, but in 1969 the Escort was being outpaced persistently by several other cars. It looked to be at its limit with the Twin-Cam engine, and Ford were desperate for a morale booster.

The *Daily Mirror's* marathon event was much the most professionally-organised of the intercontinental rallies we have yet seen. Its route was settled very early, a high quality entry seemed assured, and with the backing of Britain's largest-sale newspaper there was going to be limitless publicity on tap for the successful cars and crews.

Ford, and Stuart Turner, were never really in any doubt – Ford would be

120

Triumphant procession through Mexico City after the 1970 World Cup Rally. FEV 4H is Timo Makinen's car (5th), and FEV 2H is that driven by Jimmy Greaves and Tony Fall (6th)

entering cars in strength. It was Turner's first experience of the way every activity at Ford is governed by a budget. Only weeks after his arrival at Boreham, from Castrol, he was begging an extra £100,000 or so from Walter Hayes, to rally half way round the world. That, he has sometimes said, was as difficult as planning for victory itself!

He now recalls, with a wry smile, that it was an enormous gamble: "All I can say is, 'Thank God Ford won', or I might just have been out of a job in June 1970, just like that!"

The event would start on 19 April 1970, but by the autumn of 1969 Stuart Turner, Bill Meade and Bill Barnett were already niggling about the cars they would be using. At that stage, indeed, they didn't have a clue. In one period, almost every car made by Ford in Britain or in Germany was considered. Even though a rally Twin-Cam had been sent to South America, there were so many variables to consider, and so many different drivers' opinions . . . . .

Practice crews returned from South America with spine-chilling tales of distance, height and isolation. There were more opinions, and more horror stories, than people. The only solution was a round-table meeting with everybody present.

The venue was London's Excelsior Hotel, close to London Airport, and the occasion was the aftermath of the 1969 RAC Rally. On that day, 20 November, Stuart Turner was determined that the specification of his World Cup cars should be agreed.

121

It could be South America, but in fact this is Northern Italy. Mikkola's car is on the San Remo Prime – but shouldn't he be wearing a crash helmet?

It was a meeting without auspicious omens. Ford had had rather a poor season. Hannu Mikkola had won the Thousand Lakes, but the entire team had retired from the Alpine Rally, while the best RAC Rally result had been Ove Andersson's fourth place. Ironically, Andersson was not being retained for 1970 . . . .

There were no homologation restrictions; there were several possibilities. A German Taunus (driven by Robin Hillyar) had won the Safari that year, Roger Clark had tried out a Ford Zodiac on the Three Cities, while the Lotus-Cortina was still in production.

It was a long meeting, very long. At first the team's Finns – Mikkola and Makinen – asked for cars with V6 engines. They wanted low-revving torquey engines, not needing any tuning. Roger Clark had already tried a 'prototype' Escort in the Alpine, with the German Taunus vee-6 (of 2.3-litres), but company politics suggested that a British-made 'Essex' 3-litre might be preferable.

All the initial discussion revolved round engines, because it was engines which had ruined Boreham's London-Sydney Marathon efforts in 1968. For that reason, Twin-Cams were never considered seriously. They would have to be rally-tuned to give the desired performance, and with doubtful petrol forecast for South America the risks were too great.

The fatigue shows for car and driver, near the end of the World Cup Rally, with Gunnar Palm driving and Hannu Mikkola still finding time to wave

The BDA was considered, but rejected, mainly because (in November 1969) it was still not in production, and was quite unproved.

It was Peter Ashcroft, newly returned from Ford of Germany, who crystallized the choice. Bill Meade wanted to see either a German V6 or a BDA installed, Stuart Turner was willing to consider anything but a BDA, and Henry Taylor (then at the embryo Advanced Vehicle Operations factory) was pushing for a high-output push-rod engine.

It was Gunnar Palm and Roger Clark's views on speeds which helped. They had come back from early recces with the opinion that 120mph cruising speeds were not needed. That had been one point on which the V6 engine choice hinged. When Palm suggested that 100mph would be enough, but that easy service and repair were vital, Ashcroft's mind was made up.

"I looked at Holbay's push-rod 1600 which they were building for the Lotus Seven," says Ashcroft, "and I thought that with our knowledge of siamesed blocks we could stretch it to an 1800."

A guess, without factual backing, was that 140bhp could be guaranteed, and this was the clincher. The question of servicing settled it. Getting the head off a Twin-Cam or a BDA, changing gaskets or whatever, and replacing everything, would have taken far too long. Ashcroft, and deep-thinking drivers like Rauno Aaltonen, were attracted by the idea of an engine that, at a pinch,

123

Old rally cars never die – they just go off and win out-of-the-way rallies. After the works cars finished 1–2–3 in Hong Kong in 1972 the Ford importers (Harpers) were very glad to buy two of them!

could accept any flat-top cylinder head from any Ford anywhere in South America. It was Rauno, in fact, who put this decision to the test – his car needed a head change before going into *Parc Ferme* in Santiago, and it was accomplished in a mere 45 minutes.

Sorting out the engine took little time: "We produced three versions – an 1800, an 1840 and a 1900 – but to get the 1900 capacity we had to 'stroke' the engine as well, so I rejected that," Peter Ashcroft told me. "We developed two or three different heads, took 30 or 40 power curves to settle a spec., decided that time was short, and settled on a simple tune which gave an easy 140bhp."

Choosing the car, in the end, was a decision settled by Roger Clark. He had already won his class in the Three Cities in a British Vita-prepared Zodiac (and said it was "like being captain of an aircraft carrier"), but he had also been practising in South America. The event would be so long – 16,000 miles all told – that it was easy to assume the need for a three-man crew. But Clark had completed London-to-Sydney very happily with Ove Andersson, and was convinced that a two-man crew was enough.

Turner wanted to know if he was sure? "Sure, absolutely," said Roger, "it's high, it's horrible, and the drops sometimes are quite unbelievable. But a two-man crew in a light Escort can crack it – and I don't think I'm going to need high-altitude oxygen either!"

So that was that. Escorts would be used, wth enlarged 'Kent' engines, and with only two in the crew. The choice of other major components – five-speed ZF gearboxes, and the modified Capri 'Atlas' back axle – followed logically. The ZF box, as detailed elsewhere in this book, has had several different Escort versions; on this occasion it would have the original 'noddy' ratios, complete with an overdrive fifth ratio.

Henry Liddon and Jim Gavin drove across the Sahara, laying out the route for the UDT
World Cup Rally. Naturally they used an Escort RS2000

How to make a temporary repair for a London-Mexico Escort's axle – with angle iron. This was how two cars were kept going from France to Portugal. The dural axle brace was developed in a week while the cars were being shipped to Brazil

Turner, Barnett, and others all agree – it was this three hour meeting, more than any other, which set the stage for Ford's London-Mexico success. Comments within Ford are that if other teams had done as much analysis at that time, then they might have been more competitive. The rigid decision to use two-man crews is still seen as decisive; without it, the choice of an Escort would not have been practical.

Originally, Ford's assault was to have been with a strong four-car team. Stuart Turner, exercising an idiosyncrasy, persuaded his administrators to find a set of easily-remembered registrations, FEV 1H, 2H, 3H and 4H would be for the World Cup (and incidentally 5H, 6H, 7H and 8H were allocated to a new set of 1970 Monte cars).

Crews settled down as follows:

FEV 1H	Hannu Mikkola and Gunnar Palm	*(Telegraph Magazine* support)
FEV 2H	Jimmy Greaves and Tony Fall	(Springfield Boys Club support)
FEV 3H	Roger Clark and Alec Poole	*(Shoot Football Weekly* support)
FEV 4H	Timo Makinen and Gilbert Staepelaere	*(Daily Telegraph* support)

126   It was a formidable team, but by the time the build programme was under

way, after the Monte Carlo Rally, three more cars had been added. This made a total works entry of seven Escorts, and the 'second division' was:

FTW 46H	Rauno Aaltonen and Henry Liddon	*Daily Express* support)
FTW 47H	Colin Malkin and Richard Hudson-Evans	*(Sunday Express* support)
FTW 48H	Sobieslaw Zasada and Marek Wachowski	

Few of these names need introduction. Jimmy Greaves, recently-retired football star, might originally have been recruited for publicity, but well before the end of the event had proved to be a very capable driver; Tony Fall, however, would drive the Primes which were expected to settle the event. Colin Malkin, though very much the 'new boy', had been third crew member in the London-Sydney winning Hillman Hunter.

Bill Meade, Mick Jones, and the other mechanics, have probably never worked harder than they did between February and April. Not only did they have to build seven impregnable rally cars, but repeatedly they had to fettle a series of tired test and practice cars, build up and pack mountains of spares for airfreighting to Europe and South America, and find time to accept medical jabs, update passports and visas – not to mention preparing cars for the normal European events as well.

One of the set of 'ETWs' spent days and days at Bagshot on test, finally with Meade-invented roll bar/buffalo bar which distinguishes these Escorts from any other. Another ETW – '880G' had taken time off from a South American recce for Tony Fall to win the Rally of the Incas in Peru.

In the event, it was all a bit too much for Boreham to tackle. Initial build of the 'second division' cars was farmed out, very successfully, to Clarke and Simpson, British Vita, and Clarks of Narborough. They must have done a good job too – two finished, and the third was eliminated by a main road crash in Yugoslavia.

Bill Barnett, on his own admission, was nearly driven mad by his mountainous planning task. A 'Barnett-bible' for any European event might run to 50 pages; for the World Cup, covering six weeks, 16,000 miles and dozens of countries, it was vastly bigger, and had to be issued in several sections.

Added to the usual problems of getting valuable parts into and out of countries was that of getting rally cars through them. How, for instance, should he cope with regulations in Brazil – where importing cars was virtually impossible, and re-export almost unthinkable? How to get transit visas for his crews from the country of Guatemala, which had no diplomatic representation in Britain at all? How to plan for the fact that at least one local war, across frontiers to be used in the rally, was in progress?

Getting round the world, without cars, was hardly less difficult. As a travelling controller for the *Daily Mirror*, on several occasions I changed planes at some unlikely South American airport, and fleetingly saw tired-looking Boreham mechanics going the other way, or occasionally on the same planes.

Invariably they carried personal luggage, tool bags, and sinister-looking heavy holdalls which rattled. It was quite surprising how many major items like differentials and axle shafts passed through customs posts labelled as personal baggage!

127

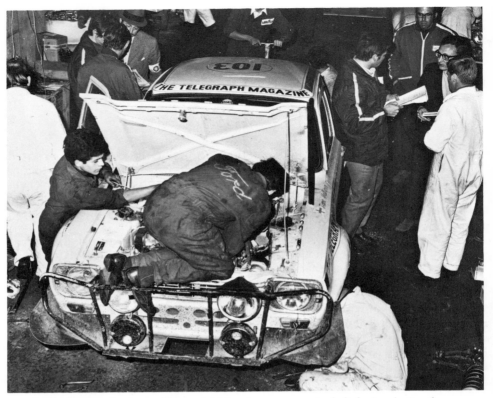

Everybody, but everybody, working on Makinen's car at a service halt during the South American section of the World Cup Rally

It is now history that the world's most difficult rally was an Escort triumph. Of seven cars entered, five finished, and the other two were forced out by accidents. An errant truck (with sleeping driver) mowed down Colin Malkin's car near Belgrade, while Roger Clark's machine was buried into the back of an innocent VW Beetle by co-driver Alec Poole. *"Five for the Fiesta"* was Ford's title for the commemorative film, and that tells us everything.

Bill Meade takes much credit for the cars' specification. For weeks he fought and fought to keep their weight down. With mechanical details settled, his other problem was to resist drivers' attempts to pile more and more details into their cars. Timo and Rauno, with ultimate reliability in mind, were the worst offenders.

Everything, after all, weighed more than standard. The axles were more bulky, the crossmember more solid, the ZF gearbox bigger than standard, and fuel tank capacity up to 28 gallons, and the spares load increased. Light alloy doors, no bumpers, and other details, all helped, but in the end the cars weighed in at around a ton – more than 200lb over a rally car's usual fighting weight.

That extra weight, unexpectedly, gave rise to a big problem. Rough Yugoslavian roads, and the jumping involved, caused the previously impregnable Atlas axles to bend. Indeed, on Roger Clark's car, it not only bent, but broke completely into two pieces. The tube had snapped away from the cast differential casing, needed much wayside welding and bodging and they made Lisbon with little time to spare. The Greaves/Fall car suffered similar problems, and the start of a major epidemic was feared.

At Lisbon, after one week's rallying, and five fairly short Primes, Mikkola's car was second, behind Trautmann's Citroen; the lowest of six factory cars, Clark's was placed sixteenth.

Not that Clark was to get any rest while cars were on the high seas. The day after arrival, he and Bill Meade flew back post-haste to England, where a dramatically-rushed development job awaited. An Escort would be sent to Bagshot, and driven round and round by Clark. Their task was to devise an axle support which would solve the tube-snapping problem.

The work itself took less than a week, and could produce only a crude solution; there was no time for elegance. If axles bent, and eventually broke, they must be stiffened externally. A rigid, lightweight, brace was needed. Not only that – it would have to be duplicated very quickly for six cars, and all would have to be taken to Rio de Janiero by mechanics.

There was no time to deal with normal customs formalities. The braces must be able to be packed into suitcases. Personal luggage was going to be suspiciously heavy – but fortunately the Brazilian authorities were in a very friendly mood that week; they were sportsmen, and were enjoying the European invasion.

Clark's repeated Bagshot high-jumps, and Len Bailey's 'blacksmith engineering' gave rise to the familiar axle brace. This light alloy plate, fixed between axle differential casting and the cover plate, and clamping to the tubes themselves, did the job in no uncertain manner. Once in the build schedule, it persisted until the end of 1975. Only then, after time to re-engineer the axle's structure, did the cautious Boreham team decide it could finally be deleted.

In that first, European, week, with 4,000 miles of rallying, the Escorts fared well – and badly. Completion of cars had been late, and rushed. Some drivers, ever-pernickety with final requests, had mechanics working late into the night before scrutineering. Inevitably, there were shake-down troubles.

Makinen's car shed teeth from its distributor drive, and then damaged its camshaft, on the very first Prime, but kept going to Monza where the engine was rebuilt. Zasada's car, though, had eaten a piston on the way to scrutineering, which meant a last-minute engine swop. Apart from the axle problems, Aaltonen's car had suffered a cracked gearbox tail cover.

Mikkola, for his part, was thundering through without a care in the world. He was so fast that at one point co-driver Gunnar Palm opened his door and threatened to get out unless the exuberant Finn slowed down! There were, after all, 16,000 miles to go!

Mikkola's problem was that although he was faster overall than Trautmann at Lisbon, several Primes had been cleanable; Trautmann had been faster on the roughest one. With a lot of sponsor's money already changing hands at Lisbon, Mikkola was not happy . . . .

From 8 May to 27 May, the event wound its way round South and Central America, with only occasional night halts (at Montevideo, Santiago, La Paz and Lima), a boat trip round the Darien Isthmus to Panama, and innumerable frontiers to be crossed. The team re-started from Rio in second (Mikkola), fourth (Makinen), ninth (Aaltonen), tenth (Fall), twelfth (Zasada) and sixteenth (Clark) places.

Drama came almost at once. Trautmann crashed his big Citroen, and

Clark's Escort was eliminated, almost before the crews were used to the South American conditions.

The event was so immensely long that one's normal perspective of time and distance was destroyed. Rauno Aaltonen's car was fastest over the Rio – Montevideo sector, only a pipe-opener, but with very handsome cash prizes.. "And so there should be," said Rauno, "after all, the mileage was longer than that of the average European event."

For him, incidentally, that had also involved giving a Montevideo policeman a lift to sort out a local gunfight and chase!

From then on, things improved steadily for Ford. On the 560 mile Argentinian Prime (and that is no misprint) Mikkola's leading Escort very nearly collected an ambulance head on, as it sped against rally traffic on its way to Andrew Cowan's accident. Aaltonen's car needed a new cylinder head in Chile, while the Greaves/Fall crew and car suffered ten punctures on the rough, very high, Peruvian Prime.

Zasada fared even worse; on the same Prime his car needed a new front strut. Ford's emergency service sited in the middle of the stage had no suitable spare. Nothing daunted, the resourceful Pole took a drum-braked standard-settings item from the Escort in attendance at that point, and wallowed off with the only three-disc-brake Escort in the world.

Greaves and Fall hit and killed a horse in Panama, but this was nothing to their earlier troubles. Near the end of one stage the wheel nuts on one wheel had sheared, and the car was driven, pushed and (against the regulations) towed for some distance on three wheels. Makinen's car suffered the same trouble, but the inventive Finn solved them by jamming a plug spanner into place where it could best help.

After the sea trip from Buenaventura to Panama, it was nearly all over, with the Escorts well and truly in command. Hours before the boat had left, there were Ford panics when Mikkola's car was found to have an empty dry sump oil tank, even though nobody owned up to draining it. Without tell-tale pools on the ground and no other evidence of sabotage, it was, and remains, one of life's little mysteries.

In the end, the finish was one very happy occasion. All the works cars, except Clark's which had started from Rio, raced hilariously through the streets of Mexico City to the finish at the football stadium. Everybody enjoyed it, that is, except Ford photographer Ken Shipton, who fell out of the boot of a moving car while taking action pictures of the winning car . . . . .

Mikkola's winning margin over the second place Triumph 2.5PI was 1 hr 18min. Aaltonen took third place, Makinen fifth, Greaves sixth, Zasada eighth to notch up an astonishing finish record. Incidentally, there was one other Escort finisher – Doug Harris and Michael Butler – who rolled serenely up to the final control, *57 hours* more in arrears than the winning car!

Whatever happened afterwards would be an anti-climax, and for years it looked as if there would never be a longer or more demanding event. Another World Cup Rally was held in 1974, of course, but attracted no important works entries of any type. Boreham loaned a single Escort (to Andrew Cowan), but he like most other competitors suffered grievous mechanical damage along with a lot of navigational trouble in the sandy wastes of the Sahara.

It would have been enough for the Escort's reputation if it had never tackled another monster event (and did not the Escort Mexico arise from the ideas incorporated in the London-Mexico cars?). However, Ford's and Stuart

Turner's eyes were always enviously fixed on success in the East African Safari. For 1971, and for the first time with Escorts, a full-scale assault was planned.

Ford, of course, knew all about the Safari. They had entered Zephyrs in the 1950s, and Anglias in the early 1960s, with some success. In 1964 a strong Cortina GT entry was rewarded by Peter Hughes' outright win, and the manufacturers' team award. Vic Preston's works-loaned cars took several class wins, but a 1967 outright victory was lost at the last hour when Jack Simonian's GT lost an argument with a wild animal.

Ford of Germany scooped the pool in 1969 with a Taunus 20MRS (Robin Hillyar), but failed miserably a year later when all three Capris were forced out.

For 1971, with Escort prestige running high, Stuart Turner was relishing the idea of a full-scale Safari attack. But not just any victory would do – he also wanted to prove that the event could be won by a European driver. East Africans had won the previous 18 Safaris, thought their local knowledge and cunning was essential to success, and were getting insufferably cocky about it.

The Escorts nearly didn't make the start at all. Ford's disastrous nine-week production line strike, over a new pay contract, came at exactly the wrong time. Apart from the problem of getting parts to Boreham, there was the fact that all budgets would have to be cut back. As we shall see in the next chapter, only the combined personalities of Turner and Walter Hayes kept any sort of programme going at all.

Works Escorts had never been 'on Safari' before, though Lotus-Cortinas had. This, plus the fact that the RS1600s were not really established as rally cars, led to a very controversial decision. Even though the Escort Twin-Cam was obsolete, this was the variant chosen for the Safari. It was a miscalculation which Boreham people are still not happy to admit. Put quite simply, the Escorts were outpaced; it was a mistake not to be repeated in 1972.

In spite of including every legal feature from the World Cup cars, which meant that the cars were very strong indeed, the 1.8-litre Twin-Cam engines were detuned to about 140bhp (on a 10.4 to 1 compression ratio). The valve burning episodes experienced on the London-Sydney Marathon by Lotus-Cortinas had never been forgotten, and East African petrol could still not be trusted.

There were no fewer than six Boreham-built cars. Originally a five-car entry was planned, but Sears Roebuck, the giant American mail order concern, came up with sponsorship for Robin Hillyar to use their 'own-brand' tyres. The cars, except for Vic Preston Junior's (an ex-Makinen RAC Rally car), were brand-new, and carried the now legendary LVX registration series.

The event, for Ford, was an almost unmitigated disaster. Singh's car seized its gearbox selectors, Clark's broke engine mountings, Makinen's had suspension damage then broke a propshaft, and Mikkola's finally disappeared with a blown engine gasket. The cars were always struggling for pace against very rapid Datsun 240Zs, but Mikkola had pulled up to within 30 minutes of the leader when the engine let go.

Two cars finished – Hillyar fourth and Vic Preston sixth – and ironically it was the 'last minute' Sears Roebuck car which produced the best results. There were two consolations – that Singh's gearbox problems, compounded by the time taken to get the box out of the car, led to Boreham's developing a quick-change conversion, and that the same car would eventually achieve enormous glory in Roger Clark's hands. But that, all that, was for 1972/73.

One of the unlucky 1971 Safari Twin-Cams (Hannu Mikkola driving) which all, later, became RS1600s

For 1972, Ford were determined not to make the same errors. Their programme was decided good and early, their decision to take RS1600s was both right and good marketing policy, and their experience even more marked. There was no way they were to be beaten for pace in 1972 – even with a bit of the obligatory de-tuning to suit African conditions, engine-specialist Peter Ashcroft and builder Brian Hart would be able to guarantee 205bhp that should 'run for ever'.

As usual, there would be a set of brand-new cars for the Safari – a quartet of the RWC . . . series – with, once again, the addition of a fifth machine. As in 1971 Robin Hillyar would be a driver, but the entry (of REV 119K – the ex-Piot Monte car) would be in the name of Mark Birley of the plushy Annabels club. Walter Hayes, in a fit of generosity, had donated the entry as a competition prize.

Practice was made easier because two of the LVX cars were still in Africa, plus a couple of rather battered Mexicos from 1971. The team – Mikkola, Makinen, Singh and Preston Junior, almost picked itself. Bill Barnett's 'Bible', if anything, was even thicker and more detailed than usual. The cars would have two-way radios for the first time, as would Stuart Turner's 'spotter' plane, hired to Ford by BillParkinson.

In 1972 there was no mistake for Mikkola. This shot, incidentally, was taken from a light aeroplane, and the car was actually overtaking it!

This time there was no mistake. The Safari is a very tough event, so Ford's five car challenge did not bring a blanket victory. Even so, with a non-African winning for the first time, and four cars finishing strongly, it was all that Turner and Barnett could have wished. This time their performance was outstandingly good. The cars, and their crews, lined up as follows:

RWC 455K	Hannu Mikkola/Gunnar Palm
RWC 456K	Timo Makinen/Henry Liddon
RWC 457K	Joginder Singh/S.Sembi
RWC 458K	Vic Preston Junior/Bev Smith
REV 119K	Robin Hillyar/Mark Birley

Once again the big Datsuns and Zasada's singleton Porsche 911S were the main rivals. A team of three Alpine-Renaults had been scratched before the start. Not that Ford were worrying about performance. Not this year. 117mph was possible in fifth gear, while first was a 30mph 'stump puller'. 8,500rpm was the BDA's safe limit, 7,500rpm more normal for endurance usage.

The seeding had put Timo's car at No. 2, and Mikkola's at No. 7 – a great advantage on this event, which promised to be a very dusty one indeed.

133

Hannu Mikkola losing a wheel in the 1972 Olympia Rally. Incidentally, this ex-Safari car started the event with RWC 456K on the tail, which is correct, and RWC 456J on the front of the car, which isn't! *(photo Hugh Bishop)*

Right from the start, it was Mikkola who set a blistering pace. Even so, Makinen's car led him at two controls, and after trouble with front struts loosening in their mounts, and a bad batch of stretching fan belts, found himself 20 minutes adrift of Hermann's big Datsun at the Nairobi rest halt. 'Junior' was behind him, but the others lagging behind that.

After the second leg, Mikkola led from Zasada's Porsche by a mere four minutes, and Preston's car still lay third. All manner of Safari problems, from punctures to wheels coming adrift, vast pot holes causing bent steering racks, and simple navigational errors, were delaying the survivors. Singh, for the second year, had been unlucky; his car had suffered the same strut problems, then flown off the road and broken the differential housing.

The third sector saw Mikkola's lead stretched to 15 minutes, Preston hanging on to third, and the resourceful Hillyar/Birley car pushed up to fifth. In the meantime, Makinen was still trying hard . . . .

The rest of the rally was a matter of pacing oneself. Zasada's deficit was increased – to 19 minutes, Preston held on, and the remarkable Annabels car elbowed its way up to fourth. Timo's drive, after many troubles, was rewarded with eighth.

There were 18 finishers – and only one of the others (Brian Culcheth's Triumph 2.5PI) was British.

Back in Britain it was bedlam. The World Cup had been one thing, but a win in the Safari was quite another. There was, after all, the beating of the tradition to celebrate. Mikkola was the first European to win a Safari, and he had done it in such a cultured manner. But let's remember, of course, that superbly mature co-driving by the experienced Gunnar Palm had a lot to do with it, while the weeks and weeks of preparation and practice had been invaluable.

The statistics make good reading. Four service support 'barges' – Corsairs – had been airfreighted out from London. Eight of Boreham's best mechanics had followed them. They achieved miracles in the bush, helped by 55 locally-manned static service points. Turner's spotter plane (with Mick Jones, Robin Vokins, Peter Ashcroft and Don Partington also aboard), had made 31 flights and spent 46 hours in the air. Ford had found out, over many years, that there was no substitute for being prepared.

The aftermath was interesting. Two of the cars were in such good condition (456K and 457K) that they were flown back to Europe, and sent off to do the Acropolis with little attention. Mikkola and Palm were feted at a lavish reception in London – where Palm to his astonishment found that Walter Hayes had decided to 'retire' him, and to give him a new job in Ford Sweden!

It was all so smoothly organised that there was no doubt about 1973. It would be another flat out attack. The only major difference would be that yet another set of new cars (the five XPU . . . series) would have the latest alloy-block 2-litre engines, and that Roger Clark would get his team place back. Peter Shiyukah, a high official in the Kenyan government, would also have one of the cars.

Like 1971, though, the trip was a bit of a disaster for the company. Only a single car finished, and that – Preston's XPU 217L – was in a lowly 14th. But in parts it was not without glory.

Right from the start, Roger Clark began to pull out a big lead. After the first leg he had more than 30 minutes on any other competitor, but this may have been too much for his car, which shortly shed its steering rack, and later consumed its alternator electrical system. Timo Makinen had an enormous accident, in which the car rolled so often that the bemused crew didn't even know which way to drive again when they got the battered Escort back on its wheels!

Hannu Mikkola, unluckiest of all, led for a time later in the event, but also suffered mechanical breakdowns, and was forced to retire. The Shiyukah entry was rarely in contention, and retired on the first day.

Since then, there has not been a full team assault on more recent Safaris. The budget was in no state to go in 1975 and a 1976 entry was cancelled in favour of more cost-effective European and African events. The Safari, like many other extravaganzas, is costing its way out of sight.

Although the factory team was never directly involved in the disastrously under-organised World Cup Rally of 1974, nevertheless a Boreham car did appear. First of all, Henry Liddon and Jim Gavin used a rally-prepared RS2000 to recce the African section – from Algeria down to Nigeria, then back across the Sahara desert to Tunis.

The same car, rebuilt, but rather mysteriously re-registered, was then loaned to White Horse Whisky for Andrew Cowan and Johnstone Syer to drive in the event.

The entry itself, apart from a handful of competitive-looking Citroens and Peugeot 504s, was of such doubtful quality that the Escort started as a very hot favourite indeed, – which just goes to prove that where long distance rallies are

Andrew Cowan's White Horse Whisky RS2000 at the beginning of the UDT World Cup Rally of 1974. Axle failure in the middle of the Sahara ruined its chances

REV 119K led a hard but happy life. Fifth on the Monte (Piot), fourth on the Safari (Hillyar) then first on the Scottish (Mikkola) — all in six months. This is journalist Hamish Cardno in the other seat

concerned you should never trust the form book. Cowan himself, Marathon winner in 1968, was certainly well up to the job of winning, but on entering the roughest roads the Algerian Sahara could provide, the wretched 'Escort broken axle' problem reared its ugly head, in spite of the fact that his car had all the very latest works modifications.

At one stage one axle tube had parted company with the differential casing altogether, and 'in all' five half shafts were needed on that side of the car. Cowan struggled on, even putting up ftd on five of the 18 special stages, and was credited with 15th position overall. Not that this was in any way close to the winning Citroen; Cowan's total penalty was more than 300 *hours!*

9

RS rampant

The only surprising thing about the RS1600's success story is that it took so long to get started. The car was foreseen in 1969, announced early in 1970, and won its first event in March, but even as late as Easter the following year the factory still chose Twin-Cam engines for their first Escort assault on the East African Safari. It was, somehow, as if Ford didn't trust themselves to do a good tuning job on the new-fangled 16-valve engines at first.

Once properly developed, of course, the BDA engine was quite peerless. While nobody had been able to make even the 1800cc version of a Twin-Cam produce 200bhp with much reliability, a stretched BDA beat that achievement within months. Once pushed even further out – to 2 litres with the aid of Brian Hart's light-alloy cylinder block – the possibilities were far-reaching. Nowadays, of course, the BDA is a favourite in many classes of competition.

At first, though, the build up to dominance took time. Inevitably it was Roger Clark who was entrusted with the first experimental car. In an Escort which had already tackled the Monte Carlo rally as a Twin-Cam (seventh in Makinen's hands), and hastily converted to BDA power, he won the 1970 Circuit of Ireland by a big margin from Chris Sclater's ex-works Twin-Cam.

Even so, for a time that was the only encouragement. Another converted ex-Monte Twin-Cam blew its engine on the Scottish, while the Circuit machine, which had meantime won the Thousand Lakes as a Twin-Cam, again blew up in the TAP Rally – poor Roger was the victim on both occasions.

Only one of the three new team cars for the RAC Rally was given a BDA engine, and guess what? Clark was the driver, and the car retired – on this occasion suffering from the epidemic of half shaft breakages which also eliminated the team's Twin-Cams.

At about the same time, and quite unconnected with the build-up of experience of RS1600s, Ford made a very important change of supplier. At the end of 1970, Boreham switched its allegiance on tyre equipment from Goodyear to Dunlop. The switch was certainly not because Goodyear were falling behind in technical development – no one could complain on that score – but for more complicated 'political' reasons.

Ford had rallied with Dunlop for many years, switching over to Goodyear from the winter of 1965/66. Towards the end of 1970, however, a most significant event took place. Dunlop decided to withdraw from Grand Prix racing – and the corollary of this was that Jackie Stewart decided to throw in his lot with Goodyear.

Repercussions were immediate, Goodyear's competition programme was obviously going to expand to cope with the ultra-professional Scot's demands, while Dunlop for their part made it quite clear that they would place most of their technical emphasis on the development of new road tyres.

Stuart Turner's conclusion was that while Goodyear would be very stretched to look after Jackie Stewart and a major rallying programme, Dunlop would now be ideal partners in the future. Therefore, with what looked like perfect bonhomie on all sides, Boreham's boots began to be shod with Dunlop tyres from the beginning of 1971.

Dunlop soon made good their promise of technical co-operation on rallying tyres. While they, and their customers, had been happy to use SPs and SP Weathermasters for some years, it soon became clear that Ford (and particularly Timo Makinen) had other ideas. Timo, now in his prime as a driver *and* as a compulsive car-improver, got stuck into an intensive rough-road tyre programme with Dunlop. The result, quite supreme for some years, was the famous M and S, of variable tread width.

After being thoroughly trounced by Porsche and Alpine-Renault in 1970, Ford didn't even bother to enter Escorts for the 1971 Monte; a year earlier they had been sure they would be using GT70s, but these cars were not ready. Instead, they chose a full-scale entry of six cars for the East African Safari, all with Twin-Cam engines. Significantly, for they had no more than 155bhp available, the cars were effectively beaten for pace.

That Safari defeat was the last straw. Whatever their lingering doubts about the 16-valve BDAs might have been, Stuart Turner, Peter Ashcroft and Bill Barnett now had to admit that the Twin-Cam's competitive days were over. Even by then, early in 1971, it looked as if the idea of a GT70 was better than the actual car – henceforth, the RS1600 with its Brian Hart-built engines would be their front-line competition car.

Historically, therefore, KHK 597J – as used by Roger Clark in the 1970 RAC Rally, and several times in Britain during 1971 – is important as the first 'works' RS1600 built from scratch at Boreham. Previous cars had all been 'conversions' from Twin-Cams.

Right away, it seemed, Ford could look forward to using *much* faster team cars – and they could also promise better and potentially race-winning performance to Ralph Broad's works-backed team. Once reliability was found, in rally use a 1.8-litre's potential leapt from around 160bhp to around 200bhp, and the rev-band increased by at least 1,000rpm.

Torque at all speeds was vastly improved, and maintained much more strongly at high rpm. For circuit racing, Broadspeed's car – actually registered MEV 34J but usually appearing on the tracks as 'RS1600' – boasted 245bhp, not far off the best of Keith Duckworth's single-seater Formula Two FVA units.

More important, even, than the engine's extra power potential was the way in which the RS1600 was homologated. Although the BDA engine used the same basic block and crank as the many thousands of Cortina 'Kent' engines, Ford made its tolerances add up differently. Instead of 1,599cc, it would be 1,601cc.

It's quicker if you go the shortest way! Gerry Marshall right behind Roger Clark in the 1974 Tour of Britain. They finished the event in the same order, with Clark winning outright *(photo Colin Taylor)*

Roger Clark only rallied an RS2000 once in the forests – in the 1974 Mintex Dales event, which he just managed to win. Roger Willis, commentating, has ruderies for the crowd to hear . . . .

This difference, a tiny two cc in round figures, and even less if the actual dimensions were quoted in miniscule decimals, did nothing for the power output, but everything for the car – instead of a 1.6-litre contender it could theoretically be a 2-litre, and *that* was inportant.

I have already pointed out that Ford were not interested in class wins, but only in outright victory. With the Twin Cams, eventually, they had a problem. The Lotus engine was inescapably homologated at 1,558cc, and the car tied to the 1,600cc class; only the increasingly rare 'prototype' classes could allow enlarged engines to be used.

With the RS1600, obviously, there was going to be no such problem. Engineering permitting, it could be pushed right out, and made as close to a 2-litre as possible.

Even so, Ford were still faced with the fact that their blocks, even in much-modified cast iron 'Ashcroft' form, were already being stretched to their feasible limit. The BDA's block was deeper and rather different from the Twin-Cam, but the cylinder spacings and the general disposition of cast iron was the same. In 1971, they knew of no way to enlarge it much beyond 1,800cc without beginning to lose out on reliability.

It was something which worried Peter Ashcroft very much. They would be going straight in to racing and rallying with 1.8-litre units, and for the future could look forward to no more than minor tuning changes – new camshafts, improved breathing, and altered carburation. To beat Porsche, Lancia and BMW at their own game the BDA *must* one day be given bigger lungs through which to breathe. More cubic capacity meant more torque, more torque meant better driveability, and this might mean fresher drivers and fewer accidents.

The short-term, in Formula Two, was serious. Some tuners refused to admit to a practical limit, and built a series of glass-fragile 1900 and 1950cc FVAs. Either they blew up for lack of rigidity if bored too far, or wouldn't revolve fast enough if given longer strokes. BMW, for their part, with 'natural' 2-litre engines, were delighted, and started to mop up all the business.

For better or worse, Ford's 1971 competition season turned out to be a very quiet one. With the GT70 in the offing it had been planned that way in any case, as far as the Escort was concerned, but in the event there was a much more depressing reason. The factory had to suffer a desperately draining nine-week strike over pay in the spring, and to keep the company on any sort of even keel for the rest of the year every department's budget was cut to ribbons.

Whatever Boreham might have planned, the accountants' cruel, if logical policies, put a stop to it. Bill Barnett spent more time cancelling events and entries than he did even organising them, and it must have tried his drivers' patience to the very limit. One of the new RS1600s sent to Finland specifically for Timo Makinen and Hannu Mikkola to use was hurredly re-called.

Ford did not, however, shut down their 'works' competition involvement completely. Stuart Turner's elevation to become the supremo for motor sport all over Europe had seen to that. To keep Boreham as busy as ever, Ford speedily expanded their European programme at the expense of a Boreham-based rallying programme – and got the separate subsidiaries to pay. It meant that for the first time any Ford of Europe company could have a race or rally car built at Boreham, for their own use.

The team's rally drivers would be kept as busy as possible. All three – Clark, Makinen and Mikkola – would get a trip to the Safari at Easter, but thereafter would almost be confined to their own countries. Roger Clark petrified the

Roger Clark's first Esso car – 'Old Gold'. For him it was an old car, as it had already done the 1971 French season for Piot *(photo Colin Taylor)*

British rallying 'circus' by turning up to do many more events than usual, establishing a pattern which is still evolving.

Boreham, at this time, built no fewer than 16 new cars in sequence – 13 of them in the well-known LVX...J series (and five of these were new Twin-Cams intended for the Safari). The other LVX cars went to countries like Belgium, Holland, Denmark and Switzerland where they spent their year racing. One – the first one, LVX 941J – was intended for Jean-Francois Piot's rallying programme with Ford France.

This car, incidentally, later achieved fame as Roger Clark's celebrated 'Old Gold' car (or 'Golden Oldie', as one wag christened it before it was finally pensioned off) but started life being built up by Johnnie Rule at Boreham. He then commuted to and from Paris to keep the car in trim, while Jim Porter was sent out to France both to organise the company's French competition programme, and to co-drive Piot in nearly all his events.

Apart from the Safari entry (described already in Chapter 8), the first half of 1971 was very quiet indeed. There was more activity later in the year but Ford's team entries were almost entirely missing.

It was a year which most of these concerned are happy to forget – and not only because of the budget cuts. It would be quite wrong to suggest that the general air of gloom at Ford affected the cars built at Boreham, but certainly the general atmosphere of rather frantically active poverty must have had an effect.

In the whole of 1971 the Boreham-based RS1600s did not win a single event on their own. The only successes were Staepelaere's RS1600 win in the Dutch rally, and for Cypriot Ford importer Chris Kirmitsis who 'borrowed' KHK 598J to win his country's own international rally.

The gloom was so persistent that Stuart Turner took the unprecedented step of calling a press conference in December 1971 to talk about Ford's future programme, where he was happy to say, most emphatically, "I would like to quash *any* rumours that we are pulling out of rallying." He then went on to list the programme of events, and the drivers already contracted to compete in them.

The accent was still very firmly on Escorts, almost entirely on RS1600s, though Gill Fortescue-Thomas would be racing a Mexico and even rallying on occasions. About the mid-engined GT70, which had not exactly covered itself in glory during 1971, there was little to say. Four cars had been built, of which one was a show car and another a development hack. There were still no plans for production, even at AVO, on any scale . . .

One innovation was that Boreham, for the first time on its own account, was intending to campaign an Escort in touring car events, rather than have Broadspeed look after everthing. Broadspeed would continue to be involved in the British series, but a new car (never registered) was earmarked for Gerry Birrell to drive in the European Touring Car Challenge. At the events themselves, Cologne's Jochen Neerpasch would control the car.

The rallying programme started with a bang. Two new cars were entered for the Monte Carlo Rally, no longer with any dreams of winning the event outright, but of annexing the Touring Car category. This they did, with Piot's BP-sponsored car taking fifth place overall, after Makinen's Pepsi-Cola-sponsored car had retired with engine troubles.

Only a matter of days later, Clark and Makinen flew out to Hong Kong, were re-united with two old works RS1600s, and proceeded to dominate the tight little international event in that far-flung corner of the Empire. Timo was first, Clark second, and local man Ted Moorat third in another of Boreham's machines. It was all very brisk, very effortless, and very satisfactory. The local Ford importers, who had sponsored the expedition, were delighted.

The 1972 Escorts were settling down into a well-proven specification, with around 205bhp from 1,790cc in rallying form, the newly-homologated triple-plate clutches, and yet another variation on the strengthened half shaft theme. After much patient testing by Roger Clark at Bagshot, the half shaft breakage bogey appeared to have been laid, and the cars were just about as reliable as any highly-tuned and abused competition car could be expected to be.

There remained the problem of 'engine stretch', and this was about to be solved in a most abrupt and exciting way. Peter Ashcroft told me the story himself: "I had gone over to Brian Hart's workshops at Harlow on some routine matter, probably connected with the 1972 Safari engines. It would be January or February 1972. Brian and I were walking through his engine build shops, which were always crowded, and I tripped over – quite literally – a block wrapped up in rags. The rags came off and I saw, or thought I saw, that it was a BDA block, but in light alloy!"

Brian Hart now takes up the story: "I hadn't even got round to telling Ford about this block, which was one I had designed myself. I say 'designed' because

143

'Esso Blue' on the way to winning the RAC Rally in 1972

there was quite a lot of difference between the cast-iron production block and this one. I had done it specifically for Formula Two engines, and specifically to get a 2-litre capacity. The 2-litre requirement came first, and the light-alloy idea was obvious for racing purposes."

Peter Ashcroft: "At first I just couldn't *believe* it. My eyes nearly dropped out. I said to Brian, 'What the hell's *that*', and when he explained I nearly blew a blood vessel. I can tell you, it wasn't more than a few minutes before we'd arranged for him to build me a full 2-litre engine, and for me to put it into a car!"

The sensational new block, in every way a private venture by Brian Hart, enabled a full 2-litre capacity to be achieved with a 90mm cylinder bore – compared with 85.6mm for the 1.8-litre rally engine and 80.97mm for the production-sized 1,601cc BDA. That was made possible by siamesing all the cylinder bores, and by altering the side camshaft/tappet chamber always left unused in the cast-iron BDA which, don't forget, was essentially a conversion from a pushrod overhead valve design.

"I took that first car to show to Stuart," said Peter Ashcroft, "and he couldn't believe it. Then we both took it to Walter Hayes, and he was incredulous too. We all knew, straight away, that we had to have it in production. Then we had to go through the whole trauma and the formalities

It isn't often one works car sees another on a stage – but here is Mikkola's brand new RS1600 ahead of Chris Sclater's ex-works RS1600 which he had won for his 1973 Kleber-*Wheelbase* 'scholarship' prize. The event is the 1973 Monte

of getting it machined, and getting it costed, and seeing if Ford could cast it themselves ..." his voice trailing off in a wistful way. "... but in the end Brian Hart made the patterns, or rather an employee of his did, modified them to our requirements, and shipped them off to Stirling Metals for the first production batch."

It was, in every way, a remarkable episode. The weight reduction – about 40 lb – was going to be very valuable both in single seaters and in the Escorts, but the big advance was going to be the possibilities of full 2-litre engines.

But as Keith Duckworth says: "I think Brian's a very resourceful bloke. I don't like siamesed-bore engines, and because the only way to get the size was to siamese I had never tried anything like this. We'd already found bore distortion and problems with our iron blocks, so I thought he was very brave. The fact that he now hard-chromes the bores instead of fitting thin steel liners is even more praiseworthy. Remarkable effort though – but I still think it's significant that only Ford themselves use the alloy block now. We sell bits for BDAs, BDFs and BDGs all over the world, and of course Formula Atlantic uses them all the time – and all of these are cast iron blocks!"

No matter. For Boreham, Brian Hart's new invention was the answer to their problems. "Funnily enough," says Ashcroft, "the first *real* advantage we

First event after the 1973/74 'Energy crisis' was the 1974 Marlboro Arctic. Markku Alen's RS1600 finished fourth after Mikkola's leading Escort had retired with obscure electrical trouble

noticed was that the car jumped so much better on rough ground. It was much better balanced. When the nose came down, it didn't seem to want to bury the engine through the crossmember into the sump-shield any more.''.

Almost immediately, and even before the engine could be homologated, Boreham's fortunes turned up sharply. The fabulously successful Safari entry of 1972 has already been described. Roger Clark and Jim Porter established total domination of the RAC British championship which had only faltered to a tiny degree at the time of writing in 1976. Roger's win in the Welsh was followed by a Mikkola-Clark one-two in the Scottish. Of more long-term importance was that Clark then took his nearly-new 'Esso Blue' RS1600 out on the Jim Clark national rally in June – and won it. That was to be expected. The news was that he used an alloy-block 2-litre engine for the very first time.

Homologation with the alloy block came in August 1972, and another interesting item approved at the same time was the rear disc brake kit including a hydraulic handbrake. As John Griffiths later remarked: "Even our drivers need to 'handbrake turn' a corner once or twice – and at the sort of speeds we are considering an ordinary cable action simply wouldn't lock the calipers. So we evolved the hydraulic system which works beautifully – just as long as we are sure to build in some 'sponge' on purpose. You can lock the wheels from at least 60mph – no problem!''

The most powerful iron-block 1.8-litre BDA rally engine ever tested at Hart's workshop was fitted to Hannu Mikkola's West German Olympia Rallye

146

Mikkola on his way to his fourth 1000 Lakes win, in 1974, with John Davenport alongside him. Note the first-time-out, tall and spindly, 15 inch road wheels

car, but it was all in vain as the car shed a half shaft complete with rear wheel at a very embarrassing point – right in front of a British photographer.

For the RAC Rally, a couple of months later, the four-car factory entry split its bet 'each way'. Two cars – for Mikkola and Andrew Cowan – kept their familiar iron-block 1800s, while the other two – for Clark and Makinen – used 2-litre alloy-blocked units, fitted for the first time with Lucas fuel injection, and boasting around 235bhp.

That event is already a legend in every enthusiast's memory. By the end of the first night, three of the cars had already retired – with engine, electrical, and transmission failures – but the survivor, Roger Clark, was securely and serenely in the lead. For three nail-biting days Clark and Tony Mason kept their two-litre car just far enough ahead of the opposition, and finally reached the finish ramp at York having re-established several reputations. But it wasn't all so easy. On the very last road section, with every special stage behind it, the 'Esso Blue' car ground to a halt at the side of the main road with a seized wheel bearing. Only the timely arrival of Andrew Cowan's sister car (retired, but dutifully acting as 'spares on the hoof') allowed a swop to take place, and Ford to get their reward after all. The margin between success and disaster can be very slim at times . . .

As it happens, the RAC Rally win proved two things. One was that the alloy engine was now reliable enough to use in endurance rallies, and that fuel injection gave no real advantage in road conditions over the ultra-reliable

Italian Weber carburettors. The engine's reliability was a great relief, for the engine's first 'homologated' appearance, in the Thousand Lakes in August, led to a farcical situation. The engine mountings pulled away from the new block, and damaged the stud fixings so much that they could not be repaired. The car finished the event – just – with the engine shored up from the sump guard by suitably carved pieces of stout fencing post jammed underneath the sump . . .

The following year, things were still rather quiet at Boreham, mainly because much of Ford's corporate effort was being channelled into the brutally fast and efficient Capris operated by Ford Cologne and raced in the European touring car racing series.

Even so, factory Escorts had a series of wins in Scandinavia, in the British Isles, and on the other side of the world in New Zealand. Hannu Mikkola drove his stout heart out to take fourth place in the Monte Carlo Rally (no Escort had ever been higher) – this time being defeated by three rear-engined Alpine-Renaults, but it was still good enough for the burly Finn to lift the Touring Category outright. Timo Makinen was 11th, and would possibly have beaten Mikkola if he hadn't lost a wheel in the middle of one flat-out special stage . . . .

That, of course, was the Monte spoiled by disqualified competitors blocking the road near Digne and trying to bring the rally to a premature end. When Timo arrived, and saw the blockage, he had other ideas. He backed off, tightened his belts, flicked on every lamp, and charged the blockage. People scattered, sure that rallying's super-star had finally lost his senses. Makinen knew otherwise – a few yards short of the blockage he swerved his Escort up a snowy bank, passed it in a spray of ice, and swept on his way, having done a beautifully judged 'wall of death' act. The Finns are different . . . .

The Safari onslaught of 1973 met with no luck at all – in stark and bitterly disappointing contrast to the 1972 entry – but two cars which retired early were refurbished and shipped straight off from Kenya to New Zealand. There they dominated the Heatway rally, gave Ford yet another 'one-two', with Mikkola and Jim Porter in the winning car.

Roger Clark won the Scottish very easily – his fifth such success – with Mikkola behind him and Andrew Cowan's ex-works car in third place. It also saw the 'works-loan' debut of Tony Pond, who finished seventh in the car which had let down Roger Clark on the Safari when he was leading the event by more than 30 minutes.

Makinen's win in the Thousand Lakes was only what people expected of him but I doubt if anyone could have expected the huge phalanx of Boreham-built machinery which turned up for the RAC Rally.

Apart from a new set of cars (the 'OOO' series) for the regular drivers, two ex-Safari 'XPUs' were loaned to Junior Preston and young Russell Brookes, Makinen's ex-Finland, ex-Monte car was loaned to Markku Alen, and Andrew Cowan had his usual *Scotsman* Escort.

It was all very smart and impressive but it didn't last long. First of all Russell Brookes rolled his car in front of his sponsors – ATV television – while Mikkola dropped *his* car off the road at the same point. Preston was outclassed in this specialist company, while Andrew Cowan's car succumbed to mechanical troubles.

Timo Makinen, though, in his Milk Marketing Board-sponsored car raced serenely into the lead, while Roger Clark struggled valiantly against African-type 'flu eventually to finish second. The sensation of the rally, however, was

Alen, who in spite of real 'cowboy' antics in towns and near spectators, managed to take third place – *after* sustaining a maximum penalty on the first day and battling his way up from something like 178th place. Even so, he nearly didn't make it – on the very last special stage his Escort flew off the road, hit a tree backwards and upside down, landed back on the track, and managed to finish with a badly damaged shell!

The miracle was not Ford's one-two-three win, of course, but that the event was allowed to run at all. The autumn of 1973, as everyone connected with motoring will remember, was the occasion of the Yom Kippur war, when Arabs and Israelis resumed the fighting of 1967 and of 1956, when the Arab oil producers turned to oil embargoes and price hoisting as their economic pressure weapon.

Within days, it seemed, Britain was supposed to be short of fuel, and the more hysterical sections of the media were screaming for the rally to be cancelled. Even after it had started, there were still calls for the event to be cancelled at half way. As if a couple of hundred rally cars would make much difference to the fuel consumption of a 15-million car nation!

Even so, the supply deteriorated, or was said to have deteriorated, and with ration cards distributed, lower-speed limits rushed into operation, and the price of fuel going through the roof, Europe found its motor sport banned for some months. At the same time, the motor industry and its customers went through a crisis – a crisis of confidence. It meant that for months the sale of new cars plummeted, and every company's profits disappeared. With them went promotional budgets for such luxuries as competitions – and Boreham's activities were suddenly under scrutiny.

Fortunately, there was no panic. Ford, more surely than probably any other concern, realised that even an upheaval as vast as this one would not stop man's desire for cars for long. Boreham would stay in motor sport, and would still be expected to win.

The lay-off gave the team some chance to do a bit of development, but strangely enough they didn't come up with any startling changes. Roger Clark had already been experimenting with a coil spring rear suspension in forestry-type rallies at the end of 1973, and the Griffiths/Ashcroft/Hart partnership was continually pushing for more engine power, but these were really just details. The fact of the matter was that the RS1600 Escort started its fifth season in much the same guise as its fourth.

The rallying programme was much the same as before, except that only one car (for Junior Preston) was sent to the Safari, and a full team was entered for the Arctic, which somehow got itself a petrol allocation in February when the rest of Europe was paralysed.

Cowan's UDT World Cup Rally entry in a Boreham-built RS2000 gave the team a bit of vicarious excitement, even though they were not involved in the event themselves. They were to have entered a team of cars, and preparations went ahead for some time in 1973, but once the event descended into confusion, route changes, and very late finalisation of everything, Stuart Turner very wisely decided to give it all a miss.

One way or another, 1973/74 was dominated by petrol. Even in June, when all threats of a petrol crisis had long since evaporated (and Europe was found to be swimming in a huge surplus of fuel because of the high prices and the reduced demand . . .), a local tanker-drivers' strike in Scotland led to the last-minute cancellation of the Scottish.

One of Mick Jones' 'cropsprayers' – set up with high suspension and 15 inch wheels for the 1974 RAC Rally. It was a non-finisher

It was at about the same time that Boreham became involved in a Polish escapade which all went sour. The deal, originally, was that Marek Wachowski (who had co-driven Zasada's works Escort in the *Daily Mirror* event of 1970) was to accept two brand-new works-replica cars, for use in Poland.

As it happened, Boreham's mechanics were too busy to build the cars themselves at the end of 1973, so the work was entrusted to Roger Clark's garage mechanics at Narborough. Eventually the cars arrived in Poland, were rallied several times, and never achieved any success. Any suggestion that their drivers, who were more used to pedalling two-stroke Wartburgs and obsolete VW Beetles than a thoroughbred car, were at fault was angrily dismissed by the Poles.

It all became very sordid and, after team drivers had flown out to Germany to test the cars (whence they had been returned form Poland), they were welcomed back to Boreham, and added to the fleet. At just the time when new cars were needed anyway, they were very useful indeed. These, for students of vehicle registrations, became the two 'SYW' cars, the only two in Boreham's long history which have not been registered in Essex. ('SYW. . .' was a London registration). One was sent out to South Africa for Roger Clark's abortive entry in the Total Rally, while the other one was saved for Hannu Mikkola to use in the RAC Rally.

Another cultured performance by Timo Makinen led to his second RAC Rally win in 1974, in this brand-new Colibri-sponsored RS1600

In the meantime, the motoring press had become bored with the sight of Roger Clark winning almost every British event just as he pleased. Even Turner and Ashcroft recognised that this might eventually become counter-productive, so they set about developing the new single-cam RS2000 instead. One hard-working car was used for testing and development for some months, and immediately after the petrol-enforced lay-off it was built up for Roger Clark to use in the British Mintex Dales event.

It was by no means standard – the chassis was almost pure RS1600, and the much-modified engine produced around 160bhp – but it was a whole lot slower than Clark's usual Esso-backed Escort. By dint of really furious driving, and with the help of one cancelled stage where he had been soundly beaten by Tony Drummond's private RS1600, Clark eventually won – by just two seconds. Later on he was heard to say that 'giving away that much performance was just too much.' Boreham must have agreed with him. They didn't pursue the experiment.

There was one highly-successful sequel. For the second Avon-*Motor* Tour of Britain, Boreham entered a couple of new RS2000s (in 1973 they had used 3-litre Capris with a conspicuous lack of success), and surprised everyone by turning up at the start with twin-carburettor 140bhp engines which were quite literally homologated a few days before the start.

Roger Clark in the very smart ex-Belgian-racing RS1600, on the 1975 Circuit of Ireland. The car was a screamer, but cooked its fuel-injected engine while leading *(photo Colin Taylor)*

With Roger Clark at his inimitable best, and Vauxhall-fugitive Gerry Marshall right with him at all times, the white-and-blue RS2000s notched up a very satisfactory victory – repeated, of course, in 1975 (by privately-entered Tony Pond) and in 1976.

There now occurred what a fiction writer would call 'The case of the 15 inch wheel mystery'. It had all started about a year earlier, and was yet another case of Timo Makinen's obsession with a particular technical change he desired. Mick Jones, who has had to withstand Makinen's suggestions, brilliant or inconclusive, since 1970, once said that stopping him was like trying to do a King Canute on the tide. In this case, the big Finn was not about to be discouraged by talks of expense and homologation difficulties. Having watched the way Saabs and Volvos floated over the loose, and across the ice, in his native Scandinavia, he thought there had to be something in the way a bigger tyre – with its different shape of contact patch – complemented a car's road holding.

Nothing daunted, therefore, he demanded – and won – a testing session on Escorts with 15 inch wheels. At the time there simply wasn't a competitive Dunlop cover to use, so his first comparisons were between 13in M and S Dunlops on Minilite wheels, and a 15in Finnish tyre on knocked up wheels. Getting the bigger diameter wheels and tyres into an Escort's restricted sheet metal arches was no picnic (and remember that they had originally been designed for 12 inch wheels), while Boreham were also forced to consider yet another axle ratio to bring the gearing back to an ideal figure.

Following that test, Makinen was quite convinced that he was quicker on the big wheels. After practising in Finland, he averred that he was up to two seconds every kilometre quicker than before. He therefore demanded, and got, a 15 inch wheel Escort for the 1974 Thousand Lakes.

Hannu Mikkola, then as always influenced by the massive personality of Makinen, agreed to do the same. Roger Clark, who had yet to try the tyres in anger, preferred to wait and see.

The Thousand Lakes was a triumph for Ford, and Makinen was sure that the big wheels contributed to it. Timo, in fact, might have won the event but for a niggardly traffic offence (and consequent penalty), so had to settle for second place behind Mikkola's sister car. This, incidentally made it four wins each for the men, and a total of five wins for the works Escorts.

Before the RAC Rally, a testing session at Bagshot on brand new Dunlop 15in wheels produced interesting results. Roger Clark was quite sure the car wasn't quicker on the big wheels, while all the Finns – Makinen, Mikkola and Markku Alen – disagreed with him. Roger lost the battle in part, but both Ford and Dunlop decided to bring along a supply of conventional 13-inchers as well. It was as well that they did!

The event itself, as in 1972 and 1973, was a triumph for the Boreham-prepared cars. Timo Makinen notched up his second win, using the only new car built for the event. As in previous years, however, it was a battle of attrition. Five works cars (including the ex-Clark RS2000 of Benson Ford Junior) started, but only two finished.

Every RS1600 from Boreham started on 15 inch wheels, but before long Roger Clark made one of his rare mistakes, found himself out of control at a point where he knew he would have been in charge on 13 inch wheels, and went off the road. He then spent three days trying to get back on terms, and finally fought his way back to seventh place; that was a chase as sternly achieved as Alen's third place a year earlier.

Clark, however, only made this dash by switching back to 13 inch wheels, and once Timo saw that he was being beaten on individual stages he made the swap himself! The supply situation was a bit complicated and there is at least one authenticated case of Makinen's car completing several stages with 13 inch wheels on one side of the car and 15 inch wheels on the other. All was well that ended well – and to keep the publicists happy the winning car drove up the finishing ramp on 15 inch wheels – but even after two more years it was only Timo who was thoroughly happy with them. The problem, of course, is that although there are gains in ground clearance, the car's ride height is increased, and the details of the steering geometry are also affected. For rough events (such as the Safari, or Morocco) the extra clearance is a positive advantage.

In the RAC Rally, the colourful display of sponsor's colours continued. Roger Clark, after all, had won in 1972 with Esso backing, and in 1973 the winning car had been decked out by the Milk Marketing Board. This time, in a singularly unflattering brown scheme, it was Colibri cigarette lighters which shared Makinen's glory.

That glory, though, nearly turned sour. On the last morning, with service cars already scattering all over the icy and foggy Yorkshire moors, both Makinen and Clark realised that their triple plate clutches were worn out and beginning to slip. Their good luck was that for the first time on an RAC Rally they were carrying two-way radio kits. Anguished calls from Henry Liddon and Tony Mason, from the main road on the run towards the forests, allowed the resourceful teams of mechanics to meet in Pickering, and for replacements to be made in little more than 30 minutes for each car. When we think of the problems of changing boxes and clutches before the ZF's fixings were simplified, we may marvel.

Rallying, of course, was never Boreham's only activity, even though it was their major interest. The RS1600, more than the Twin-Cam, was suited to circuit racing, and to rallycross where conditions suited it.

Rod Chapman, Ron Douglas, and ex-steeplechase jockey John Taylor all benefited from Boreham's help and expertise. From time-to-time a pensioned-off rally car would 'disappear' – whereas in fact it probably continued to race in front of millions of TV watchers, in unregistered rallycross form.

John Taylor's car was eventually supported by Haynes of Maidstone, his local Ford dealership, often with Boreham-inspired components. Their efforts were rewarded in 1973 when Taylor won the prestigious European Rallycross championship.

By then, though, rallycross was beginning to go wrong. As so often before, it was the pressures of factory involvement which caused it. European car makers began to pour money into this new form of TV spectator sport, and with this the drivers' manners deteriorated. Bumping and boring, more worthy of the local 'banger' stadium, became the order of the day, and very quickly turned Ford away from the 'sport'. Stuart Turner made a few choice comments about 'works-backed dodgem car racing', and wanted nothing more to do with it.

On the race tracks, the RS1600 immediately made its mark. Ralph Broad in Britain, and Cologne-backed cars in Europe, soon put the RS on the front row of touring car grids, and made them potential winners at any distance.

All of which was a bit counter-productive for Ford, as the Escort's principal European competition came from Ford of Cologne! The German Capris which eventually proved to be supreme were fast, but none-too-reliable until Peter Ashcroft had been seconded to Jochen Neerpasch to help sort out the Weslake-modified engines' problems.

The busiest Ford driver of 1971 was certainly John Fitzpatrick. Not only was he entrusted with the Broadspeed car on British tracks, but he was also Cologne's leading driver in the European Touring Car championship. I have to say that on paper Broadspeed's own record looked better than that of Cologne, but this remark needs severe qualification. The British series was for short sprint-type races, while the European series went in for anything up to 24 hours.

In Europe, Fitzpatrick's car recorded a string of retirements, usually due to mechanical breakdowns or accidents. On three occasions, however, the RS1600's performance was so outstanding that it could have won outright. In the end it won outright just once – at Jarama at the end of the season, when Fitzpatrick was partnered by the young Jochen Mass (later an accomplished Grand Prix driver) – but it led the Monza round for a time until a puncture forced it down to fourth, and led the Nurburgring Six Hour race until the last 30 minutes; the culprit on that occasion was the axle.

In Britain, 'RS1600' sometimes had the legs of the Camaros and Mustangs, but usually had to bow to superior power – Dave Matthews, however, in the works-backed Broadspeed 1300GT was usually fast enough to dominate the 1,300cc class – as it had ever since 1968.

For 1972, Broadspeed's efforts were limited to a 1300GT for Vince Woodman (in the big car category Broad was to dabble with development of a 3-litre BMW Coupe on behalf of the Munich factory), and Ford's European aspirations were channelled through Gerry Birrell and a Neerpasch-managed RS1600.

The Broadspeed effort was less successful than usual, in spite of the obvious power of the Lucas-injected engine – mainly because of mechanical problems and one particularly horrifying write-off shunt at Oulton Park near the end of the season.

Gerry Birrell was Stuart Turner's 'golden boy' in every respect. Not only was he a young and outstanding driver in any sort of car from saloons to Formula Two single-seaters, but he was already an expert 'car-sorter', and development/test driver. Apart from his high-speed ability, Gerry was being employed by Ford on handling and roadholding development for the AVO Escorts. What he was up to was kept under wraps during 1972, but surfaced – as the RS2000 – the following year. Tragically, by then he had been killed in a Formula Two race at Rouen.

Although Ford were to win the 2-litre class in the 1972 European Touring Car championships, they needed semi-detached factory cars (like the Sony-sponsored car campaigned by the Dutch importers – LVX 949J) and even privately-prepared cars, to ensure this for them.

Birrell's best performance in the 260bhp Hart-tuned car was his first, at Monza, when the RS1600 finished third overall, six laps behind the winning Cologne Capri. Seventh at the Salzburgring and a class win at Brno were Birrell's next two results, but after that Cologne tempted him into one of their 320bhp 2.9-litre Capris, with altogether outstanding results.

The Capris, in fact, took up so much of Ford's European racing effort later in the year, that the Escort did not run again after July. In 1973, Capris again dominated the scene, and Boreham's involvement was muted. Ralph Broad, having burnt his, and BMW's fingers in the pursuit of premature homologation of the Coupe, turned to the more fruitful subject of Capri suspension development, after which Cologne raced them in more and more bitter conflict with BMW. The urge was not only because of factory and nationalistic reasons, but was also that Cologne's manager Jochen Neerpasch had been enticed over to BMW in 1972 to jack up their racing programme, and to pit the new lightweight CSLs against the Capris that he knew so well.

Stuart Turner and Mike Kranefuss, for their part, went one better (as Neerpasch knew they would – the project having been started before he abandoned ship). Keith Duckworth and Mike Hall, at Cosworth, were developing a 400-plus bhp 3.4-litre conversion of the British 'Essex' vee-6 unit to make the Capris even more formidable.

This, you might think, had little to do with the Escorts, but its effects were important to this story. So expensive, and so far-reaching, was the Capri effort of 1973 and 1974, that all thoughts of a works-backed Escort racing programme had to be severely trimmed. In Britain, for both the British and European series, Stuart Turner's solution was to works-loan a beautifully-prepared 2-litre RS1600 to the Ford dealership of Norman Reeves Ltd, for Dave Brodie (of 'Run Baby Run' fame) to drive.

It was a crowded season which Reeves planned, as the one car had to do

155

Staepelaere and 'Jimmy' leaving a forest track into the cobblestone hairpin on a Special stage on the 1974 Rally 24 Hours of Ypres

both sets of races. Brodie took second place at the Race of Champions meeting in March, and fourth at the Silverstone *Daily Express* meeting a few weeks later, but his European forays went unrewarded. Tragedy, but happy deliverance, came at Silverstone in the Grand Prix meeting. Dicing hard for second place with Dave Matthews' Broadspeed Capri, Brodie's Escort was involved in a horrifying high speed accident just before the Dunlop bridge. All three drivers involved, mercifully, eventually made complete recoveries, but Brodie's car was written off, and – with it – Boreham's 1973 programme of racing.

In the event, Ford's heavy reliance on the Capris came to naught. The energy crisis on the one hand and the sheer overwhelming superiority of BMW and Ford over any other type of saloon car, made sure that the 1974 European series died on its feet. This, coupled with the fact that the CSI rather abruptly decided to change the rules for 1976 (and 'outlaw' the optional multi-valve cylinder heads) made the warring German teams the proud possessors of obsolete, if very exciting, dinosaurs.

Mike Kranefuss, to his great credit, had hedged his bets cleverly, with money and technical support, if not with actual cars. For 1974, very impressed by their independent showing in earlier years, he had decided to give Cologne's factory backing to the Zakspeed racing Escorts, and their boss Erich Zakowski.

Zakowski, a Prussian German with workshops at Neuhausel, not far from Cologne, took on a Ford dealership in the early 1960s, but first became

156

Zakspeed took on the mantle of 'works' cars in 1974 after Cologne withdrew their original Capri efforts. This car, usually driven by Hans Heyer, won the European Touring Car Championship and never lost a class. It even won the Nurburgring Six Hour race outright

interested in 1968, being vastly impressed by Ralph Broad's achievements with the new Escorts.

At first he prepared his cars by buying parts from Broadspeed in England, and it is no coincidence to this story that one of his first cars was driven by – Mike Kranefuss. By the time Zakspeed began to appear in international touring car races, his cars had already taken several German national titles. For 1974, with more and more of the Escort's special parts and preparation emanating from Zakspeed themselves, an assault on the European Touring Car championship was serious.

That season was more successful than Zakowski, and Kranefuss, could ever have hoped. Because of the economic recession which followed the hoisting of petrol prices all over the world, there was only demand for six events in the ETC – at Monza, Salzburgring, Vallelunga, Nurburgring, Zandvoort and Jarama. Zakspeed's performance is easily summed up – their cars won *every* class contest, and once – at Nurburgring in July – won outright after six gruelling hours. Not bad, surely, for one car which not only won the European championship but also found time to win the German national title at the same time?

The car, immaculately prepared, and sporting Castrol and Radio Luxembourg sponsors' colours, used a 275bhp alloy-block engine, with Lucas fuel

157

injection. The rest of the chassis and its special fittings was all very familiar, with the ZF gearbox and 'Atlas' axle installed, along with the usual radius arm and Watts linkage location. What is interesting is that Zakspeed were using 15in wheels just as soon as regulations and homologation would let them do so – with rims of no less than 11.5in (front) and 14in (rear).

Individual champion was Hans Heyer, an ex-Dutch, German and European karting champion from the 1960s, who had graduated to the team via private, works-blessed, then full works Cologne Capris. Driving for Zakspeed for the first time in this tremendously successful 1974 season, Heyer won his class four times and was second once – then capped off his season by taking a works Capri to outright victory at Jarama, when the Zakspeed car was second overall.

The team's other regular driver was Dieter Glemser, but it was Grand Prix driver Jochen Mass who unwittingly helped to give Zakspeed their outright win at the Nurburgring. With the two Zakspeed cars running first and third overall near the close of the event, *and* nose-to-tail though a lap apart in overall standings, a BMW CSL Coupe which was rapidly overhauling the two after earlier trouble, caught the two cars up on the last lap.

Purely by accident, and there is nobody willing to admit otherwise, when the BMW made its passing manoeuvre it collided with the second (Mass) Zakspeed car, and went off the road. All oblivious of this, until he saw a clear rear view mirror, Heyer swept through to outright victory. Co-driver Klaus Ludwig, in the pits, could hardly believe it.

The Zakspeed team's performances were so consistent that they had clinched the championship after only five events. Incidentally, in that Nurburgring event they reduced their lap time to 8 min 51 sec – it is worth rubbing in the fact that this was with a 2-litre saloon, and that the time would have constituted a Formula One lap record only 11 years earlier.

It was a fitting climax to seven years of Escort racing and rallying competition, and Ford celebrated it in no uncertain manner by circulating the press release and picture of a *very* high-jumping car with all the championships won that year plastered on the side of it. However, an end was in sight, and a beginning. Everyone 'in the know' already knew it – the old shape was dead and a new shape was about to arrive.

Ford were already preparing a neat little publicity booklet to be titled *'The car that won't stop winning',* and they were hoping they wouldn't have to retract for a good few years yet.

10

After the RS1600~
follow that!

With that magnificent and remarkably assured fifth consecutive RAC Rally win to celebrate, the end of the 1976 season signalled the close of the first two successful and incredibly varied years of 'works' competition with the new-shape RS1800s and RS2000s. Those two years proved, though Ford supporters had never doubted it, that the Escorts were still as competitive as they ever had been. In the RAC Rally, the Escorts were never even matched by Opel, Lancia, Fiat or Saab. The biggest problem seemed to be that the cars from Boreham were often likely to be beaten by privately-prepared cars!

Winning events – races or rallies – with the new cars, was no more than Ford would have expected to do. However, what they certainly did not enjoy was the number of occasions that the team cars were forced to retire, often with mechanical ailments which had been identified some years earlier. The cars might now be looking more modern, and going faster than ever, but they were certainly less reliable than before. This was a trend that Boreham was anxious to reverse in 1977.

As far as Boreham is concerned, the end of 1976 also signalled the end of an era. After seven years in the team, through good times and bad, Timo Makinen was not retained for 1977. In his place came the younger (by six years) Swede Bjorn Waldegard, the man who in the Lancia Stratos had given Boreham as much trouble as anyone else in recent years. In an incredibly hastily re-prepared car, he took a fine third place on the RAC Rally – Lancia having withdrawn their Stratos entry in a fit of pique when they heard he was not to re-sign for them.

Changes to the domestic rallying team were also announced at the same time. For weeks, during the autumn, the rumour factory was busy – who would be driving for Ford in 1977? Predictably enough Russell Brookes was given one car. The second, less obviously, went to Andy Dawson (who had turned down a 'rolling shell' arrangement for 1976). Dawson had been struggling to make a Datsun Violet programme competitive throughout 1976. Billy Coleman went off to Ireland to do his own programme.

The team should have started the 1975 season with a bang, but things did not quite work out like that. When Timo Makinen's Colibri-sponsored RS1600 completed Ford's RAC Rally hat-trick in November 1974, it should have been a magnificent swansong, the last fling of a dying breed. In any respectable film script this would have been so. By then, of course, it was a very open secret that existing Escorts were obsolete, and that new-shape cars would appear in the New Year.

According to theory, Timo's win should have been the last RS1600 appearance. Things didn't quite work out like that, not because of new-car problems, but because enough of the new cars were not rally-ready in time. There were other RS1600 victories to come. Even so, from that November day when the mechanics returned to Boreham, the accent was on 1975-shape cars.

The new Escort — new in styling, and with a revised model line-up — was announced in January, and went on sale in March. But there were shocks for the enthusiasts. Everyone assumed that Mexicos, RS1600s and RS2000s would figure in the line up. Ford management had different ideas. The new Rallye Sport cars would be vastly different.

Even before the new Escort was announced, shock news came from the AVO building. The production lines were being closed down, and no more Rallye Sport cars would take shape there! Not only that, but it was made clear that the Mexico and the RS2000 would disappear from the lists, if only for the time being.

Of course, this meant that the value of 1974 'old-shape' Mexicos and RS2000s went through the roof for a time. It also meant that homologation expert John Griffiths was faced with a problem — getting early approval for cars without serious production facilities to back his application.

I don't think anyone was happy to see the FAVO lines closed down, least of all Walter Hayes and Stuart Turner. Aveley, after all, had brought the possibility of quantity-production 'specials' within range of Ford customers when no other production plant was capable of tackling the job. But both men, above all, are ruthlessly logical in business, and had to accept that in 1975 there looked like being a lot of spare capacity for building 'specials' on the Halewood and Saarlouis tracks. The very production chiefs who had turned their backs on the Mexico in 1971 were now anxious to build anything that would keep their tracks full. That was in 1974 — whether they would say the same of the cars in a crowded and popular 1977 Saarlouis factory was another question altogether.

The looks of the new car might be new, but under the skin all was very much as before. The same, that is, if we recall that the original Escort's floor pan, rear damper positioning, and spring/damper rates were all revised for the 1974 models. This little lot, and the rear anti-roll bar which went with it, were carried over for the Mark 2 cars.

Boreham were quick off the mark. When the new Escort was shown to the press at the Dorchester Hotel in January 1975, a mock-up of a competition-prepared RS was on show, complete with RAC Rally numbers, badges, and Timo's name on the front wings. Wheel arch extensions, bibs and spoilers were all new (but very familiar now).

Because this was the rally-prepared version (though it was not a runner at that time) it had the full-house Hart-built 2-litre engine, and the ZF five-speed gearbox. It was not until we read the small type of the announcement that we realised that the basic production machine would be mechanically different. Its new name, the RS1800, gave the game away. The engine, still with its light-

First time out for the RS1800, and a first time win too! The old firm of Clark and Porter winning the 1975 Granite City rally. For its next event the car would get its new sponsor's livery

alloy cylinder block, now had an enlarged (86.75mm) bore, a single down-draught double-choke Weber 32/36 DGAV carburettor, and a capacity of 1,835cc.

The gearbox, though four-speed as before, was new – the casing was like that of the RS2000, but the ratios were from some of the Ford Granada models. Neither the basic engine nor the four-speed gearbox were intended to figure strongly in 1975, but Boreham already had their eyes on the future. The International Appendix J regulations, governing type of motor sporting activity, were due to change as from the beginning of 1976. It was only reasonable, then, to see that Boreham had foreseen the need for a larger capacity engine (there would be severe limits on the amount of boring out that could be done), and a strong four-speed gearbox (a complete gearbox swop would also be outlawed).

Showing the new RS1800 was all well and good, but the problem was that Ford had to get it homologated. This they did, smoothly and without drama, by claiming evolution from the older models. In that the same floor pan and suspensions were carried over they had a point, but with a completely new bodyshell, gearbox and much modified engine, not to mention a new model name, Ford can think themselves fortunate that approval was gained so easily. Even so, from the first of January 1975, they were in business.

161

Pre-Welsh Rally preparation 1975. Russell Brooke's new car takes shape, while Roger Clark's car gets its new Cossack colour scheme. Two more RS1800 shells, in the background, wait their turn

For the moment, however, the Mexicos and RS2000s disappeared altogether. A few RS1800s were built at Halewood in the spring of 1975, but production was eventually moved to Saarlouis, where the new FAVO-type cars would also be built in 1976. Production was at a low rate, enough for homologation to be creditably maintained, but probably not to be compared with the height of the RS1600 boom in 1971 and 1972.

Boreham, as usual, preferred to build up their own competition cars from scratch. That first show car had been born in Boreham, and led an incredibly busy life right from the start. Originally it was sent to the Brussels Show looking like a Zakspeed racer, then converted for the British launch to look like a Boreham rally car. Later still it actually would become a competition car (for Gilbert Staepelaere) – but the show business and publicity came first!

Boreham's first job was to build a set of forest-spec. cars. Naturally Roger Clark would get the first, but two more RS1800s were going out on loan to Billy Coleman (RAC Rally Champion in 1974) and to Russell Brookes (a British Leyland employee!). The fourth would be for Timo Makinen, and Staepelaere's car was meant for a European programme.

In the meantime, though, the obsolete RS1600s bridged a gap. Billy Coleman 'borrowed' Clark's old Esso car, and won the Circuit of Ireland in it. Clark himself turned up in a very smart ex-Belgium racing Escort, complete

162

Anatomy of a rallying RS1800

New shells for old — one way of updating your old RS1600 or Mexico

'Cossack Mk I' on its way to winning the 1975 Scottish Rally. Perhaps the spectators will stand farther back next time?

with lowered race-type suspension and a very hot engine with fuel injection. This let him down (as had his old car on the Mintex Dales), and led to much soul-searching both at Boreham and in Brian Hart's workshops.

In the Marlboro Arctic, three cars (including two ex-Makinen RAC Rally winners) started, but had no success. In January, too, an RS1600 loaned to Andy Dawson to tackle the Tour of Dean had been parked outside his hotel overnight, and was promptly stolen!

Whoever nicked XPU 220L must have been an expert, because starting a 235bhp Escort on a cold damp night is no picnic – and he must also have known that all works Escorts shared the same door and ignition keys. The Welsh police had a very confusing time in the next few weeks trying to find the car. We can be quite sure that within hours it was stripped, and the parts dispersed.

The loss of this Thousand Lakes winner suddenly found Boreham short of cars, which made completion of the new set even more urgent. The first win, appropriately enough, went to Roger Clark, who took a virgin-white RS1800 smoothly ahead of a championship field in the Granite City Rally. A few weeks later, this time with the same car resplendent in Cossack decals, he steered the

'Cossack Mk II' winning the Manx Rally in 1975, in tarmac-suspension guise. But it was a leopard which changed its spots . . . .

RS1800 to its first international win – in the Welsh Rally. With Rockey's on-loan RS1600 behind him and Brookes' new Mk 2 fifth, it could fairly be described as a Ford-dominated weekend. Billy Coleman's car let the side down by snapping a steering knuckle when in second place.

The Scottish was another Ford 'steam-roller' demonstration, with three of the consecutively-registered cars in the top places. Tony Pond's Opel then intervened, but Timo Makinen's brand-new RS1800 took fifth. The only break in symmetry was that '702' was second and '701' was third!

Makinen's car had a disappointing run, not finally solved before a Boreham rebuild. The big Finn's complaints of 'lack of power' were only noticeable to the tune of a few horsepower – but a well-flattened exhaust system might have had something to do with it.

John Taylor drove the wheels off the famous old OOO 96M in its last appearance, but the significance of the Scottish was how stable the new cars looked. Suspension changes between Mk 1 and Mk 2 shapes included the use of much longer rear axle radius arms, and the high-speed ride was much more predictable than before. What was a bit worrying was that after only three events (one of them a short national), both Clark's and Coleman's cars showed

165

By Monte time in 1976, KHK 983N was an unsponsored white car again, and gave Clark a troubled fifth place

every sign of beginning to crease at the scuttle. This tendency was nothing like as pronounced as with the last Lotus-Cortinas, but by comparison with the indestructible old shells it was rather alarming.

One thing was sure – the new cars were very fast. Clark described his experiences as being "the same ride with a different view" (the extra visibility due to enlarged windows was really very noticeable), and quoted maximum speeds of around 115mph between the trees, and lifting off at more than 9,000rpm in fifth to spare the engine.

Meanwhile, back at Boreham, Mick Jones, Tom Walkinshaw and Roger Clark were beavering away at improvements for tarmac-spec. Escorts. The RS1600 cars had mostly been successful in the forests, or in the rough, where lots of oversteer and ample ground clearance is desirable. With an ambitious tarmac rallies programme planned for 1976, a different set-up would be needed where the grip was high and the surfaces smooth.

Two new cars – KHK 982N and 983N – took shape, and after Clark and Walkinshaw had spent many hours at Cadwell Park, Snetterton and elsewhere, the new arrangements were pronounced satisfactory. At the rear a Panhard rod was added to the location linkage (a differently positioned rod had been in the original Twin-Cam suspension of 1967, but discarded before announcement), while at the front a pair of compression struts replaced the less satisfactory location provided by the anti-roll bar. The new cars, too, were much lower than usual. As Mick Jones once told me: "We used to build Escorts so high that I used to call 'em bleeding crop-sprayers . . . ."

In the meantime, Clark had suffered a very disturbing few hours in Europe on the Circuit of Antibes, when the high-speed Alpine roads showed up all the deficiencies of the old suspension. In the end his misery stopped when a front wheel came off, though it nearly deposited him and his car over a fresh-air kerb in the process.

The first proof of the pudding came a few weeks later in the Isle of Man for Clark, and in France for Makinen. 983N, suitably re-sprayed Cossack red for the occasion, gave Clark his much coveted win in the Manx, where he wiped the floor with a selection of Porsches. New-fangled Dunlop racing 'slicks' helped, but the expression on Clark's face at victory celebrations tells its story too. He now had an Escort for every occasion.

So too, did Makinen, but 982N's engine let him down in the course of the Tour de France, when it burst asunder. Makinen, who had just taken the overall lead, was not amused.

All in all, it had not been Timo's year, thus far. His forest-spec. car had been sent to Finland for the Thousand Lakes Rally, where both he and Hannu Mikkola were looking for their fifth outright win. Mikkola duly got his, in a rather remarkable 1600cc Toyota, while a disappointed Makinen had to settle for third place. There was, however, one other interesting pointer about the event. Peter Ashcroft had arranged to lend Timo's Finnish-championship Escort Mk I to a brave young man called Ari Vatanen, whose Opel exploits were already well known.

Vatanen, with journalist Geraint Phillips riding shot-gun, started in dramatic fashion by setting fastest times in four of the first six special stages – then made a simple driving error and dropped off the road on the next! It was a short performance, but outstanding enough for him to be offered a new RS1800 to drive in the RAC Rally.

However, if September had been a good month, October was undoubtedly one to forget. The two tarmac cars were entered for Italy's prestige event, the San Remo Rally, where the accent is on careful practice and sheer unadulterated car performance. Makinen's car, in particular, had a very hot engine indeed (around 260bhp from two litres), and even when faced with the Lancia Stratos it was expected to be a potential winner.

Ford's other problem, apart from winning the event if they could, was that Roger Clark might *just* be able to get to the start of the British Lindisfarne national rally (inportant to him in the chase for RAC Championship points), With this mind, Stuart Turner had authorised a combination of fast power boat, helicopter, company private jet, and fast car, to sweep the intrepid Clark and Jim Porter from San Remo to Northumberland in a few hours.

The one thing the team could not have expected, happened. Dunlop, to their eternal embarrassment, suffered a breakdown of their tyre-carrying truck on the way down through France. Nothing, not even extraordinary hiring measures, could get the very special racing 'slicks' to the start on time, and the outcome was that the Escorts had to start a fully-fledged international event without spare tyres. Worse – even to make the starting ramp at all, it was necessary for the team to buy Klebers for spares.

The result was predictable. Makinen suffered punctures on the very first

167

The Allied Polymer Group picked a lucky car to sponsor. On its first event LAR 801P won the RAC Rally of 1975 for Timo Makinen . . .

stage, and Clark ran out of rubber only minutes later. Both were back in their hotels in a couple of hours. The only consolation was that Clark could get back home, win the Lindisfarne without breaking into a sweat, and almost ensure his 1975 RAC Championship win.

After that débâcle, only a landslide win in our own RAC Rally could restore Dunlop's reputation. Fortunately for them, and for Ford, they produced a very advanced new tyre – the A2. This tyre, very significant indeed, as the first real rallying advance in rubber for some time, combined the best in racing construction with rugged reliability.

More important was the fact that it did not rely on a chunky tread for grip, looked for all the world like a wet-weather racing tyre, and transformed the normally oversteering Escort into a much more precise-to-drive projectile. It made a change, at least, from Timo's obsession with 15 inch wheels, and when linked (exclusively at first) with the Escorts was expected to change the tempo of rough-road rallying.

Boreham had also found time to build a trio of brand new cars for the event, so Clark's smart Cossack livery found itself on its third car in six months. Makinen had the APG combine for his sponsors, and the young blond Vatanen was supported by Capital Radio.

The result was everything Ford could have hoped, and more than they expected. With little drama apart from a leaking sump pan near the finish, Timo Makinen drew away to complete his RAC Rally hat trick (and Ford's

168

. . . and in 1976 Ari Vatanen won the RAC Rally Championship in it, in spite of several expensive body-bending accidents

fourth successive Escort win), while a desperate Roger Clark urged his very troublesome new Cossack car into second place.

Ari Vatanen, on the other hand, found notoriety after a good first day's drive by getting his Escort out of control at more than 100mph in the Clipstone forest, and rolling it into a ball of scrap between the trees. Both Clark and Makinen, according to eye-witnesses, almost joined him.

Even so, it was a great climax to a splendid first year for the RS1800, especially as Gilbert Staepelaere had, as usual, mopped up several minor internationals in Europe on behalf of Ford. Gilbert, being in the rather less privileged 'second division' of works drivers, had had to make do with the ex-Makinen Colibri RS1600 for the first part of the season, but made the transition with no fuss and exemplary success.

As in the late Mk 1 days, so in 1975, neither Boreham nor Cologne had anything directly to do with saloon car racing. Rallycross, too, was out, in spite of the huge potential TV publicity. Boreham, and particularly Stuart Turner, had long since lost interest in events where bumping and barging were as vital to success as having the best cars.

They compromised by giving John Taylor and his Haynes-sponsored car a lot of support. Taylor, as ever, was *the* Briton to beat in rallycross. In certain weather conditions, and always assuming that he could elbow his way to the front at the first corner, his Escort was quite unbeatable.

The racing scene saw Zakspeed once again operating on Ford's behalf, with

Russell Brookes, like Vatanen, expects a lot from his Escorts. HHJ 702N had a charmed life, but even in this battered state it won the Scottish Rally in 1976

an immaculate-looking and nicely prepared RS1800, vividly painted in Castrol sponsor's colours. Zakowski, as always, relied completely on Britain for engine and gearbox supplies, but was making more and more of his own chassis parts. Zakspeed it was who developed the full-length and very stylish wing extensions also found on the Boreham 'tarmac' cars in 1975 and 1976.

Zakspeed, like Broadspeed in England, always operate from their own self-contained workshops, but Mike Kranefuss and Stuart Turner were very happy to nominate them as full 'works' cars. Through no fault of theirs, however, Zakspeed's appearances in International races with the RS1800 were very restricted. The Touring Car Championship, moribund after 1974, and with no support from the big battalions, made no sort of impact at all. Most of the scheduled events were cancelled due to lack of entries. Hans Heyer and Finotto took an old-shape RS1600 to the Monza 4-Hour race in March, where they took a splendid second place, but the RS1800's only event was the Nurburgring 6-Hour where, driven by Hans Heyer, it retired.

As an important consolation, Zakspeed sent a single RS1800 all the way to South Africa for the non-championship Kyalami 1000km race, and surprised everyone but themselves by beating the entire field – BMWs, 3-litre Capris and

Brookes' second Andrews-sponsored car looking very smart and purposeful on the Manx, where it retired with gearbox failure

all. A few years earlier this would have caused astonishment, but since the world was by now thoroughly used to 2-litre Escorts beating every other car in the events, it got no more than the usual headlines.

Another consolation, important to Zakowski locally, was that his cars dominated the German National racing championships in their customary fashion.

January 1 was a very important date in 1976 for Ford. This was not because it signalled the start of another busy season, but because it meant that a new set of the FIA's homologation rules came into use. In effect it meant that the carefully-developed RS1600s and RS1800s had become dinosaurs, without a future – at least not in their existing form.

It was not an unexpected move, but it was unwelcome. The FIA had been considering tighter control of their regulations for some time, and their object was to cut down on the fiddling, and the high-cost low-production options which some manufacturers were using. Ford, no less than any other, were happy to homologate extra equipment which would improve the cars' performance; unlike some of their competitors, however, they made sure that supplies were available for private owners too.

The name of the game is sponsorship. The Tour of Britain cars in 1976, before the 'off' – Makinen's Ralgex car, Vatanen's APG car and Clark's Wigham Poland car posing for the camera

Appendix J Group 2 was much more restrictive for 1976 and beyond. It meant, for instance, that a Group 2 Escort could no longer use its ZF five-speed gearbox, its full 2-litre engine size, or its dry-sump lubrication system. The fact that many manufacturers with well-developed competition cars (and no alternative projects on the go) mightly instantly be forced out of motor sport, prompted the FIA to compromise.

The ruling was simple. All Group 2 cars from 1975 would automatically be eligible for Group 4 events in 1976 and 1977. After the end of 1977 they would be banned altogether. Ford, therefore, could carry on using their Escorts in 1975 form, *and* further improve them, for another two years. In the meantime they would have to produce a 'new Group 2' specification.

It also meant that they would be forced to compete directly against such exotic machinery as Lancia's limited-production Stratos. A less-competitive manufacturer, with his eye on class and category wins, would have quailed at the thought, Ford, however, shrugged this off. Class wins were of no interest to them – outright victory or nothing was what counted. They were therefore meeting the Lancias on level terms in just the same way.

As far as the Zakspeed racing team was concerned, they had to build Group 2 cars at once, because European Touring Car championship events were for that sort of car. Rallies took anything from Group 1 to Group 4, so this gave Boreham little pause for thought. Zakspeed, and Cologne, had a problem.

The problem was not so much a matter of engine power, or of gearboxes – they thought they could deal with this – as of lubrication. The new Group 2 insisted that a car could not have a dry sump system unless it was built with one as *standard*. Ford and others (including, of course, the expensive Jaguar

172

project) were therefore faced with using conventional 'wet' sumps again. In Ford's case, this meant going back to 1969, and losing six years' development.

Even though the sumps could have their shapes changed, could be baffled, and could otherwise be modified, the fact remained that the engine oil had to be stored below the engine. That, in itself, was not critical, but the fact that the oil would now be subject to the vagaries of centrifugal force was frightening. Under the very high cornering forces which a modern 'slick' racing tyre could develop, the oil would rush up the sides of the sump pan, and the oil pump pick-up (which could no longer be pressure fed) might well start sucking in air.

Engine failures looked likely, and in spite of the work which went into avoiding such calamities, this is precisely what happened. Not only Ford, but other manufacturers, found that it was almost impossible to get their oil to the engine's bearings without making the system illegal, and a whole series of failures duly occurred.

By June, Zakspeed had not managed to finish a single race, and were faced with astronomical re-building expenses. They withdrew in a huff. Alec Poole, in the Boreham-loaned car entered by Derek MacMahon, fared rather better, and even finished sixth at Mugello and third at Brno, but still had his share of disasters. It was only towards the end of the season, after a lot of fruitless experimentation, that the engines built by Brian Hart became anything like reliable. In 1977, the FIA finally bowed to intense pressure from the competitors, for it was not only Ford, but Jaguar and BMW, for instance, who were in deep trouble, and dry-sumps were re-admitted.

Fortunately for Boreham, and the rallying team, this problem did not arise. Though John Griffiths was told to get on with the development of a new Group 2 build specification, Peter Ashcroft was happy to compete in Group 4 with well-proven cars for the next season at least.

Not that the year started without incident. The main excitement was away from the tracks. At Ford's annual motor sport press conference in January, Peter Ashcroft revealed that he had hired Ari Vatanen's services for the season, and that he would be driving the ex-Makinen APG car in the British rally championship. This caused howls of dismay from his audience, who wanted to know why an un-known (in Britain) Finn should take precedence over Russell Brookes? At the end of the season, with Vatanen having won the championship (and, admittedly, also written off two cars!), they might have changed their tune. There were also shouts of "What *does* a British driver have to do to get into the works team, then?" to which Stuart Turner's answer was, "He must start beating Roger Clark regularly."

Barracking apart, the big news at the conference was that the new-shape Mexicos and RS2000s were at last available, but built in Saarlouis, and that the factory had found enough financial backing to tackle a more ambitious international rallying programme. Brave words were spoken about the events to be tackled, but it is as well that they were not all detailed. After all, when I started the writing of this book in January 1976 the Safari cars were partly built – but by the end of February the entries had been cancelled!

That was not an omen, but merely an admission of common sense. A team of Safari cars, backed properly, could not effectively be entered at less than £20,000 a car. No rally in the world, apart from another Marathon which would be quite a different project, costs remotely as much. Sponsorship had been expected to help close the financial credibility gap, but when this did not turn up in time common sense overcame sentiment and the Safari entry was

173

Vatanen's APG-backed RS2000 won the 1976 Tour, making it three wins in a row for RS2000s. That is John Taylor's Haynes-sponsored car right behind him

withdrawn – all, that is, except for one car for local hero Vic 'Junior' Preston to drive. The new cars themselves (one actually being Vatanen's RAC Rally crash-rebuild) came in very useful in Portugal and Morocco, and – later – in Australia.

The national season, and the British championship, can be summed up easily. For Ford there was complete domination, with Vatanen, Brookes and Roger Clark in the top three places. Leyland Cars' TR7s weren't competitive enough early enough, while Andy Dawson's efforts in the Datsuns were hampered by the 12,000-mile supply line to Japan.

It was not a season completely without incident. Very surprisingly, Roger Clark had two accidents – the second of which was caused by early-morning driver error. Ari Vatanen's driving went from strength to strength during the year; he won his first International, the Welsh, in May, and went on to dominate the Manx in September. In the meantime, his rallying led a charmed life. His poor car rarely finished without one destroyed corner, he had a bad roll in the Ulster rally, and another one to finish off the old shell in the Castrol 76 (even so, the long-suffering machine was then due to be rebuilt for Safari practice in 1977!).

Russell Brookes, too, did his reputation a lot of good, and his cars a lot of harm. He led the Welsh until the last morning, then flew off into the trees, won the Scottish after rolling on an early stage, and suffered mechanical breakdowns in other events. Throughout the season he always appeared behind the same registration number, but from April, effectively, had the makings of two RS1800s whose mechanical parts were swopped about in some confusion.

In the forests, the cars were always impressively reliable. Billy Coleman's car, prepared as always by Thomas Motors of Blackpool, was less successful, probably because it lacked the truly dedicated preparation of the other three cars. There was no doubt that Boreham, by now, could build very fast and very strong 'forest racers'. The problem, perhaps, was that they had concentrated on this breed to the exclusion of all others, and to gain that strength they had allowed the weight to creep up.

The weight problem was serious. The homologated weight in January 1975 was 810kg (1,785lb). Stripped out race cars could approach that, but a well-protected rally car was much heavier. An endurance car (built, say, for a Safari) will probably weigh between 950 and 970kg (2,095 and 2,139lb). Russell Brookes, when rebuilding one of his 1976 cars, took the trouble to weigh a complete axle assembly fitted with the dural brace and the axle skids; he was astonished to find that it weighed more than 250lb. "No wonder", said Russell, "that the Bilsteins get hot!"

Weight, or rather getting rid of it, was a major pre-occupation in 1976. I once called in at Boreham, and found Norman Masters pottering purposefully round Roger Clark's Cossack car with a drill and variety of bits in his hands. How much did he reckon to save eventually? About 100lb, he thought.

The back axle for 1976 was usually built without its brace, but on the other hand it had thicker and stronger axle tubes than before, and the suspension Panhard rod had recently been specified. Although the brace was fitted for the rough events, Peter Ashcroft is not at all convinced that it is necessary any more. Not only that, but the fact that a brace was fitted, and a set of gaskets leaked, was directly responsible for Ford's poor showing in the Southern Cross rally in October.

The other major problem, solved only towards the end of the year, was engines. As prepared at the end of the 1975 season by Brian Hart, a minimum of 245bhp was guaranteed. The same engines, in more effective chassis in 1976, gave persistent trouble. Look at the record:
Monte – Makinen's car retires with a blown engine
Firestone – Clark's car retires with a blown engine
Morocco – Clark's car retires with a blown engine
Thousand Lakes – Makinen's car blows an engine before the start
Southern Cross – one car needed a new engine flown out before the start
Manx Rally – Clark's car blew an engine in practice.

In nearly every case the problem was cylinder head gaskets, and in each case this failed at the back of the head. It took months of detective work (the pressure being such that there is *never* enough time for leisurely and persistent testing) to discover that cylinder head nuts at the rear of the engine, well masked by stiffening ribs, were now beginning to yield to enormously high compression pressures. Boreham hope that that one is now well and truly laid to rest.

Even so, the Boreham cars' overseas programme was never without its

Ari Vatanen 'totalled' this car against a tree in the 1975 RAC Rally, and Timo Makinen had no more luck with it in Morocco. It blew its axle in the Southern Cross, so one wishes Ford New Zealand better luck with it!

disasters. The pundits were quick to jump in with both feet, saying that it was because the team was out of touch. A little less loud-mouthing and a bit more analysis would have shown up something rather different. Murphy's Law was incredibly active at Boreham in 1976.

In the Monte, for instance, there was no way that Clark or Makinen could be expected to beat the Stratos team, but they could expect to beat everybody else. In the event Makinen's car blew its engine, and Roger Clark's car (the ex-Manx winner) was slowed by faulty damper settings. No matter what was tried, and set after set of dampers were fitted, the car was picking up wheels, and losing time on every hairpin. Clark finished fifth – itself a stupendous achievement, but Walter Rohrl's Opel was fourth. Not until the team got back to Boreham did they find that the Germans had supplied wrongly-calibrated Bilsteins *with the up-to-date markings!* It had never happened before.

In the Firestone Rally, held in Spain, Timo Makinen was surprisingly beaten into second place by a local twin-cam Seat 1430. No excuse really, though

Makinen thought he had practised enough. Afterwards it was revealed that the local hero had also practised various stages in the hope that they would be used as 'secret' sections. They were – he won.

Morocco was a disaster for the team, as both cars retired. Once again the unfortunate Makinen suffered repeated gearbox failures through a case of mis-alignment which only became obvious after the event.

There was triumph after another disaster in South Africa. Timo's Total Rally car should have been the Preston Safari Escort, suitably refurbished, but it was only about a week before the start that it became clear that it was still ship-bound, on the high seas. An incredibly rushed re-build of an ex-Firestone Rally car (which had also been mildly crashed by Pentti Airikkala in a recent British event) in *four days,* allowed a substitute to be rushed out to South Africa by air.

"Everybody in the place was working on that one," Mick Jones told me, "and when I loaded it into the hold of a Jumbo at London Airport I wouldn't have been surprised to find someone locked in the boot, still working away!" For once Murphy's Law was confounded. Makinen took the car straight from

177

the plane to scrutineering, then drove it serenely to a fine win for Boreham – as it happens, his last ever. Roger Clark, in a locally-prepared and slightly-slower car, was second close behind the flying Finn.

Even in the Thousand Lakes, the Boreham jinx struck again. Timo, driving with all his old fire and precision, led the entire event away from the start, but after only a handful of stages his car began to be slowed with elusive misfiring. Contaminated petrol was the culprit – but it was only Boreham's luck that nobody else seemed to suffer. Ari Vatanen, for his part, wrecked a brand new car when distracted by an intercom failure.

The Southern Cross debacle was almost the last straw. As in every event they tackled during the year except the Monte, the works Escorts had started as favourites. True to form Makinen and Clark led in the early stages. Both then suffered back axle failures caused by a gasket failure between axle brace and axle casing.

Even in Britain, the jinx was present. Vatanen's APG car, leading the Scottish rally, suffered crown wheel and pinion failure on the second morning. This fault is so unknown that Boreham service cars never carry repair kits. The subsequent antics of the mechanics in persuading a private owner to sacrifice his 3-litre Capri axle (3.09-to-1) to put where a 5.3-to-1 Escort ratio should be, turned the Esso film *Scotch and Dry* into a comedy classic.

The Tour of Britain, for Group 1 cars, was a triumph for Vatanen but a near-disaster for Boreham. Four brand-new RS2000s, initially prepared by Haynes of Maidstone, carried different sponsorship. Two of them, driven by Clark and Makinen, retired on their first and second circuit races respectively. Their clutches, of what ought to have been an impeccable specification, literally exploded. The new sponsors were not at all amused. Ari Vatanen, the ever-fortunate young Finn, swept sweetly on to win for Ford. His APG car, need I say it, had a different type of clutch. Ari, in 1976, was having that sort of a season.

Only one event remained to tie up the year – the RAC Rally. But before that, there was heartening news for the factory in other directions. Zakspeed, making their annual pilgrimage to South Africa, took a pair of RS1800s (without the penalties of wet-sump installations) to the Kyalami 1000km race. The old firm of Heyer and Ludwig finished a splendid second overall, but even that must have been a disappointment to the ambitious Zakowsky, as his car had won the event outright in 1975!

In November the news was more about people than about cars. Peter Ashcroft finally decided that the time had come for Ford and Timo Makinen to part company – a decision brought about purely on the grounds of personal incompatibilities, and not on driving skill – and this caused enough of a sensation. Ashcroft then caused an even bigger furore by flying off to Sweden, and signing up Bjorn Waldegard to take Makinen's place. Waldegard, master of the Stratos like nobody other than Sandro Munari (and twice winner of the Monte Carlo rally in Porsches), told Lancia that he was leaving them. The Torinese management were so piqued by this that they instantly withdrew his RAC Rally entry. This then allowed Ford to scratch around, reshuffle their resources, and to find an Escort for Waldegard to drive in the team even earlier than expected!

With the 'Silver Jubilee' RAC Rally looking to be as fast, exciting and closely-contested as ever, Ford's entry from Boreham was all keyed up for its attempt to win for the fifth consecutive year. All the form books, and all the suggestions, were that the Escorts might be overwhelmed by both Fiat and Lancia, while the possibilities of the new 16-valve Saab 99s could not be discounted.

Boreham's first problem was one of cars. What had started out in the spring as a neat and compact three-car entry had eventually mushroomed into a positive army of Boreham-owned machines. Some, it is true, were loaned out for the occasion, but the fact was that five machines were under the direct control of Peter Ashcroft's team, and another five were present in one capacity or another.

Two brand-new RS1800s (for Clark and Makinen) were joined by Vatanen's heavily-rebuilt Thousand Lakes machine. Markku Saaristo, who had driven an RS2000 so brilliantly in the Thousand Lakes, was to have the same car in the RAC Rally. So far, so good. Bjorn Waldegard then joined the team, and in two hectic weeks another car was found for him. The Makinen Total Rally winner (which the South African Jan Hettema was to have driven), was hastily refettled.

How the other five were allocated bears examination, because it was typical of the way a modern factory gets the most use out of its team. Brookes and Coleman had their usual 'loan cars', David Sutton was lent an RS1800 to prepare himself and for Simo Lampinen to drive, Peter Clarke (a Ford Rallye Sport dealer) was asked to prepare and enter another ex-Tour of Britain RS2000 for Kyosti Hamalainen, and finally the South Africans were provided with Roger Clark's long-suffering '1976 season' Cossack car.

The results, as I am sure every Escort owner will not need reminding, made all the effort worth while. At the finish, in Bath, it was a very emotional occasion, for not only did Ford manage to win for the fifth year in succession, but they did it in such good style, *and* with the delighted Roger Clark in the driving seat!

For the first part of the event, though, the entire event was led by Pentti Airikkala, driving a privately-built RS1800 for the David Sutton team. Airikkala's abilities are not in doubt, and frankly the Ford management were not at all worried about being matched by a private car. As Peter Ashcroft said during the event: "At least this proves that there is *nothing* special about the works cars. A customer can make his just as fast and just as strong as our own, if he can afford it. But I have to admit that this means spending a lot of money. Make no mistake of it, though, David Sutton's workshops build very fine rally cars."

Airikkala, though, suffered engine problems in the West Country, spent a lot of time fettling the car in Weston-Super-Mare, and was excluded for being outside the time limit. A protest was registered about what was a difficult-to-understand decision, and Airikkala carried on, but his car later suffered a burnt out clutch, which settled the matter.

The Ford factory cars, too, had mixed fortunes. Timo Makinen, desperately keen to prove that Ford had been wrong to drop him, made a very rare and uncharacteristic mistake on only the second stage, rolled the car, and bent the chassis so much that the transmission failed. Ari Vatanen, too, established an early and expanding lead, but struck engine trouble by the first evening, and was forced out by midnight.

Roger Clark, delighted with an "absolutely gorgeous" new car (his words, not mine), soon found his way into second place behind Airikkala, and Waldegard showed that his own abilities and only a single three-hour testing

Timo Makinen's car going into temporary orbit on the 1976 Thousand Lakes, which he led until contaminated petrol slowed him to fourth place

session in another Escort had allowed him to be competitive. Russell Brookes and Billy Coleman, too, were well placed, though Brookes' fuel-injected car suffered the ubiquitous head gasket failure before the second day dawned. Simo Lampinen went off the road, Saaristo later emulated him (but not terminally), and Coleman's car was rammed by a non-competing car on an open road section, but carried on looking rather crumpled.

With Airikkala's challenge gone, and after Clark had stamped his enormous personality on the event yet again, the chances of this quite unprecedented fifth win for Boreham grew firmer and firmer. Clark, quite uncharacteristically, was looking phenomenally fast and even a bit ragged at times, but he was also unquestionably the master of the event.

He rolled in to the usual celebrations at the finish in Bath, and a highly-charged emotional response. Not only had he not been expected to win this event, but there were people ready to say that he was 'over the hill'. Clark's response to that was that he personally thought he had been over the hill for years, but he still enjoyed proving the opposite!

It was a fitting climax to the year, not just because Roger Clark won the event, but because Ford proved everything about their cars. Not even the 'homologation special' engineering of the Fiat-Abarth 131s, nor the mid-engined magic of a Lancia Stratos, could beat a healthy Escort. It proved, yet again, that the Escort was, and probably would be for some time, the most versatile competition car in the world.

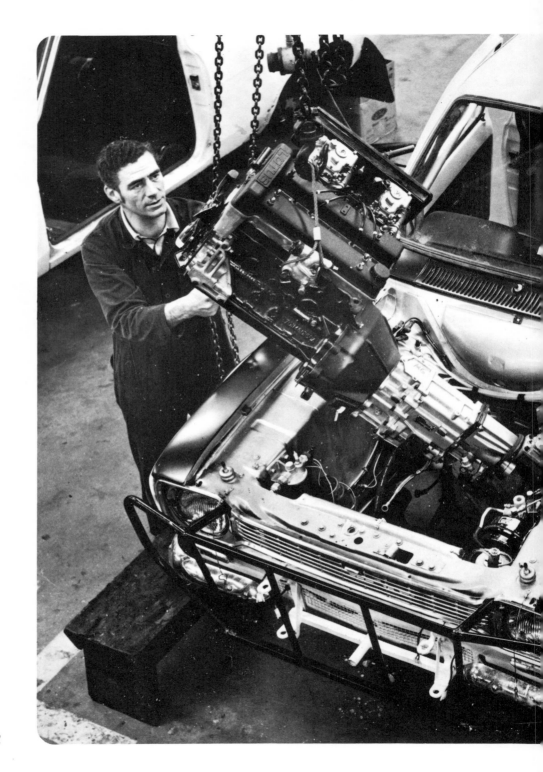

11
Building a world beater

A Safari-tune Twin-Cam dropping into one of the last of the Twin-Cams which Boreham built. That is a 5-speed long-shift Z F gearbox fixed to it

Factory-prepared Ford Escorts, waiting on the grid at a race track, or at scrutineering before a major rally, always look immaculate, brutally-efficient, and magnificently-prepared. What looks right usually is right, and the results usually prove it. The effort, in making *sure,* takes hundreds and hundreds of hours. Building a works Escort is a long, complex, carefully-thought-out, and incredibly detailed business.

Boreham have been building the world's fastest Escorts for so long now that you would be excused for thinking the process came automatically. Nothing could be further from the truth. Every event, and every week, something in the car is being changed. Last year's RAC Rally car would look very similar to this year's – but the mechanics and the drivers would know where improvements had been made.

Building a world beater starts from a body shell, but before that it starts with the entry to an event. There is, need I emphasise it, a world of difference between a car built for the Tour de France and one built to tackle the Safari. A ground-hugging race car would be quite unsuited to tackle Morocco, or South Africa, where one of Mick Jones' 'crop-sprayers' would be more at home.

So let's assume that a new car is to be built, and let's also assume that the event and its driver are already known. So where is the build sheet? Where is the detailed specification that a mechanic needs to start assembling parts from which to build up the car?

For some years, until the late 1970s, there wasn't one. It might sound old-fashioned, but memory worked equally as well. There would be problems, of course, if any of the dozen mechanics were asked to prepare any of the dozen or so cars on the fleet at any one time. Production-line preparation has been tried – notably in 1969 to 1971 – but caused more aggravation than it was worth. Roger Clark, for example, was asked to drive left-hand-steering cars because the rest of the team were all continental drivers. It made flow-line building possible, but it made Roger rather unhappy.

From about 1971 to 1977, Boreham's method was to encourage one mechanic to know all the whims and fancies of a particular driver, and to know how he wanted the car set up. Not that he could look after every stage of build on every car, but he would usually be there 'at the death.'

Robin Vokins, recruited by Stuart from Abingdon in 1969, is the Timo Makinen expert, while long-serving Norman Masters looks after Roger Clark's rally cars. Clark, indeed, is so confident that Masters knows exactly what should be done to his cars, that he rarely sees the cars before he arrives at the start of an event. His Cossack cars, used exclusively in British championship events, lived at Boreham between events. It is nothing for Clark to arrive at scrutineering after his car, kick the tyres, and enquire amiably of Norman Masters if everything is in order? His first drive in the car since a rebuild is often the moment when he takes it up the slope of the starting ramp.

The build sheet, usually, was in a mechanic's head, though its basic details have been ingrained into every Boreham's instinctive working pattern for some time. When I asked Robin Vokins to show me the last formal sheet he had used, he scratched around on his bench, and eventually found a much-modified three-page dossier about the Safari cars – the date on the form was 1972, and this was 1976! To be fair, when he was building up a 1976 car he also had a scribbled list of Makinen's latest preferences – hung up on a nail, sandwiched between a movement order for his next trip abroad, and the latest centre-fold from *Playboy*.

Even that list, terse and undetailed by any standards, was in special Boreham gobbledygook: "Axle with light brace . . . Timo's usual seat . . . ZF long extension with short stick . . . Timo's electrics . . ." – which all meant something to Robin Vokins and the others, if not to an outsider.

The method of Boreham's operations has changed radically in recent years – with the watershed really marked by the 'energy crisis' of 1973. Before that time, when the company had more staff than today, most of the special jobs were tackled at Boreham. Afterwards, with the total workforce greatly reduced, many jobs had to be farmed out. In one case, at least, a specialist – Terry Samuell – left Boreham, but took the contract to build and rebuild ZF gearboxes with him.

At the time of the World Cup Rally in 1970, more than two dozen mechanics crowded themselves into the building. Nowadays, even though the post-crisis days of 1974 are well past, Mick Jones has only a dozen mechanics.

Whatever the FIA's intentions about competitions cars, there isn't a single works competition department who start preparation by taking delivery of a complete car. Not, that is, unless it is to be built to the most milk-and-water of Group One regulations. That doesn't mean that a competition Group Two or Group Four machine is a cheat, or a one-off fiddle – it is merely that Boreham has found a better way. The better way, for them, is to start from the beginning – from a bare body shell.

Even the preparation of the shells, a time-consuming business, is contracted out. With regulations which allow greatly modified and improved rear suspension systems, and because the ZF gearbox is that much bulkier, altering a body is a big job.

For the real birth, the real genesis, of a new Escort competition car, we have to go right across London, to the Old Woking workshops of Gomm Metal Developments Ltd. Here it is that Maurice Gomm and his three sons control a thriving specialist business which might at any one time be building a Formula One monocoque, a 'dream car' for a film or TV series, and a whole new series of modified Escort shells.

Gomm himself is a sheet-metal specialist from way back when, who was first introduced to Ford via the Lola GT and its development into the GT40 in 1963. Since then he has never looked back, and Ford keep him very busy. Len Bailey, who was closely connected with the GT40, Mirage, GT70 and other specialised racing cars, also got involved in Alan Mann's racing programme from the very beginning.

It was Bailey who devised and shaped the now-well-known Mk 1 Escort wheel arch extensions, and it was Gomm's 'Tinkers' who shaped the first examples. Incidentally, there is no truth in the rumour that Transit van wheelarch extensions were used – ever. Several thousand sets have now been sold, almost all of which have been neatly pressed by a Midlands concern.

By 1970, and the rush of works preparation for the World Cup Rally, Gomm's workshops took over the bulk of Boreham's body shell build. Well before the end of the 1970s, Boreham was also taking some supplies from Gartrac, and occasionally from Safety Devices.

The Mark 2 shaped Escort needs less work than the original car – both because it was re-styled and re-engineered with competition in mind, and because items like the wheelarch extensions and the spoilers are bolt-on items made in reinforced glassfibre.

185

The Mintex Dales single-cam RS2000 engine, with twin Webers and a hot cam

Even so, the Ford Sport bulletins issued in recent years show the amount of detailed thought that goes into improving a body without making it 'illegal' for motor sporting purposes. The production body shell, made by Ford at Halewood for British Escorts, and at Saarlouis for German versions, is perfectly strong enough for its intended use, but where the regulations allow it there are numerous ways in which the shell can be further stiffened, lightened and modified.

Apart from the detail and painstakingly scrupulous checking of welds, the additional welding and brazing, the big jobs tackled by Mo Gomm's workshops are the installation of the rear damper 'turret' kits which accept the vertical Bilstein dampers, the addition of fixing points for rear suspension radius arms, the Panhard rod mounting brackets (since the beginning of 1976), slipper bearings for the latest type of leaf spring and the re-shaping of the gearbox tunnel and its mountings to accept the ZF gearbox.

Added to this is work to provide fixings for dry sump oil tanks, the re-positioned petrol tank, a second brake servo in the back seat area, and other details.

Last, but very important, is the installation of the Safety Device full roll cage, which is now mandatory even on national rallies. Incidentally, the forward pointing 'Llama' bars, used on the 1970 World Cup Rally bodies, have never again been used for any other application. Also thought of as a precaution against shell racking, they have been found surplus to requirements even in

Brand new for the RAC Rally, OOO 97M gets chassis treatment before the engine slots in

rough conditions – and in most cases the regulations ban their use.

Even a Gomm-prepared body shell has limits to its life, so it has been Boreham's policy in recent years to prepare brand-new shells for the RAC Rally, for the Safari, and usually for any other major championship-attacking car. A properly-built Escort shell can withstand unbelievable misuse, even involving major accidents, before getting beyond repair.

Ari Vatanen's championship-winning RS1800 of 1976 is a case in point. That car was brand new for the 1975 RAC Rally where, sponsored by APG, it was steered expertly to a first-time-out victory by Timo Makinen. After that gruelling debut, and with APG's blessing, it was committed to contesting every event – 13 before the RAC (when he would get another new car).

It had quite a life. A winning car five times, second once and third on three occasions, it failed to finish three times. In those five wins were the Welsh and Manx Internationals. On the Scottish it was forced to retire (with a smashed differential), but it had several accidents. A roll on the Ulster was so major that the car really ought to have been treated to a new shell. Only the fact that time was so short (and because Vatanen had also rolled the only alternative on the Thousand Lakes a week earlier!) meant that it had to be extensively re-skinned and knocked into shape. It visited the scenery in nearly every event (Vatanen is that sort of Flying Finn!) and was finally rolled into retirement on its last event in October.

Even so, it was an astonishingly resilient car, which suffered regular and

There really isn't much space under an Escort for the ZF gearbox

Single-piece prop-shaft, short radius arms, axle skid *and* brace, all date this as a 1973/74
RS1600. The latest cars have much longer radius arms

Ken Wiltshire wiring up the complex loom of a new Boreham rally car

compassionate repair without complaining. With an early Escort one usually saw signs of old age in cracks and breaks at the base of the screen pillars, and with the later cars the tell-tale signs were usually that the front 'chassis' legs started to fold up underneath the scuttle panel.

All rally cars seem to take on a set early in their life, but the really hard-working ones eventually give up the hard struggle. At that stage, incidentally, they are usually sold off to private owners, who pay good money for them. There is sentiment in these things, for sure, but Boreham's mechanics cannot usually see the attraction of buying one of their cast offs.

An even better example of toughness was Roger Clark's first 'Esso Blue' car of 1972 and 1973. In fifteen months it tackled as many events, and was only re-shelled once (after Clark had rolled it in a filming session at Boreham!); during that time it won 12 events, including the 1972 RAC, 1972 Manx, 1973 Welsh and 1973 Scottish Internationals. The other eight wins were all in RAC nationals.

Boreham hold no enormous float of already-modified body shells. Their new-car building programme is always carefully worked out, and reviewed   **189**

This was an RS1600, but RS1800s are much the same. The petrol is stored in a rubber bag tank, behind the light alloy covers, and the dry sump oil reservoir is in the tail

frequently, so that Mo Gomm can allocate his facilities accordingly, but to allow for the occasional big accident (and even works drivers have them – at times) there may be one or two in stock, either at Old Woking or at Boreham.

There are hundreds of important components in a car, but the three most vital, in the Escort's case, are the engine, gearbox and the back axle. Of the three, only the axles come in for any measure of work on the premises.

Boreham used to be equipped with every facility for preparing, and renovating, its own engines, but for nearly ten years they have not done so. At almost any time of year there is steady flow of 16-valve BDA engines between the competition centre and a small factory in Harlow New Town – Brian Hart Limited. Hart himself is an ex-Cosworth employee from way back, and Keith Duckworth has paid him the ultimate compliment by telling me that he is *still* sorry that he could not persuade the balding young man to move up to Northampton with Cosworth Engineering in the mid-1960s.

Hart was a very successful Formula Three and Formula Two driver, who seemed to thrive on very very fast circuits, but – he admits – suffered quite a bit from sometimes being in the same team as Jim Clark. "Anyone's ego would suffer if they had to compare their performance with those of Jim!" quips Hart

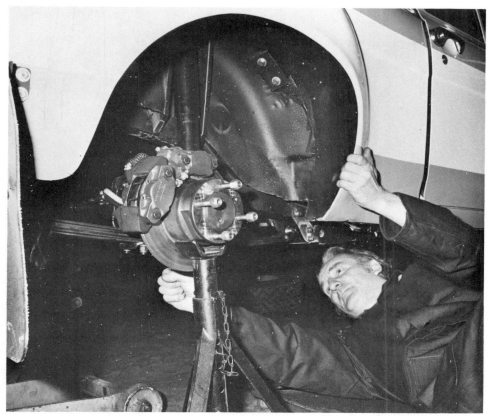

Rear disc brakes, twin-calipers per disc, big vertical Bilstein dampers, leaf springs and radius arms are still typical of the Escort rally car. Only an independent rear suspension conversion would improve the traction compared with this

today. By the end of the 1960s, with his own active racing career over, he had started a modest little business as an engine builder/tuner. The fact that Keith Duckworth thought so much of the still-young Hart helped, but Hart's connections with Peter Ashcroft were also valuable.

By 1970 Brian Hart Limited were already doing some work for Boreham. "I suppose we came in strongly with the arrival of the BDA. We did some work with Boreham on Twin-Cams, but they still had their own engine shop at that stage. They moved on completely to RS1600 from 1971, and I have been building engines for them ever since."

Hart is modest. Not only does he prepare race and rally engines for the works, but he also tackles production of 'normal' RS1800 engines for dispatch to Saarlouis where the RS1800 is manufactured.

From Boreham to Harlow New Town takes less than an hour, and it is a trip that 'Reg' Redgewell knows well. The distance is not great, and the atmosphere in both places is the same. The Hart workshops, like those at Boreham, are too small, in no way luxurious, but get on with their job very efficiently.

The 'offices' – which means space for Brian Hart himself, a designer and one secretary – are upstairs, above a glossy tape-controlled machine tool or two.

Zakspeed-developed spats help get the heat away from the brakes on high-speed tarmac-rally or race Escorts. Rauno Aaltonen is leaning into the car, asking for details *(photo Martin Holmes)*

Petrol injection and adjustable strut tops on this works car show that experiment and improvement are still being sought *(photo Martin Holmes)*

The contrast, not deliberate, is obvious. People can get by without the ultimate in surroundings – the money here is spent on the machines. Sound-deadening – except around the dynamometer cells – is nearly non-existent; getting an interview with the gaffer is a noisy business.

For many years, BDAs were supplied to Boreham, and to many other customers. Hart supplied engines to Zakspeed on many occasions, and of course also designed and built his own very successful four-cylinder engines for Formula 2, Formula 1 (in turbocharged form), and hill-climbing.

"But for an out-and-out 2-litre racing formula you need a proper 2-litre engine, not the 'converted' BDA we had to use for so long. That explains why I went ahead with the 420R."

Thus Hart dismisses his own, his very own, Hart 420R Formula Two engine. You would be excused for thinking there was a lot of BDA hidden away inside the similar profile – and you would be wrong. Dead wrong.

The 420R is two inches longer than the BDA overall, with unique cylinder spacings, bore and stroke, and almost everything except the basic breathing arrangements. But why do I even bother to mention this? Hart explains:

"There are some details in my 420R which are not idealised for a pure racing engine, even though we get more than 300bhp from 2-litres. The problem was that while I was designing it, Stuart Taylor kept on saying 'Don't forget to make sure it could be fitted into an Escort!'."

After a pause for my mind to stop boggling, Hart carried on in that slightly bemused, matter-of-fact, way of his:

"Yes, really. At one stage the 420R was a definite contender for the job of powering an RS1600 replacement, in de-tuned form. But not any more, for the usual economic reasons. If it was, I wouldn't be telling you, would I?"

I have already explained how it was Brian Hart who designed the light-alloy cylinder block for his own racing purposes before Peter Ashcroft even knew about it. It was this block, more than anything else, which kept the Escorts competitive for so long. At 1,800cc, and around 205bhp, the iron block engine was at its rallying limit, and the Escort was about to be engulfed by its opposition.

Nothing will drag out of him the admission that he is other than a competent engine builder. His test beds, and the 420R engine, all tell you that he must be a designer/tuner of enormous merit as well. Hart may not boast for himself, but certainly proud of his staff. He also makes no bones about the vast contribution still being made by Cosworth.

"Cosworth supplies nearly all the cranks, rods, cams, valve gear details, and other bits and pieces to all of us. I admit it, readily. Some of the other tuners would have you believe they do their own machining. But all they have is a plain van collecting bits from Northampton!"

Do Boreham give him a logical build programme? Does he have enough time to build engines in a leisurely manner any more?

"A couple of years ago it was better, when the works weren't doing as many events. From 1976, certainly, the pressure has always been on. You can't really carry a BDA as excess airline baggage, but I reckon Mick Jones would have liked to, once or twice.

"There is no big bank of engines, either at Boreham or here. They don't come back from a rally, pluck another lump down off the shelf, and send the old one back for a rebuild. No way. If they have ten days to re-prepare, it means we have less than a week!"

One of several rear suspension systems used on works rally cars – coil springs and a Watts linkage in 1973 *(photo Martin Holmes)*

Apart from Hart's achievement in nudging the rally engines' power up from 225bhp in 1972 alloy block form, through 235bhp in 1973 and 1974, to a guaranteed 245bhp for 1975/76, 255/260bhp by 1979 (with up to 272bhp in full-house tarmac-specification, fuel-injection, tune) he has made remarkable strides in reliability.

High-output 2-litre BDAs got themselves quite a reputation for blowing cylinder head gaskets, and for cylinder liners which tended to move around a little. The second failing almost automatically led to the first. Some tuners still lined their BDAs, but it was Brian Hart Limited which developed the liner-less, hard chrome bore engines which solved the problem – not Ford themselves. Light-alloy blocks without liners, at those sort of speeds? Even General Motors had difficulty with their first Vega engines at first, but Hart had solved the BDA's problem.

And let's make it clear. You couldn't blame the original BDA design for this. It is, as Hart hastens to point out, one of the problems of an engine stretched to its limit to take advantage of capacity classes.

The Hart-prepared engines have reached such a pitch of reliability, power and flexibility, that Boreham still think there is more power in there, to be winkled out for future improvements. As John Griffiths told me:

"The engines have to do stages, trickle off through towns and traffic jams, *and* we expect them to start up in *parc ferme* at 4am, with water on the ignition leads, and on dirty old racing spark plugs. All the drivers use 9,000 and

9,500rpm. If they miss a gear it's nothing to see more than 10,000 on the rev-counter tell-tales – and the engines can still do a full-length International! Remarkable. Remarkable."

Behind the engine is the gearbox, and here Boreham have a rather easier time. Whereas the BDA has been stretched and tuned right away from the original concept of the engine, the ZF gearbox is at least built with huge torques in mind. Anything built by a reputable West German firm to withstand 2½-litres of Ferrari power should, one assumes, be able to deal with the best in BDAs.

All the best ZF rallying gearboxes find a home in a small workshop in Rainham. ZF build them in Germany, and there is a ZF subsidiary company in Nottingham, but racing preparation and modification is in the capable hands of just one man – Terry Samuell.

Terry's ZF business, like Topsy, just grew and grew. He was a mechanic at Boreham in the 1960s and early 1970s. When the ZF gearbox arrived on the Escort scene in 1969 it was an unknown quantity. Soon, and he still isn't sure how it happened, Terry Samuell became the rebuilding expert at Boreham. More significantly, he also noticed that the private owners usually had to come back to Boreham for advice with their own ZF problems.

When the Ford man-power squeeze set in a few years ago, he did not hesitate for long. With the full agreement and encouragement of Ford's motor sport management, Samuell left – and took Boreham's ZF gearbox maintenance business with him.

"Mind you," says Terry, "I soon thought I had dropped an awful clanger. I started up my own business just before the summer, and after a brief spate of activity the orders just died away. I thought I had made a dreadful mistake, and even took to driving a lorry for a week or two. Then, thank goodness, everybody came back to rallying, the orders started rolling in, and I haven't had time to relax since!"

Probably only Samuell understands all the permutations of ratios, quick-change modifications, updates and cross-referencing to non-Ford users which make this particular gearbox such a valuable 'building block.' His notebooks, started the day he set up shop from home in Rainham, can give you the detail of any gearbox and any modification he has carried out in three years.

"When XPU 220L was stolen in Cardiff early in 1975, I was able to tell Boreham within minutes what gearbox number to look for, and I know that Brian told them as quickly about the engine. The bloke who did it must have been very naive – – surely he *must* have known we'd have a record?"

Keeping up with a driver's little ways is only part of his expertise: "Timo went through several phases. Once he liked the short rail box, then he liked the long rail. Nowadays he prefers the long rail with the short gear lever!"

Quite a few of the improvements to a ZF were developed by Terry Samuell at Boreham – such as the light alloy sandwich plate between selector housing and main box, and the changes to selector slide materials, but he makes no claim to the quick-change methods.

"That was done by Mick Jones and several of Boreham's mechanics. At first, with the ZF box as built in Germany, it took anything up to three hours to change one in the workshops, and at the side of the road it was impossible. There wasn't much space around the bell housing and the tunnel, and to get all the fixings we have to drop the engine, and *that* meant dropping the front suspension too!

195

"Now, with very simple changes we make the box to be split from the bell housing very fast, and even at the side of the road, in the dark and in the rain, the job is possible in under 20 minutes."

Regarding ratios, nowadays Terry has no problem in remembering. Just about every application is covered by the '025' assembly, or 'race/rally' box, with top gear direct and bottom gear 2.30 inside the box.

Not, by the way, that there is even an element of quantity-production about the job. Terry Samuell's business *is* Terry Samuell, he has no staff. "That way I always know who to blame if anything goes wrong!" Only a handful of gearboxes are rebuilt every week. There are only so many hours in a week, so the ZF's reliability is welcomed down Rainham way.

Back at Boreham, then, build-up starts when the Gomm-prepared shell is trolleyed into place. There is only room on the shop floor for ten or so cars, and there is only a single ramp. All shells start out by being white. In the good old days before sponsorship became important, they rallied white too; nowadays the sponsor's paint-job is an important part of the preparation.

Spraying on the major colour is easy, but the sign-writing and the decoration is different. Boreham have a tame sign-writer, who has now stopped being amazed by Boreham's requests. After all, when you have painted a Cossack horseman by hand on the bonnet of Roger Clark's car, or made Timo Makinen's RAC Rally car look like a passable imitation of an *Evening Standard* delivery van, what else is there? What could be more incongruous than a Milk Marketing Board supported car with 'Are you getting enough' written upon it, or a muddy-brown paint job meant to look as much like a cigarette lighter poster as possible,

Stacked against the walls are odd bonnets, boot lids, doors and spoilers. In a hectic period it is amusing to try to match panels to embryo cars. Things get so confused at times, with number plates being removed so that the rear deck can be spruced up, that even a mechanic loses touch. "Hang on mate," Johnnie Rule once said in answer to my query, "we'd better look at the licence disc to make sure!"

At Boreham, with so much success behind them, and a publicity machine which allows them to be as well-known as the drivers, the mechanics need very little direction. Not that they ever would, with an extrovert anarchist like Mick Jones as their foreman. Don Partington, for instance, specialises in electrics, but could still build up a complete car. Norman Masters, inevitably, is linked to Roger Clark's cars.

In theory you don't rush the preparation of a car for the Safari, or for the RAC Rally. Up to six weeks is the ideal period for an all-new car to come together – but things rarely happen like that. Makinen's Total-winning machine of 1976, for instance, was re-prepared from slightly-damaged condition in four days when the car he should have been driving failed to arrive in South Africa.

A new car to replace a successful 'old nail' might take a very long time to be finished. As Norman Masters recalls: "When Roger started his Esso programme in 1972, he was supposed to have a new car. He started by using the Old Gold car in February, but it was the Scottish Rally in June before Esso Blue finally made it." Mechanics, like most successful businessmen, speak in their own lingo!

The pressure, with so few mechanics, is intense. The less-modified machines, like the set of Mk 2 RS2000s for the 1976 Tour of Britain, start preparation

The oil leak which lost Ford the 1976 Southern Cross Rally – from both Makinen's and Clark's differential housings. Henry Liddon, with time to spare having retired, took the photograph

somewhere else; those cars, incidentally, were entrusted to the Ford dealership of Haynes of Maidstone. Boreham preparation did not begin until 10 days before the start!

An outsider, looking on at Boreham, would be sure that a particular car could never be ready. Even a week before an important, and immovable, shipping date, a rally car looks as if it has been gutted by a gang of vandals. But no one seems to worry. Once the ever-valuable Reg has delivered an engine from Harlow New Town, and a gearbox from Rainham, the sign-writers have done their stuff, and the panels and lamp bars are collected nearby, the jig-saw soon takes shape.

Even so, it is a fact of life that no rally car (at Ford or anywhere else) is *ever* ready until the day it has to leave. Some of Ford's most successful results have been achieved with Escorts delivered at the start on a transporter, and theoretically 'running-in' for the first few hours.

In the end, of course, what must never be forgotten is to allow Ford's system to catch up. The car might have come together at Boreham from a collection of parts supplied from Saarlouis or Halewood, but it still needs a proper chassis number. That a works car is exquisitely hand-built, whereas all the others come together on a moving track, makes no difference. The parts are the same, as is the result. Even so, the system allows a few personal little wrinkles. You can usually recognise a works RS1600 or RS1800 by its vehicle number: ..9901 to ..9905 have been very popular in recent years.

Boreham mechanics can recognise their own handiwork, and somehow the many 'replicas' built elsewhere are different. Even in 1974, when Roger Clark's mechanics built two RS1600s for Poland, all from factory parts, the result was not quite the same. When the cars were brought back to Boreham for use in the 1974 RAC Rally, Boreham found many differences.

The 'replica' business, too, is big business. Resourceful private owners copy *anything*. After XPU 220L had been stolen, Boreham's staff gave Welsh police careful detail of some fittings which were unique to the works. One such was the latest in oil tanks – of which only a half-dozen had been made by Mo Gomm's workshops. Boreham found otherwise within days – the police kept ringing up and saying 'We've found it' – only to be told that the car they had discovered was well-known to Boreham and respectably privately-owned! The copyists had been busy, and Boreham didn't know it.

All the best fairy stories, of course, tell you that brand-new cars are built for every event. There might be isolated occasions, somewhere in the world, where this has happened in the past (Mercedes-Benz in Grand Prix racing in the 1950s?). but it certainly doesn't apply at Boreham. A look at the Appendices shows just how hard some cars are made to work – whether for racing or rallying. A few – a lucky few – which have gloriously won one event, are retired for exhibition use. The rest look forward to at least a season of campaigning.

Boreham's secret, not even a secret if you had time to hang around long enough and watch the painstaking way the mechanics go about their job, is that they can turn the most unlikely-looking wreck into an immaculate race or rally car. Only the most comprehensive accident leaves them in despair, but it is still remarkable what a new body shell can achieve. I doubt if any Escort has been crashed at such speeds as Ari Vatanen's brand-new car in the 1975 RAC Rally – LVW 690P was as good as dead for weeks, but it re-appeared – miraculously re-born – in the spring.

Although Boreham's basic preparation philosophy – of 'buying in' ready-prepared body shells, engines, and transmissions – never varied from 1968 to 1979, there was something of a revolution in build methods in the last few years. In 1976, Peter Ashcroft had been given clearance to develop a World Championship effort, and in 1977, to help him achieve this, he appointed Allan Wilkinson as the team's resident engineer.

In the late 1960s, Wilkinson had worked with Ford in Germany, and earlier in the 1970s he had not only been involved in AVO development at South Ockendon, but had raced his own Mexicos in British events. In 1977, his brief was, quite simply, to develop the RS1800 still further, so that it could win the World Championship. No radical innovations were likely to be approved, but he would have to see that the cars became more reliable, and more versatile; in particular, the car's tarmac handling would have to be improved.

The major changes took time to appear – the most powerful 16-valve engines, with fuel-injection, were not blooded until the Autumn of 1978, and the effective back axle differential oil coolers were not ready until 1979 – but the most immediate improvements were made in preparation. Wilkinson, an industry-trained engineer, rather than an enthusiast (he had not even been

198

involved with rally cars before moving to Boreham), noticed that the cars were effectively being built 'by hand', without specification sheets, and often without reference to other cars intended for the same event. It didn't seem logical to him, and even though he knew that it seemed to have worked well for years, he insisted that it had to be changed. The one mechanic/one car/one driver relationship, he thought, might have been cosy, but he didn't like it.

"It wasn't the way I saw us succeeding in the future", Allan said, "if only because there *could* have been occasions where spares held in one barge wouldn't fit one of the cars."

Within weeks, therefore, things began to change. Even while the 1977 Portugal cars were being prepared (one new car, STW 130R, for Waldegard, and two ex-RAC rally rebuilds for Clark and Vatanen), standardisation set in, and this process was ruthlessly extended in the months which followed. Soon the traditional method of preparation, where a mechanic kept his own build sheet 'in his head', was scrapped, while formal (and very detailed) specification sheets began to be issued.

Not only were certain key dimensions specified, and written down, for the first time (the length of the steering column being a typical example), but the first moves were made to standardise the layout of electrical wiring looms, control positions, and the layout of components (fuel tank, spare wheels, oil tank, and other details) fitted in the boot compartment.

The major administrative change of 1977, however, was not to the cars themselves, but to homologation. In effect, if not in fact, the Escort RS1800 was dropped, and a new model, the Escort RS, took its place! The difference, as far as Boreham was concerned, was not noticeable, though the result was most satisfactory.

In the first edition of this book, completed in 1976, I pointed out that the RS1800 faced a major problem. New homologation rules, due to be enacted on 1st January 1978, meant that the car would no longer to able to run as a full Group 4 car, but that it would have to revert to Group 2 status, and that this – among other things – meant that it would have to run with an 1,866cc engine, a wet sump lubrication system, a four-speed gearbox, and standard (road-car) suspension pick-up points. There was no doubt that this would have ruined the car's competitiveness, probably permanently.

Boreham's solution to the problem was masterly. Peter Ashcroft, and his homologation expert, John Griffiths, reasoned that several hundred works-replica Escorts had been built since the new-shape car was introduced in 1975, and that because of AVO's well-developed parts-supply business almost all of these cars used the same basic specification.

Accordingly, the brilliantly successful strategy was to discard the RS1800 before it was rendered uncompetitive, and to homologate a 'new' rally car. The new car was to be called the Escort RS, and for homologation Boreham had to convince the authorities that more than 400 of them had been produced. In view of the fact that Boreham themselves had already commissioned 25 new-shape cars (including four new machines being built for the Safari, at Easter), and that clones seemed to have sprung up all around the world, no-one argued with this claim.

The basic specification of the 'new' car was precisely what Boreham wanted, which is to say that it incorporated the full-house dry-sump 1,975cc engine, the multi-plate clutch, five-speed ZF gearbox, and Atlas axle, together with five-link rear suspension, adjustable struts, four-wheel disc brakes, wheel arch extensions, and a full roll cage. Nothing was missed, nothing was found wanting, and no compromises had to be made by the team in the next three seasons. The 'new' car was homologated on April 1 1977, under FIA Approval No. 650, and it was this Escort derivative which was finally dropped by competitive teams at the end of 1981. It would not be exaggerating to suggest that this master stroke of homologation was the key to Ford's success in the Escort's final years, equally as important as the assembly of the fine team of drivers.

There was still, of course, the bogey of British Type Approval, which no manufacturer could avoid. With effect from April 1978, every production car had to be put through a whole series of tests to satisfy the legislators, not only to prove that it was strong enough to be sent out on the roads, but that its exhaust emissions were low enough, its noise levels limited, and that many other safety features measured up to the required standards.

Since the Escort RS1800 was only ever a *very* limited-production machine (How many road cars *were* built? I have never been able to find out), Ford decided not to Type Approve it, and it was officially withdrawn from production before the end of 1977. For a time it seemed that Boreham would not be able to register any new cars after April 1978, which explains why WTW 569S was first registered in November 1977, and why no more new cars came into existence until May 1979; the four 'new' 1979 cars, in fact, came into existence as Escort Sport 1300s, briefly registered, then gutted and re-created as secondhand Escort RS models!

Boreham's mechanics, and the drivers who so bravely pushed their cars to the limits, did not care to get involved in such legal niceties. They were only interested in winning, and in looking for the next detail improvement to their well-loved machines.

All the effort, and all the back-breaking toil, is worth it when 'your car' wins its next event. Ask the Boreham mechanics, and they will agree. I have lost count of the times I have witnessed an all-nighter developing before a major event because some prima-donna driver is demanding changes. I have also marvelled at the way a problem can be solved in the pits, or at the side of the road, with championships and a lot of money hanging on the result. The chequered flags, and the sprayed champagne, make it all worthwhile.

12

Ford~versus~Fiat, 1977 and 1978

In 1977, media interest in world-class rallying perked up considerably. It was easy to see why. For several years, there had been no effective competition for the World Championship for Makes, which was in any case an under-promoted series. Suddenly, however, in 1977, Ford showed every sign of being able to match Fiat and Lancia, the principal protagonists, and they looked to be determined to fight it out with the Italians throughout the year.

In the next few years, indeed, World Championship rallying was really all about the running battle between Ford and Fiat, between Boreham and Turin. The record books show that Fiat, with the 131 Abarths, won three times (1977, 1978 and 1980), while Ford won only once with the Escorts (in 1979), but the contest was by no means as one-sided as it might appear. In 1977, and again in 1978, Ford might so easily have taken the honours – and in 1980, of course, Fiat had the field to themselves.

In the first two years, 1977 and 1978, there were both major and minor changes at Boreham – to the Escorts, to the team of drivers and staff, and to the way the programme was organised. Looking back, with hindsight, I nominate 1976 as the season in which Ford came tentatively back into the World Championship, though with little success, 1977 as the second 'learning year' when so much of the season was still new to Peter Ashcroft and Charles Reynolds, and 1978 as the season which could so easily have been successful for the Escort if the programme had not been stifled by a long company-wide pay strike. Before 1977, the Escort was still something of a 'forest racer', which could not match its opposition in every type of event, but after 1978 it was a potential winner everywhere.

In 1977, Boreham's tactics seem to change as the year progressed, for at the start of the season they promised team entries in only five World Championship rallies, but eventually took part in eight of them while Ari Vatanen was flown out to New Zealand to drive an ex-works Escort (LVW 690P actually, re-registered and owned by Ford New Zealand) as well. During the year, seven new cars were registered (and several more were re-created from old machines, following crashes), and there were four famous victories.

201

Charles Reynolds, Peter Ashcroft's right-hand-man at Boreham in the late 1970s and early 1980s. That is a list of 'car movements' on the wall, to the right

The problem for Peter Ashcroft was that all those four wins were in rough-road events – Safari, Acropolis, 1000 Lakes and Lombard-RAC – where the specification of the Escort was easy enough to settle. The problems – and there *were* problems in 1977 – came on tarmac events, where the handling was not right. Looking back to an *Autosport* feature I wrote in November 1977, I see that I said: ". . . it still comes as something of a shock to realise that the cars still fail to shine on tarmac events even after ten years of rallying ... There is nothing wrong with an RS1800's behaviour on the loose, and it is now high time that a suitable tarmac specification was finalised. But if Boreham has an Achilles heel at all, it is one of lack of time. There never seems to have been the time to detach a car, a couple of drivers, and a suitable mountain of settings, to get the important question sorted out. But if the RS1800s are to be better than the Fiats everywhere next year, this will have to be done."

For Ford, and the Escort, it was a season which started well, matured in a most exciting manner during high summer, but which somehow fell to pieces in the autumn. After the Acropolis, and the first six events (out of 11), Ford and Fiat had won two events each, with Lancia and Saab winning the other events, but because Ford had also been second twice and Fiat second only once, the Escort was leading the World Championship. Thereafter, it was Fiat all the way, with three more wins and a second, to Ford's two wins and a third. The disasters for Ford came in the San Remo and Tour de Corse events, both of which Fiat won, and both of which exposed the Escort's development difficulties.

The Escort achieved its second famous victory in the Safari in 1977, when the winning drivers were Bjorn Waldegard and Hans Thorzelius, in STW 201R (nearest the camera). Team manager Peter Ashcroft is standing between Waldegard and Roger Clark

It all looked so promising at the start of the year. The driver line-up was outstanding – Bjorn Waldegard, Roger Clark and Ari Vatanen forming the 'first team', with Russell Brookes having a British-championship car, and other drivers like 'Junior' Preston being drafted in for special occasions. Allan Wilkinson joined the staff as Boreham's first full-time development engineer, and there was a bigger budget than ever before.

After a gap of four years it had been decided to send a team of cars to the Safari once again, and because the cars had to be built up from scratch at the same time as those for Portugal, there was no time to enter Monte Carlo and Sweden. At this time, in any case, Peter Ashcroft had come to admit that the Escorts could not match the Stratos in the Monte, so it was not purely a pragmatic withdrawal.

In Portugal, *Autosport's* Henry Liddon described the three Escort drivers as 'Grace, space, and pace', but left the reader to work out which title belonged to which of Waldegard, Clark and Vatanen! The record shows that Markku Alen's Fiat 131 Abarth won the event, with Waldegard's Escort (STW 130R) second. The fact that the Escort lost at least 10 minutes with four punctures (but lost the rally by just four minutes) tells its own story ... Clark's car failed him, while Vatanen crashed his car, while leading, *after* the end of a special stage.

The Safari, for which four brand-new heavyweight cars were prepared (STW 200R, 201R, 202R and 203R), was the wettest East African event on record,

'Dealer Team Ford' in operation, Lombard-RAC rally 1978, with the author (drenched, in anorak), discussing the damaged tail of Bjorn Waldegard's Escort with a rather bashful driver

which cut down on the speeds achieved, but made route finding and sheer survival more problematical than usual. Only one Escort finished, but that was enough, for Bjorn Waldegard won outright, by 35 minutes from Rauno Aaltonen's Datsun.Ford were so delighted that they immediately took the winning car (STW 201R) off Boreham's fleet, and made it an exhibition car, which it remains to this day. The fact that STW 201R eventually re-appeared on another car, for the 1978 1000 Lakes, is just one of those endearing mysteries for which most British rallying teams are sometimes noted . . . .

Bjorn Waldegard, Peter Ashcroft's star signing at the end of 1976, had completely paid off Ashcroft's investment by this time – third in the 1976 Lombard-RAC, second in Portugal, and a winner on Safari, but he then rubbed it all in by winning the Acropolis from Roger Clark, both using their re-prepared Portugal cars. As for Vatanen – poor Vatanen, he crashed his car on the pre-event classification test! At this stage, incidentally, POO 504R had started three rallies and been crashed on all of them; it was rapidly becoming a 'jinx' car, which only Hannu Mikkola would rescue from ignominy in 1978.

In the meantime, the meteoric Vatanen had been sent out to compete in the Rally of New Zealand, in an ex-works car now identified as IF 870, against no fewer than three works Fiats. It was one of those occasions to be remembered as epic: Vatanen had several accidents totalling 36 minutes, yet kept the battered car going, and still managed to finish second overall, just 95 seconds behind Baccheli's Fiat

The occasion was the Safari of 1977, but Bjorn Waldegard had many reasons to smile in three happy years with Ford, including winning the Drivers' World Championship in 1979

So far, so good, but on the 1000 Lakes at the end of August (which Escorts had already won several times), there was a quite unexpected bonus. Vatanen and Waldegard had their 'usual' European rough-road cars, while a third machine – POO 489R – which Ari had been using in Scandinavia throughout the season, was loaned to Kyosti Hamalainen of Finland. Fiat, for their part, entered no fewer than five cars, all 131 Abarths.

As usual, the 1000 Lakes was fast and furious, with most cars retiring. Two of the Escorts kept going (Vatanen, poor man, was in POO 504R again, so somehow we expected him to retire!), but only one Fiat survived. Miraculously, it was Hamalainen who won the event, with Salonen's Fiat second, and Waldegard, driving steadily, third.

A 'semi-works' Escort for some years, though always built and prepared outside Boreham, was John Taylor's Haynes of Maidstone car

Now it all began to go wrong for Boreham. Not particularly because they liked the idea, but because they were now determined to win the World Championship, they sent two ex-Safari cars to Canada, for the Criterium de Quebec, for Roger Clark and Ari Vatanen to drive. Fiat, equally determined, entered no fewer than five cars. Once again it was an event of attrition, with three of the Fiats retiring with engine trouble, but unfortunately two of them survived to win, and take second place. Ari Vatanen's Escort (STW 200R) dominated the event until his car was sidelined in mid-stage with failed engine electrics, while Roger Clark finished third overall. This was ridiculous – with eight of the 11 World Championship events held, Ford were leading Fiat by just two points!

But not for long. The next outing was San Remo, on Fiat's home ground where not only was practising allowed, and where Fiat entered no fewer than six cars, but where the 131 Abarth's handling promised to be ideal. Boreham sent just two cars – one for Vatanen being a refurbished practice car from 1975/76, the other being a brand-new machine for Bjorn Waldegard. The Swede, who had won for Lancia in 1975 and 1976, was looking forward to it. Both cars had coil spring rear suspension, and new damper settings front and rear, but bitter experience soon showed that their handling in the wet was atrocious. Vatanen's car crashed on the second night, and Waldegard also survived a shunt costing 10 minutes, to struggle home fifth, 14 minutes behind the winning Fiat of J-C. Andruet.

There was still time, however, to regain the advantage, for Ford also had two entries in the Tour de Corse of early November, another specialist 'tarmac-plus-notes' adventure. Fiat entered four 131 Abarths, Fiat-France another three (one being for a striking young lady called Michele Mouton – we knew nothing about her then . . .), while two official factory Lancia Stratos cars also turned up. Against this, Ford offered Waldegard's rebuilt San Remo car for Jean-Pierre 'Jumbo' Nicolas to drive, and POO 505R, reconstructed in tarmac form, for Russell Brookes to use. POO still kept to leaf spring rear suspension, but VHK 74S retained coils; both cars had compression strut front suspension, and 5.8:1 final drive ratios.

It was a brave effort, but it was to no avail, as both Escorts cooked their overworked rear axle differentials, though at one stage it looked as if Nicolas (third at half distance) might take the second place Ford needed to keep the Championship alive. But in the early morning of a Corsican November, it was all over for Boreham, when a trail of oil led to the back of 'Jumbo's' smashed diff. Darniche's 131 Abarth won the event, and Fiat clinched the 1977 World Championship for Makes.

For the Escort to win, and dominate, the Lombard-RAC rally a few weeks later, was merely a consolation, for they had always been expected to do so. There was one brand new car, for Bjorn Waldegard (which carried sponsorship by British Airways), in a massive seven car entry. Waldegard won – easily – from Hannu Mikkola's Toyota Celica, with Russell Brookes, Roger Clark, Andy Dawson and Kyosti Hamalainen in the next four places, all in Boreham-owned cars. Dawson, who had been rallying KHK 982N throughout the season in the UK, was unlucky not to take third place, having one 'off'. The best Fiat 131 finish, incidentally, was Lampinen's car, in seventh place.

In Britain and in Europe (where drivers like Russell Brookes and Gilbert Staepelaere continued to win their own 'speciality' events – Staepelaere in his faithful JJN 974N, and Russell now with a choice of two cars) the Escort was still *the* car to own, and no-one argued with it. The big discussion among rallying enthusiasts, and journalists, centred on the Escort's showing all round the world in the 1977 season. Could it have won – should it, indeed, have won in spite of all the tribulations of the second part of the season.?

Peter Newton of *Autosport*, writing a very thoughtful review of the season suggested that there had not only been mistakes in preparing the cars, but an inexplicable choice of drivers in some cases, but summarised the problem as being, in the end, one of money. After pointing out that Ford only had one tarmac car in any case (VHK 74S), he wrote that: "Fiat used a total of just over 20 cars throughout the entire season, but Boreham had nowhere near double figures . . ." In fact, the records show that 11 Boreham cars were used, but the point was still well made.

In the meantime, in any case, Peter Ashcroft had not only retained his company's confidence for 1978, and secured a big budget for the 1978 season, but he had also pulled off a real coup, by persuading Hannu Mikkola to rejoin the factory team of drivers. If Ford were to win the World Championship, they needed drivers who could win in all conditions – 'pace note' or 'secret', tarmac, loose, or winter conditions, and although Peter Ashcroft knew that Roger Clark was still a British folk-hero, he also knew that Mikkola was even quicker and more versatile.

Ford approached Mikkola at precisely the right time, for even though the Finn had not been happy to be dropped by Boreham at the end of 1974, he

This could be nowhere but Kenya, with Waldegard's brand-new Escort RS on its way to winning the wettest Safari on record in 1977. His was the only 'works' Escort to finish, on that occasion

also realised that he must soon choose to move on from Toyota, where he had spent two happy years. The heavy Celicas, which had only barely been competitive of late, were due to be hit very hard in 1978, when new homologation rules would outlaw their optional 16-valve engines.

In every way, therefore, Ford's line-up of drivers for 1978 was probably the strongest in the world, for how many other team managers would have loved to see Bjorn Waldegard, Hannu Mikkola, Ari Vatanen and Roger Clark 'in the first team', with back-up men like Gilbert Staepelaere, Russell Brookes, and – at times – John Taylor also available?

In spite of this, however, the season was not to be as successful as that of 1977, sometimes because of sheer bad luck, but in the end because of a long and bitter pay strike which afflicted every department of Ford of Britain, and paralysed Boreham from the end of September to the beginning of December.

At the beginning of the year, though, the strategy was clear. Having won the Safari in 1977, and made their point, Ford saw no need to go to Kenya again, especially as it was such an expensive exercise in money, cars and manpower terms. Nor would they tackle the Monte Carlo (a wise decision, as it transpired, for a private Porsche 911 won, and the weather caused all manner of upsets), or Bandama.

Instead, they would tackle the World Championship head on – and, by implication, Fiat head on, too – with further developed Escorts, now expected

Only weeks after winning the Safari in 1977, Bjord Waldegard repeated the trick, by winning a fast and dusty Acropolis, with team-mate Roger Clark second

to be suitable for all events. At the start of the year, incidentally, when Peter Ashcroft and Stuart Turner jointly announced Boreham's plans, they were at pains to suggest that there was no question of Championship-chasing, though as in 1977 it rapidly became clear that extra involvement would develop once the position vis-a-vis Fiat was established. In January it was suggested that Boreham would only tackle five events – Sweden, Portugal, 1000 Lakes, Quebec and Lombard-RAC – but that "it is possible that we shall expand this international involvement slightly as the season progresses . . ."

At the time all this was being planned, there was mixed news from the rival Fiat-Lancia camp in Turin. The good news, as far as Boreham was concerned, was that the two rallying teams seemed to be merging, and that the Ferrari-engined Stratos was being 'retired' while it was still amazingly competitive, but the bad news was that this meant that all the Italian giant's efforts could now be concentrated on the refinement of the 131 Abarth saloons.

For 1978, too, there was to be a much more determined factory assault on the British series. Russell Brookes had won the championship in 1977, having only tackled it alone, but with cars prepared and maintained a long way from Boreham. Now, for 1978, not only were his cars to be prepared at Boreham once again, but he would also be joined by cars for Hannu Mikkola and Roger Clark! It was not just that Ford wanted to make sure of their UK domination, but that they could see the serious, and growing, competition

The Escort started the 1978 season well by winning in Sweden, in its current 'Castrol' sponsor's livery. Waldegard was the driver *(photo Hugh Bishop)*

from Vauxhall (with the new Chevette HS) and BL (with the V8-engined TR7 coupes).

In the UK, the team was almost entirely successful, the result being that Hannu Mikkola became Champion, from Russell Brookes, Roger Clark, and John Taylor – all in works-backed Escorts! Hannu won four of the seven events (Welsh, Scottish, Burmah and Lombard-RAC) while Russell won the Circuit of Ireland, using the special tarmac car (VHK 74S) first used in San Remo and Corsica at the end of 1977. A virtuoso performance by Pentti Airikkala (Chevette HS) in the Mintex defeated all the Escorts after Mikkola's car had broken its differential (guess what – it was POO 504R!), and on the Manx BL's brutally powerful TR7 V8 won, on the tarmac surfaces for which it was ideally suited.

The minor miracle of 1978 was that Hannu started winning rallies in POO 504R, after it had started, and retired from, several events. He won the Welsh and the Scottish, Castrol-liveried, at something of a canter, then won the Burmah (in Scotland) in the same car, now sponsored by Eaton's Yale by courtesy of the regulations, after tieing for the victory with Russell Brookes. He also had a subtly different 'tarmac' POO on the Manx, led it for some hours, then crashed at high speed when he picked up a puncture.

As for Roger Clark, it seemed that he was slowing down, ever so slightly, compared with earlier years. Roger always used to say that if rallies started on the second day he would never have lost one, and in 1978 this certainly seemed to be true, for he put up a series of splendid charges towards the end of the events. The results, however, tell their own story: using the same (new-for-1978) car, WTW 569S, he took 4th, 4th, 2nd, 2nd, 3rd and 4th in six events – and in the Lombard-RAC he rolled his car into retirement.

The Escorts notched up many successes in Europe, notably in the hands of Staepelaere, who destroyed his old car in mid-season, and came back to take more wins in the autumn, before finally announcing his retirement. In a season governed by marketing, as much as championship, considerations, he won four European championship events – Lucien Bianchi, Haspenguow, Warsaw and Bosphorus – and retired having won more international rallies than any other 'works' Escort driver.

There was also a partially successful European effort centring around Jean-Pierre Nicolas, mainly in STW 200R, a specialised 'tarmac' Escort, but 'Jumbo' actually had no outright wins in the car. This, in fact, was an Escort identity which caused much controversy during the year, for at one time the registration number seemed to appear on different cars – one a heavyweight rough-road car (it had been new for the 1977 Safari, let's not forget), the other a tarmac lightweight, first used by Hannu Mikkola in the 1978 Circuit.

After that, to quote an *Autosport* correspondent, ". . . it has been used as follows: June 4, Charles Samson, Scottish, RHD; June 16, Jean-Pierre Nicolas, Antibes, LHD; June 23, Ypres, Gilbert Staepelaere, LHD; July 1, Nigel Rockey, Jim Clark, RHD . . . it would be rather funny trying to explain it to Swansea's computer."

Nobody, in fact, tried, for this was the result of the 'numbers shortage' brought on at Boreham by a packed programme, the onset of British Type Approval, and a shortage of identities. Let's say no more than that other companies did it, sometimes even more intensively, that everyone understood why it should be necessary, and that no-one doubted that each and every Escort built at Boreham was genuine, and authentic. Identity? What's that? It merely makes life difficult for an historian like me . . .

In World Championship events, Ford started their season well, but not quite well enough. Having ignored Monte Carlo (in which Fiat finished fourth), they went to Sweden, where Mikkola and Waldegard completely dominated proceedings in the Castrol-backed machines (WTW 568S and 567S, respectively). Having ignored the Safari, they then went off to Portugal, where an impressive ding-dong developed between the leading Escort (Mikkola) and the leading Fiat (Markku Alen).

It had been a major Boreham effort, for four cars had been sent out to practise, and four started the rally. Waldegard and Vatanen broke halfshafts, while Jean-Pierre Nicolas finished a creditable third, but before the final night of 12 very fast, well-practised stages began, Hannu trailed Alen by just 11 seconds! What followed was the most competitive rallying of the year, for after ten of these stages, Mikkola had cut Alen's lead to just a second. Then, on the last stage of all, Mikkola cut a rear tyre on a rock, punctured, and limped in to finish second, nearly five minutes adrift. But the spectators will talk about that duel for years to come . . . .

Having committed such a big effort to Portugal, which was a full four weeks later than usual, Boreham could not send cars to Greece for the Acropolis, so they must have been delighted to see Billy Coleman finishing seventh in one of David Sutton's Boreham-replica Escorts. Instead, they sent four cars to

Finland for the 1000 Lakes rally, which Hamalainen had won in 1977, but had all their hopes shattered when Mikkola's and Vatanen's cars both broke down, and Hamalainen had one disastrous stage when his car (STW 202R) punctured, rolled, then punctured another tyre in the process, eventually struggling home in eighth place. In Finland, as in Portugal, it was Alen who won – and Fiat had now won three consecutive World Championship events.

The rest of the reason then rapidly went wrong. Ford decided not to send cars to Quebec after all, though they had originally scheduled a full team entry, and Fiat won their fourth WCR round on the trot. Plans to go to San Remo instead foundered when the sponsor (thought to be Publimmo) withdrew, and a firm intention to tackle the Tour de Corse was suddenly hit when Ford were plunged into a long and ultimately bitter strike over pay, by the AUEW trades union. Since Boreham's famous mechanics had all become members of this union, they had no alternative but to join the strike, which began on 26 September, and to sit it out. They found themselves in the galling position of not wanting to strike (and, it must be said, not agreeing with it), having to picket their own premises, knowing that partly-completed cars were immobilised. They knew, full well, that if the strike was not settled very soon, the Tour de Corse entries would have to be cancelled, and that in due course the traditionally large entry in the Lombard-RAC event might also be in danger.

There was one item of cheer for Boreham at about this time, however, for a car had been sent ahead, to Cyprus, for Roger Clark to drive. This machine, the 'rough road' STW 200R last used by the Australian, Greg Carr, on the Burmah rally in Scotland, was quite strong enough to stand the tracks and twists of the Mediterranean island, so that Roger won outright, in spite of having his windscreen shattered by a rock hurled by a rival's co-driver!

But the chase for the World Championship was over, as Fiat won yet again – in Corsica this time – and although Ford finished second to them in the points table, it was really a crushing defeat – by the time Fiat came to Birmingham to start the Lombard-RAC rally, they had won five events to Ford's one.

In spite of the strike, which still dragged on, and was not actually to be settled until the week after the Lombard-RAC rally, Ford, and Peter Ashcroft, were determined to put up a good show in the event. To do this, Ashcroft and Charles Reynolds, with a lot of help, official and otherwise, farmed out their drivers to various 'dealer teams', and arranged for them to be managed by non-Ford personnel; the author, indeed, was co-opted to run the unlikely combination of Roger Clark, and John Taylor, in Haynes of Maidstone cars.

Because Ford won the event – their seventh straight victory in the RAC – how they did it deserves some telling. In the end, all six regular UK team drivers (which, in this context, includes John Taylor) started the event, running in three two-car 'dealer teams'. David Sutton ran Mikkola and Vatanen, ostensibly in his own cars, Haynes of Maidstone ran Taylor and Clark, while Andrews Heat for Hire/Russell Brookes ran Brookes and Waldegard. So much, as it were, was for the press, and to keep ruffled feathers happy; those in the know, which included Boreham's union members, knew that it was much more complicated than that.

The fact was that Mick Jones and Allan Wilkinson had been able to spirit several partly-prepared cars out of Boreham before the strike began, and the cars which turned up at the Birmingham start were by no means as 'private' as

'Dealer Team Ford' triumphant in the 1978 Lombard-RAC rally, when David Sutton ran cars for strike-bound Boreham, and Hannu Mikkola won the event. The registration number hides the identity of a famous old Boreham machine

they looked. Mikkola's car, for example, carried one of David Sutton's registration numbers, but was actually a re-creation of the 'tarmac' STW 200R (and was never seen again with its SJN 830R identity . . .). Vatanen's car, and the two Haynes cars were genuine non-Boreham machines, one being a regular David Sutton 'hire car', the identity of which would survive even into the Rothmans era of the early 1980s, the other two being John Taylor's regular machines.

Of the two cars run by Russell Brookes' mechanics, one was brand-new, for him, and one was WTW 568S, supposedly sold off to Thomas Motors of Blackpool, for them to build for Bjorn Waldegard. The truth was that Brookes's new car had been part-completed at Boreham before the strike, 'sold' to Jeff Churchill in that state, finished off by Brookes' mechanics, and subsequently sold properly to Churchill for his use in 1979.

WTW 568S, in truth, which carried Eaton's Yale sponsorship, never went anywhere near Blackpool, but was prepared by the redoubtable Mick Jones in his garage at home, near to Boreham. After the event, incidentally, it went back to Boreham, was straightened out, and was genuinely sold off to Ford New Zealand, where Hannu Mikkola won the 1979 Motogard WCR qualifier.

In spite of the complications, and the subterfuges which had been necessary, the result was a triumph for Ford. Peter Ashcroft, Charles Reynolds and Mick Jones were always around to see fair play, and teams of non-factory mechanics did the rest. At the end of the event, the 'dealer team' Escorts finished 1st, 2nd, 3rd and 7th, with Hannu Mikkola and Bjorn Waldegard up front as usual. Ari Vatanen's car was disqualified when the co-driver missed a passage control, and Roger Clark's machine suffered a ruined clutch, a blown head gasket, and hitting a massive gate post (caused by the no-clutch phenomenon), all within the space of an hour. Every Boreham enthusiast was delighted to see the result, just as they were delighted to see that the Fiats were completely outclassed.

It was, at least, an up-beat ending to a very disappointing World Championship season for Ford, not only because of the victory itself, but because it had been possible to prove to the world that Boreham-replica cars could be constructed very quickly, and effectively, to take the place of the factory cars. No more proof, surely, was ever needed of the Escort's homologation legality, or of the way in which it could so easily be built, and fettled, by private teams?

In some ways, of course, the strike of 1978 was a blessing in disguise (though when I first put this point to Peter Ashcroft, he grunted that the disguise had been very effective indeed at the time!), for it allowed a time for reflection, a time for planning, and – forAllan Wilkinson at least – a time to continue the standardisation, and refinement of the cars. Not only the tarmac handling of the cars, and the fuel-injection systems (Lucas or Kugelfischer both being used in 1978), but the commissioning of more special tarmac cars for 1979, and final settlement of the suspension settings.

It all looked very promising for 1979. But *that* season needs a complete chapter to itself.

13

World Championship
Year~1979

In all the best adventure stories, success comes at the end of the day, almost –
but not quite – too late to save the Good Guys. Sometimes, just occasionally,
it happens in real life too – it certainly happened to the Boreham-built Escorts
in 1979. After 12 competitive years, the works cars and drivers surpassed
themselves. Not only did Ford win the World Rally Championship for Makes,
completely annihilating Fiat along the way, but the team's star drivers, Bjorn
Waldegard and Hannu Mikkola, also dominated the first official World
Drivers' Championship as well. On the other hand, it comes as something of
a surprise to note that the Escorts only won three of the seven British
Championship rounds.

It was probably because the 1978 season had been such a disappointment,
that everything inevitably came right in 1979. One real bonus to come out of
the lengthy Ford strike in 1978 was that staff men like Peter Ashcroft, Allan
Wilkinson and Mick Jones had all had time to sit down and think, and to plan
ahead. Even though Ashcroft originally denied that Ford were going all out to
win the World Championships in 1979 when he held a press conference in
January, it was always clear that the programme was more ambitious than ever,
and that there was a great deal of flexibility in Charles Reynolds' event
planning.

Throughout the season, however, there were two complications. One was
that it became widely known that the existing Escort's days were numbered (a
new front-wheel-drive model was on the way), and the other was that work
continued at Boreham on the development of the smaller, front-wheel-drive
Fiesta. On the horizon, too, were two other dark clouds – the impending
change of homologation regulations which promised to outlaw the Escort RS
in its ultimate form, and strong rumours that Audi were developing a new
four-wheel-drive Supercar, the Quattro.

However, one ideal way to sum up the Escort's amazing 1979 World
Championship season is merely to quote a few vital statistics. The Boreham-
built cars contested only eight out of the twelve rounds during the year, but
won five of them outright, and finished second on the other three occasions.

215

Usual pose for Hannu Mikkola *(left)* **and Arne Hertz in their Escort RS days – picking up loads of trophies for winning, yet again. The occasion was Portugal in March 1979**

Not only that, but there was a clear moral victory in the Monte Carlo, where spectator sabotage (resulting in a blocked road) robbed Waldegard at the last moment, while on the 1000 Lakes Mikkola's car led until near half-distance until the engine let go. There was ample evidence that the Escort was supreme in most conditions though, in fairness, I should admit that every one of the five victories was in a mainly loose-surface event.

It was a season-long performance which needed massive backing, not only in money and material, but in men and motor cars. Ford themselves never admitted to the scale of budget involved, but the number of cars involved was always obvious. Even by using the rather shaky method of identifying cars by registration number, there were no fewer than 18 different machines. However, taking into account the inevitable re-shelling operations, and the complete re-creation of more than one old car, virtually from scratch, I can account for at least 23 cars!

Even so, there were only four ostensibly new cars during the year, and several of the existing identities were really quite old. Four of the cars (MTW 200P, POO 489R, POO 504R and POO 505R) all dated from 1976, and ten more had first been registered in 1977. As already explained, because of the restrictions of Type Approval, not a single new car had been commissioned during 1978. It was a fact, hilarious though it might seem, that three cars had to be put through the MoT test for three-year-olds during the season!

It was the sort of year where there was, at last, scope for some specialisation, where cars could be prepared for a particular purpose; this was nowhere more obvious than in the creation of three *very* individual 'tarmac' cars. For the

WTW 569S not only won the 1979 Lombard-RAC rally – Mikkola's second, and the Escort's eighth – but notched up yet another victory for the sponsors, Eaton's Yale. This was the car kept by Boreham, for comparison purposes, while the RS1700T was being developed in the early 1980s

Monte Carlo rally, Hannu Mikkola and Bjorn Waldegard were each given one of these machines (each, in fact, carrying the identity of an existing car), with the third scheduled for use by Russell Brookes in Britain and Europe. Not only were these cars much lighter than any other Boreham Escort of the period, and more squat, with extended wheelarches and ultra-wide wheels and tyres, but they also had revised suspension, including radically changed geometry, engines sitting back and down to improve weight distribution, and a great deal of special attention to tarmac 'racing'. Perhaps we will never know just how different these cars were – but certainly no other Escort has ever gone, and handled, in quite the same way. A great deal of weight had been eliminated – the Monte cars weighed about 2,000lb, compared with up to 2,300lb for a forestry-stage car – and I have the distinct impression that the whole of the passenger cabin had been settled down considerably on the suspension.

Even so, the experiment was only a mixed success. The Monte cars, which achieved second and fifth places, were never used again during the year (and were then sold off to Publimmo for 1980), while Brookes' car (GVX 489T) was crashed three times in four events, but won the Manx rally on its only successful outing.

In 1977 and 1978, Allan Wilkinson's aim had been to standardise the build of the cars, and in 1979 he extended this, while keeping specialised fittings for special circumstances. The monstrously powerful 1978 'tarmac' engines were improved still further for 1979, for with Kugelfischer fuel-injection they developed up to 272bhp at 9,000rpm. Up to mid-season the World Cham-

217

GJN 126T was the last brand-new car built in Boreham, and was used by Bjorn Waldegard, in Eaton's Yale colours, in the 1979 Lombard-RAC rally. This combination finished ninth after all manner of dramas

Ford's unluckiest outing of 1979 was in the Monte Carlo Rally where Mikkola (seen here) struck trouble with the ruthless French police, and Bjorn Waldegard's sister car was beaten to the flag by six seconds

This was one of the 1979 Monte cars, showing off the standardised boot fittings evolved under the direction of Allan Wilkinson in 1978 and 1979. The only 'extra', later in the year, was to find space for the rear axle oil cooler and fan

pionship cars all used injection, but there were still problems, and for the 'rough' half of the year they all reverted to Weber carbs, losing between 10 and 15bhp.

To add to the life of the transmission, the differential oil cooler first tried on Jean-Pierre Nicolas's car in 1978 was fitted to most team cars in 1979. This comprised a Serck radiator mounted in the boot, and connected to the differential by armoured, flexible, piping, with air ducting from the outside of the bodyshell, and a thermostatically-controlled electric cooling fan drawing air through the system. Temperature reductions were dramatic, and they put an end to axle problems.

Brakes, tyres, and suspension settings were still under development. In 1979, for instance, the semi-wet-racing treaded Dunlop A2 tyre, once considered a real breakthrough for smooth forestry-stage driving, was displaced by softer and more grippy M & S types. The softer the tread, however, the quicker the wear – team drivers, who were not having to pay for their extravagance, tended to ask for new covers at least every 20 miles of stage motoring, if they could find the time!

The biggest rush of car preparation came early in the year, not only because of the proximity of Monte Carlo, Sweden, Portugal, and the Acropolis, but because the two cars for New Zealand had to be finished very early, and sent out by ship. It explains, for sure, why the Monte cars were neglected, outside the workshops, for months, after they returned, and it also explains why three all-new cars had to be built up for the Acropolis, as there was no time (or spare cars) to re-prepare existing machines.

For the first and only time in Boreham's Escort preparation history, these

219

The Escorts completely dominated the Rally of Portugal in March 1979, with Hannu Mikkola (in POO 504R) winning from team-mate Waldegard, the rest of the entry being 20 minutes behind. The cars carried no sponsorship on this event

cars were actually based on the identity of existing 1300 Sports, rather than created completely by Boreham themselves, for this was the only way to create a 'new' Escort RS, which had no separate Type Approval certificate. As the series co-ordinator of a 1300 Sport championship for Ford at this time, I well remember receiving a call from Charles Reynolds to tell me that major components (like 1300cc engines, transmissions, and back axles) were all available 'at the right price' as a result of this manoeuvre.

The season was not without its disappointments. In the first event of the year, Waldegard and Mikkola clearly had the legs of every other car except Darniche's Stratos at first, and completely outclassed the Fiats. Ford led until the very last moment, even though Mikkola was penalised after the police had complained about his driving on the open road. On the final night, however, Waldegard was gradually overhauled by the flying Stratos, but the final indignity came on the penultimate stage when, running first on the road, Waldegard rounded one corner to find the road blocked by boulders. Co-driver Thorzelius had to get out of the car, and heave the boulders aside, before the Escort could continue – and that was that. In the end, the Escort lost by a mere six seconds.

Waldegard put his Escort off the road on the very first stage of the Swedish event, which was not a bit like him, but the team were still unlucky not to win outright, and repeat their 1978 showing – it was beginning to look as if there was a jinx on the likeable Swede once again! From Portugal, which followed, the team's fortunes changed.

The Escort RS 'works' cars carried Rothmans sponsorship for the Acropolis in 1979. Hannu Mikkola's car, seen here, was forced to retire with engine failure, but Waldegard's Escort RS won by more than 30 minutes!

Waldegard's second outright win of 1979 was in the Canadian Quebec rally. POO 505R – or, at least, its identity – led a busy life for three years at Boreham

In the last months of 1979, POO 504R finished well on two World Championship events –
third, in Rothmans colours, in Quebec, with Ari Vatanen driving, and second, converted to
right-hand-drive, in Andrews colours, with Russell Brookes driving in the Lombard-RAC rally.
And to think that this particular POO had once been considered a jinx car!

Portugal was a real walkover, with Mikkola and Waldegard finishing first and second, while Waldegard notched up his first win of the year in Greece, with Roger Clark (deputising for an unwell Vatanen) making a rare appearance; In New Zealand, two locally-registered cars (both, however, having been prepared at Boreham earlier in the year), finished first and third. Three wins in three events – quite suddenly Ford were leading the World Championship by a distance, with Fiat already outpaced, and Datsun struggling.

Normally, Ford could have been expected to win the 1000 Lakes rally, if Mikkola and Vatanen had enjoyed normal luck, but Hannu's Escort engine blew a cylinder head gasket, and Vatanen had to settle for second place, after one near accident had frightened him badly. Alen's Fiat won (his third win in four years), and Bjorn Waldegard finished third.

Three weeks later, however, Boreham chalked up another overwhelming victory, when Waldegard and Vatanen finished first and third in the Canadian Quebec event, in the ex-Portugal cars, and although Timo Salonen's Datsun finished second, this effectively ended the Championship chase for the year.

It was then, immediately after Quebec, that Mike Kranefuss dropped his bombshell, when he announced that Ford would be pulling out of international rallying at the end of the season! "We have been active as a major participant in international rallying for 17 years without a break. There is hardly an event of significance we have not won, and we have won a number of these several times . . . A rallying "Sabbatical" will give us the opportunity to proceed with vehicle development, aerodynamic research, and work on new engines which combine performance with economy."

In the short term, this meant that a great team would soon be split up (*Autosport* headlined their comment: "Four world class drivers out of work"), but in the long term it meant that the Escort's competitive days were numbered, and that there would be a lengthy pause before a competitive car from Boreham could be made ready. What actually happened – or, more precisely, what did *not* happen – is related in some detail in Chapter 15.

When the announcement was made, Ford's World Championship position was secure, for they had 120 points, to Datsun's 94 and Fiat's 59, while the only competition facing Waldegard (103 points) and Mikkola (71 points) in the drivers' series came from Markku Alen (40 points). The results of San Remo and the Tour de Corse, which followed, made no difference to top placings, except that they confirmed Ford as the Makes champion for the year.

There was just one more event in the programme for Boreham, and all concerned set about doing it in style. For the 1979 Lombard-RAC rally, which was based on Chester, no fewer than six cars were prepared, all to the same immaculate, and familiar, forestry-specification. Two of the six were brand new (one obviously so, with a new identity and all, the other being a re-creation of a venerable old machine which had seen hard times recently), but all were clearly out to win, and backing them up, as ever, was John Taylor's car, sponsored by Haynes of Maidstone. As was becoming normal on these cars, there were different sponsors' colours for different cars, most notable being Eaton's Yale colours for Mikkola and Waldegard, and Rothmans colours for Ari Vatanen.

The result was an absolute triumph, with Mikkola notching up his second, and the Escort its eighth, successive RAC rally win. It was, in truth, a real steamroller of a performance: at half-distance, the works cars held the first three places, with two other cars inside the top ten. At the end of the event, where only 74 of the 175 starters actually reached the finish, no fewer than six of seven 'works' Escorts cruised home – in 1st, 2nd, 4th, 6th, 9th and 10th places. Only the luckless Roger Clark was forced to retire, when the engine on his favourite Escort, POO 505R, failed.

Because Mikkola won, and Waldegard could only finish ninth, after a mechanically troubled run, it also left the drivers' series wide open, for there was still one event left in the season (Bandama, in the African Ivory Coast), and he could be overhauled by Mikkola. But Ford were not proposing to attend.

The result was that both of Ford's stars were released to drive for Mercedes-Benz (who sent a team of 450SLC coupes), that Mikkola won that event, with Waldegard second, and that Waldegard became rallying's first official World Champion Driver, by a margin of one point – 112 to 111. It had been *that* close.

After the Lombard-RAC rally, there was exhilaration, and there was sadness too, for everyone – drivers, Ford staff, press and spectators alike – all realised that they were participating in the end of an era. What had seemed unbelievable when the announcement was made in September, was suddenly seen to be coming true. We were witnessing the break-up of a phenomenal team.

Although the Escort RS1800 had officially been out of production for two years, the Escort RS 'homologation special' was still a current model, and new examples were still taking shape all over the world. Even though most of us knew that a new transverse-engined front-wheel-drive Ford Escort would be launched in less than a year, we also knew that Ford, officially, did not want to carry on rallying with a dying breed of car.

Back at Boreham, drivers were being released from their contracts (or were they . . .?), and existing Escorts were being refurbished before being put on sale. Only one car – Mikkola's 1979 RAC rally winner – was to be retained, for comparison, and back-to-back testing, with whatever was next to be developed.

But was it really the end of the Escort in World Championship events? We only had a few weeks to wait, to find out.

14

The 'David Sutton' cars ~ 1978 to 1981 Eaton's Yale and Rothmans sponsorship

Strictly speaking, of course, few of the cars run by the David Sutton team were truly 'works' Escorts, but as the drivers were often directly contracted to Boreham, and the cars had sometimes been sold off to Sutton from Boreham, the edges became very blurred at times. In 1980 and 1981, for sure, most people looked on the Sutton operation as quasi-works, although supported by generous outside sponsorship as well.

Sutton's links with Ford, and Boreham, were long-established even before he started running Hannu Mikkola on the factory's behalf in British events in 1978. Indeed, he ran an Escort Twin-Cam for Timo Makinen as early as the 1968 RAC rally, during the Escort's first season. In the intervening years, a car built in his workshops became the nearest possible machine to a 'works replica', and there were several occasions on which he was 'loaned' drivers for a particular event. On the 1976 Lombard-RAC rally, the Sutton team was even in the happy situation of leading the entire factory team, *and* the rally, until the last night, with Pentti Airikkala as their driver.

The links became more formal in mid-1978, when Ford needed to continue running a car in the British series for Hannu Mikkola, but found that they did not want to divert effort from the World Championship programme. POO 504R, which Mikkola had already used to win the Welsh and the Scottish, was decked out in the blue colours of a new sponsor, Eaton's Yale (who supplied forklift trucks and truck axles to Ford, so it all made commercial sense), and loaned to Sutton for the rest of the season. In 1979 the Sutton-Mikkola-Eaton's effort redoubled, and in 1980 an even more ambitious programme was mounted, sometimes with help from Eaton's Yale and sometimes from Rothmans (who had been prominent on Ford works cars during 1979), both at home and overseas. All this, however, was just the prelude to a truly massive operation in 1981, when the David Sutton team was exclusively backed by Rothmans, who were quite determined to produce a World Championship victory out of it all. It was a remarkable 'arm's length' relationship involving no more than drivers on loan, the use of service vehicles, and sometimes the invaluable expertise of individuals from Boreham like Peter Ashcroft and

World Champion in 1981, but an Escort RS hero since 1976, was Ari Vatanen (left). His co-driver in that Championship year was David Richards, and the sponsors were Rothmans

Charles Reynolds. Works Escorts, or merely works-blessed? For sure, they were complete replica cars, although all the 1980 and 1981 machines were built, from new, at Acton. We can argue over detail definitions for some time, but I doubt if any rallying enthusiast would want to divert the Eaton's Yale and Rothmans cars from the definitive study of this great car.

While Ford was still actively involved in rallying on its own account, David Sutton's efforts on its behalf were limited to British events – yet still resulted in outright wins in the 1978 Burmah, the 1978 Lombard-RAC, and the 1979 Welsh, all the outright wins being to the credit of Hannu Mikkola. Mikkola should also have won the Scottish in 1979, but went off the road on the first corner of the first stage after a night halt, later admitting to having been "sleeping . . . ."

Well before the end of 1979, Sutton had made an agreement with Peter Ashcroft for 1980, not only that he would find gainful employment for Hannu Mikkola and Ari Vatanen whenever, and wherever, possible, but that he would be able to buy ex-works cars for use as recce machines in the future, and that he would also have the pick of the parts bins at Boreham. As David has since told me: "We went to Boreham with lots of Transit vans to empty the stores! In the second year (1981), Boreham also continued to supply us with special bits like the 5.3:1 diffs, and the 'Len Bailey' halfshafts. My programme though, was built around a middle-of-the-road specification, without the last five horsepower or super technical details being important."

Davis also reminded me that he never had a massive budget for on-going development, which explains why his late-1981 cars were really no better, and

UYY 256S was once nicknamed 'Black Beauty' when originally built by David Sutton's team, but in 1980 it became a rough-road car for the Rothmans/Sutton team. Throughout the Acropolis rally, in which Ari Vatanen gained his first outright World Championship victory, it hardly ever seemed to be travelling in a straight line!

certainly no faster, than his 1979/80 models. He insists, however, that they were all very strong, and very reliable, as a look at the 1981 running record confirms. "If Ari hadn't done so much for us, in terms of crashes, we would be looking even better." In those two years, however, Sutton finally sorted out the Lucas fuel-injection (helped along by Terry Hoyle as his chosen engine builder), though he admits that he could never make much sense of the handling of an Escort with 15in road wheels.

Not that it was all plain sailing, for at the end of 1980, not only did Castrol

PLY 829W was always an unlucky Sutton/Rothmans car, for it rarely finished an event. In the 1981 Monte Carlo, Vatanen suffered a blown engine . . .

. . . while in Portugal he crashed it spectacularly, after exciting progress like this

pull out of major rally sponsorship, but Dunlop too, which not only left Sutton's team sitting on bare rims with dry oil tanks, but left them looking for funds into the bargain, for Castrol had effectively been paying the salaries of the drivers in that year. It says much for Sutton's cunning and expertise, and for his standing in the business, that he was quickly able to attract help from Duckhams and Pirelli (both of whom stayed loyal to him when he switched the team to Audi in 1982).

In the winter of 1979/80, David Sutton's mechanics built up a total of six new cars, four being brand-new, the other two being re-creations of tired old machines. During the season, the team tackled five World Championship rallies in Europe, the five Sedan British Championship rounds, plus the CS (Spanish) and Cyprus events.

The way to sum up that first season is to say:
World Championship: One win, three 2nds, one 3rd.
British Championship: Three 1sts, five seconds (in five events!).
Other two events: One 1st and one 2nd.
No wonder that the sponsors, and the factory, were delighted!

In Europe, though, the season started very badly indeed, when both the Rothmans-sponsored cars, driven by Mikkola and Vatanen, crashed at the same corner of the same stage, ending up side-by-side in the trees! That was the bad news – the good news was that both were rebuilt for the Acropolis, where Ari Vatanen used UYY 256S (once known as 'Black Beauty' in a previous existence) to win his first World Championship event. The rest of the year was a sequence of second places, including the Lombard-RAC rally where Hannu Mikkola was beaten by Henri Toivonen's Talbot Sunbeam-Lotus.

To round off a busy season, Ari Vatanen took a car to Spain for the CS Rally (his British Championship car), and finished second, while Roger Clark was invited to drive the famous old car, STW 201R, in Cyprus, where he won in spite of having a well-publicised rumpus with another competitor. 201R, in its original existence, had graced the car used by Bjorn Waldegard to win the Safari in 1977 . . . .

The team's performance in the 1980 British Championship was quite outstanding, and as near to a 'steamroller' performance as we are ever likely to see. Suttons built up two new cars for it (EUW 938V and 939V – sponsored by Rothmans and Eaton's Yale respectively), which won three of the five rounds, and notched up second place on every one of them. No wonder I headlined one of my magazine reports "Business as usual for Mikkola"!

At the end of 1980, as I have already mentioned, there were major changes in almost all respects – except that David Sutton retained some cars and drivers. Eaton's Yale, Dunlop and Castrol all pulled out of rallying, probably for the same reasons – that it was all becoming very expensive, and because they had really achieved their marketing and publicity objectives. I should also point out, too, that the Mk 2 Escort, on which all these RS cars were based, had been dropped from production in July 1980, and had been replaced by a new design of Escort, with front-wheel-drive, a transverse engine of a new type, and with hatchback body styling.

For 1981, therefore, there was really no justification for Boreham to continue supporting David Sutton so strongly – but it is to their great credit that they continued to do so, not only morally, and in spirit, but by continuing the loan of vehicles and equipment.

The outcome was that Rothmans decided to take over the funding of

One of Ari Vaṭanen's finest drives of 1981, on his way to winning the Driver's World Championship, was in the Acropolis rally, which he won for the second year in succession, and when the Escort RS won for the fourth time in five years

virtually the entire team, with generous help from Pirelli (for tyres) and Duckhams (for lubricants) though there was no fuel contract of any sort. Even though the Escort RS was officially obsolete, the David Sutton team planned to build new cars as and when required. Rothmans made it quite clear that they wanted to win the World Championships, and the British series (which they were sponsoring as well!), and to do so they hired three drivers – Ari Vatanen, Pentti Airikkala (enticed from Dealer Team Vauxhall) and Malcolm Wilson. David Sutton has always confirmed that the team's effort was mainly behind Ari Vatanen, and that new, or newly-shelled, cars were prepared for him for every World Championship event he tackled during the year.

There was no doubt that the Rothmans-Sutton-Escort RS assault on rallying in 1981 was a very professional operation, even if some old-fashioned members of the media (yes, I was one, at times) complained of the 'overkill' attitude which prevailed from time to time. There was an end to the greasy overalls and scruffy anoraks of the past, and information simply poured out of the companies.

Everyone now knows that as a result of the 1981 programme, Ari Vatanen won the individual Drivers' World Championship, but that Ford finished behind Talbot and Datsun in the Championship for Makes. All in all, Vatanen started ten World Championship rounds, winning three of them (Acropolis, Brazil and 1000 Lakes), and finished second in two more (Sweden and Lombard-RAC). On the other hand, it was not a season without incident, for the intrepid Vatanen crashed his cars into retirement on the Portuguese and Argentinian events, damaging his San Remo machine when in sight of victory, and crashing his Ivory Coast car so severely that the team took hours to rebuild it so that he could finish ninth and last, 22 hours *(hours* – not minutes) behind the winner!

Even so, the Sutton/Rothmans/Vatanen combination was always com-

The very last of the Sutton/Rothmans Escorts, backed to some extent by the 'works' team at Boreham, was VLE 756X, brand-new for the Lombard-RAC rally of 1981. Ari Vatanen finished second overall, and clinched his personal World title. The car then went on display at the National Motor Museum at Beaulieu

petitive when not beset by accidents and Acts of God. Vatanen had to give best to the four-wheel-drive Quattros in Sweden, San Remo and the Lombard-RAC, and his engine let go on the Monte, in what David Sutton now describes as a 'jinx car' (PLY 829W). Support all round the world came from Airikkala and Malcolm Wilson, though neither won events for themselves. The strangest entry of all was in the Ivory Coast, where the mechanics fettled a single-cam practice car, for John Taylor and one of the Sutton mechanics to start, and use as a 'chase' car after Vatanen; as it happened this car failed almost as soon as it left the starting ramp, and Vatanen had to face the rigours of Equatorial Africa alone.

The position in the Drivers' World Championship was so tight that Vatanen was two points behind Guy Frequelin after San Remo, eight points behind after the Ivory Coast, and needed a very high placing in the Lombard-RAC to clinch it. Right at the end of the year, therefore, the Sutton team built him a brand new car (VLE 756X) in a classic, conventional, forestry specification, and sent him out to do battle.

There was no way that Vatanen's old-style Escort could beat the four-wheel-drive Quattro of Hannu Mikkola in very slippery conditions, so he had to settle for a secure second place, more than 11 minutes adrift. Frequelin, for his part, did not finish the event, which meant that Vatanen's crown was assured.

Back in Britain, there was massive involvement on every round in the Rothmans-RAC Open Championship. Compared with 1980, however, it was not by any means as successful, though Airikkala won the snowy Mintex, while Vatanen took time off from his travels round the world to win the Welsh in EUW 938V, which was probably the most successful single car to carry Rothmans colours, though Pentti Airikkala besmirched its reputation by crashing it on an early stage in the Manx rally in September!

At the end of 1981, however, it was all over, for Rothmans took their vast promotional budget to a new team – Opel – and effectively brought the Escort RS's rallying career to a close. Perhaps it was a little unfair of them to point out that the Escort's basic design was 14 years old by this time, for it had been good enough, and versatile enough, for Ari and David Sutton to provide the World Championship which they had sought, but it was certainly true that the car was no longer getting any quicker.

The saddest sight of all, perhaps, was the advertising which appeared in the motoring press during the winter. David Sutton elected to keep EUC 958V for himself, and for his step-son to drive in the future, while Rothmans took over the last car of all (VLE 756X) and put it on show at the National Motor Museum at Beaulieu, but everything else had to be sold. As for the rest, cars, engines, trailers, parts and even service vans were all sold off, to a value of more than £250,000.

Early in 1982, however, this was not quite the end of the story – as the final chapter makes clear.

15

RS1700~the Escort that never was

If all had gone well with plans laid in 1980, a new type of rear-drive Escort RS should have been rallying in 1982, and a major team attack from Boreham should have started in 1983. But, as I am sure nearly every Escort enthusiast knows, the programme to develop a new car ran late, and the project was abruptly cancelled in mid-March 1983, just before a run of 200 'production cars' was due to be built, and immediately after Stuart Turner had begun his second stint as director of European Motor Sports. This book would be incomplete if I did not at least sketch out the way that the new car, to be called Escort RS1700T, was conceived, and how it came to be cancelled.

The search for a replacement really began in 1977, at about the time the World Championship effort became more serious than ever. The small new front-wheel-drive Fiesta had already been launched, and (although the model had not yet been finalised) the decision had already been taken to replace the 'classic' Escort by an all-new front-wheel-drive car, having a transversely mounted engine and an end-on gearbox. At that time, though, four-wheel-drive cars were still banned from rallying, and in any case no-one was known to have one under development.

In 1977 Peter Ashcroft, Allan Wilkinson, and the team drivers were all convinced that their new car would need rear-drive for the best handling and traction to be achieved, though it was also assumed that such a car would have to look like a mass-produced Ford, superficially at least; management had not thought it necessary to lay down a rigid policy.

In 1977, therefore, work began on two prototypes, both being based on the new Fiesta's bodyshell. One was a mid-engined machine of what we would now call Renault 5 Turbo type, and was to be designed by Len Bailey, while the other was to have a front engine, and rear-mounted gearbox/final drive transaxle, and was to be designed at Boreham. The Len Bailey car was to have a transverse engine behind the seats, while the Boreham car was to have a fore-and-aft engine ahead of the passengers. In each case, merely 'to get the show on the road', normally-aspirated BDA engines were employed. By the end of that year, although much study, and design work, had been completed (with

233

The prototype for a new generation of Escorts was this front-engine/rear-drive BDA-engined Fiesta, completed in 1980, using some Escort front panels and front suspension (*photo Martin Holmes*)

the 'Boreham' car intended to use a much-modified Hewland Formula One transaxle at first), the project was shelved while development of the classic Escort RS continued.

There was a further diversion in 1978/79 when there appeared to be a short-lived revival of interest in front-wheel-drive rally cars. In spite of the fact that all previous experience suggested that massively powerful f.w.d. cars could not be made to be competitive (even the Saab 99 Turbo, which won some events, had found its limits by 1979), Ford allowed themselves to be diverted into the building of BDA-engined front-drive Fiestas. The conundrum was further complicated by Mike Kranefuss in mid-1979, when he confirmed that a new rear drive car could, in fact, be developed without the company's new front-wheel-drive 'image' being damaged.

After Ford had wound up their old-style Escort's rallying career by winning the 1979 Lombard-RAC rally, some time was spent in fettling all the company's stocks of rally cars before selling them, such that by the spring of 1980 only one machine – WTW 569S, the car which Hannu Mikkola had used to win the last event – had been kept, for comparison purposes.

Even up to the summer of 1980, when back-to-back tests were carried out in Welsh forestry stages between WTW 569S and the front-drive BDA-engined Fiesta (one of the distinguished drivers being Stig Blomqvist, whose exploits in Saabs made him *the* expert on front-wheel-drive), Boreham thought that they might be able to make such a Fiesta competitive, but since the old car proved to be much more effective, they decided to abandon that idea.

In the meantime, the first rumours of a sensational four-wheel-drive Audi Quattro had begun to circulate, and the car itself had been launched in March 1980. Audi said they intended to mount a serious rallying programme with this car, though some observers (the author included) wondered if 4WD would fare any better than it had when tried on the GP circuits at the end of the 1960s.

The 1980 rear-drive Fiesta, conceived way back in 1977, was fitted with a Hewland Grand Prix car type of transmission, with the box itself behind the line of the final drive *(photo Martin Holmes)*

Another significant event came at Bandama in December 1979, when a four-wheel-drive car (a Range Rover, actually) competed in a World Championship rally for the first time.

Boreham made haste to start developing a rear-drive car again, almost a year after they had announced their intention to withdraw from rallying to produce a new car, and originally finished off the two Fiestas. Little ever became of the mid-engined 'Bailey' Fiesta, but the 'Boreham' car, now coded P1, was finished off, complete with Escort RS front panels, cross member and strut-type front suspension, very neatly welded to a Fiesta passenger cabin. There was a conventional propeller shaft to a modified Hewland FGB400 five-speed gearbox which was mounted under the rear floor pan.

In the meantime, Allan Wilkinson had left Boreham, at very short notice, to go to work for Team Toyota Europe in Cologne, and it was not until September of that year that a new engineer, ex-Porsche designer John Wheeler, arrived to take up the challenge of a new car. By the late autumn of 1980, Boreham's submission to Ford's board of directors was that a new front-engined/rear-drive rally car, of which 200 had to be made, should be built on the basis of the brand-new (front-drive) Escort three-door body shell, and the board gave its approval for this. It was at about the same time that Karl Ludvigsen, a distinguished motoring writer, and ex-Fiat USA Public Affairs chief, joined Ford, as Vice-President, Governmental Affairs and Motor Sport, Mike Kranefuss having gone off to liven up a corporate racing programme for Ford of Detroit.

The big decision of 1980 was to develop a rear-drive rally car from the basis of the new front-drive Escort hatchback. This car is prototype P4, with a normally aspirated 2.0-litre BDA engine being installed for fitting checks

Several big decisions, jointly taken by Ludvigsen, Peter Ashcroft, Charles Reynolds and John Wheeler, were taken in the next few weeks. Firstly, it was decided to build the new car with torque tube transmission, which is to say that a stout aluminium tube (which enclosed the propeller shaft) was to link the front-mounted engine to the rear-mounted transaxle; next, that Hewland should be commissioned to produce an all-new, five-speed transaxle, with the gear casing ahead of the final-drive itself; and finally, that the engine itself was to be a turbocharged version of the ubiquitous BDA design. (Such engines had already proved themselves in Zakspeed's Group 5 'silhouette' Capris in German racing, and there seemed to be little doubt that up to 350bhp could be guaranteed for long-distance rallying.)

Other engines, incidentally, had also been considered. The new Group B Regulations imposed minimum weight limits for different sizes, and it seemed that the 2.5-litre capacity limit was ideal for the new car. This could be achieved by using a 1.78-litre BDT which, with turbocharging (and a capacity multiplication factor of 1.4:1), had an 'official' capacity right on that limit. The alternative was to use enlarged Pinto engines with new 16-valve cylinder heads, which were coded T88s, or even enlarged Hart 420R engines, which were the 'hill-climb' derivatives of Brian Hart's famous Formula Two engine. Pinto and Hart alternatives were dropped when the difficulty of having at least 200 units made became obvious.

Aggressive nose of the RS1700T prototype shown to the press in mid-1981, complete with four headlamps, and NACA-type air intakes in the glassfibre bonnet panel

During 1981 the work intensified, with P2 and P3 being mock-up shells to be used for engine packaging and styling changes respectively, P4 being the first running *muletta* with a Porsche transaxle, P5 destined to be the first car shown to the public, P8 and P9 being 'road car' prototypes, but P7 and P10 being the first full-house rally test cars. P7 had a Hart engine, and P10 had a BDT, both originally running with much-modified Hewland FGB400 transaxles running 'back to front'. The project also acquired a code name – 'Columbia' – reputedly from that of the first successful United States Space Shuttle of the period.

P5, still incomplete, was shown to the press in July 1981, when it was named RS1700T, and company spokesmen suggested that it might be in rallying by mid-1982, and that the 200 'homologation' road cars would be assembled at Ford's mainstream Escort plant at Saarlouis in West Germany. Considerable detail restyling of the Escort shell had been done by Ford Cologne, and new panels such as the ducted bonnet, the front and rear spoilers, and the 'skirting' at the sides were fashioned from glass fibre. At one time it was thought that all 200 'homologation' cars should be sent down the lines at Saarlouis in a concentrated burst of effort, so that they could be inspected on the spot by FISA officials.

The ill-fated RS1700T's problems all centred around the need to build so many cars, and to have them comply with every sporting and legislative requirement. Hand-building them at Boreham, in small numbers, would have been easy enough – by the spring of 1983, indeed, the numbers had grown to nearly 20 in any case – but the amount of certification work involved was

Early loose-surface testing of an RS1700T, in a picture which shows off the special styling details incorporated. Note the non-standard bonnet panel, and the centre-lock wheels

crippling. Unlike every other rally car developed by Ford, the design *and* the certification work was all centred on Boreham. Not even Rod Mansfield's Special Vehicle Engineering department (which produced cars like the XR3 and XR4i models) was involved at first.

Meanwhile, there were two discouraging developments out in the world of rallying – the burgeoning success of the four-wheel-drive Audi Quattro, and the seemingly rapid progress of the Lancia Rally from prototype to homologated production car. Later, of course, the Quattro was seen to have flaws, and limitations, while Lancia revealed that their new mid-engined machine had been under wraps for many months before launch, but it was really all too late to lift the gloom at Boreham.

In the meantime, Boreham went testing, with P7 and P10, to stages in Portugal, used only days earlier in the 1982 Rally of Portugal. P7 used a 2.3-litre 'hill-climb' Hart engine, and was registered WVW 101W, while P10 had a 1.8-litre BDT, and was registered WVW 100W. Ari Vatanen and Pentti Airikkala both drove the cars, and enthused over their potential, but Ari crashed the Hart-engined car, which caused the testing to be curtailed. Later in the year, more testing was carried out, in Wales and elsewhere.

But still the RS1700T was not ready for production. The mid-1982 launch date came and went, as did the revised estimate of 'first competition' in the autumn of that year. Later, it was hoped that the 200 cars would be built at the start of 1983, and the final estimate was that they would be assembled in March, with homologation planned for 1st April, 1983. The car's first event, it was suggested, would be the Tour de Corse, in May. In the meantime, Ari Vatanen was released from his contract, to go off to drive for Opel (and Rothmans). Ford started 1983 still without a Group B car, and now with no front-line driver either.

The fast disappearing tail of an RS1700T prototype, with the dust cloud confirming that this was a rear-drive car

In the meantime, Cosworth built more than 200 engines, Hewland built the same number of transaxles, Abbey Panels produced much revised sheet metal for the 'chassis' components, and glass fibre body panels were also stockpiled. Just at the time that the cars should have been produced at Saarlouis, however, they were sidelined once again. It is said that the pre-production build-up to the new Orion notchback saloon had something to do with it.

By this time there were two definite schools of thought on the RS1700T's prospects, both inside and outside the company. One view was that it would never be able to beat the Quattro and other projected four-wheel-drive cars like the Peugeot 205 Turbo 16, and the other view (to which the author subscribed) was that the rear-drive turbocharged Escort could be outstanding on some events, and competitive on others. The success of the Lancia Rally in 1983 may have caused some people to think again about the so-called 'invincibility' of the Quattros.

None of this, however, could save the RS1700T, which got caught up in a revolution at Ford. During February 1983, Karl Ludvigsen moved on, and subsequently left the company, his replacement as Director of European Motor Sports being Stuart Turner, back from a lengthy sojourn in the Public Relations division. Then, on 14th March (beware the Ides of March?), the company not only cancelled the entire RS1700T programme, but the C100 Group C (Cosworth engined) endurance racing project as well.

The motoring press, as one might expect, was astonished at first, then mainly critical. *Autocar's* closely-reasoned piece, however, came closest to an honest analysis. Starting by asking the rhetorical question: "What on earth is going on at Ford?", the writer then went on: "It is hard to believe that Ford, or Turner, would cancel everything without an immediate replacement strategy. But it seems unlikely that they will have any direct participation in

239

Ari Vatanen, finding time to wave to the cameraman, tested an RS1700T extensively in Portugal in the spring of 1982. WVW 100W, prototype P10, had a turbocharged BDT 1.78-litre engine and a Hewland gearbox installed at the time. Another car, WVW 101W, had a 2.3-litre Hart engine installed for comparison purposes; Vatanen crashed that one!

world-class events for the next couple of years. It will take that long to develop, build and homologate a Group B car to replace the RS1700T . . . ."

Autosport went somewhat over the top when they suggested that cancellation looked like a 'total vote of no confidence'. It was much more likely that Turner's fresh approach had decided that time was slipping away from the RS1700T, and that it had no long-term future. His press statement, in fact, was crystal clear:

"Having spent some time looking hard at our existing plans, I have become convinced that we are not moving in the best direction if we are going to resume our former position in international motor sport . . . . Make no mistake – we shall be back, although not with the cars we have under development at the moment."

Autocar's editorial ended with the plaintive remark that: "No doubt Stuart Turner knows what's going on . . . ." I feel sure that he does. A man of his reputation was surely not drafted into such a job, at such a time, merely to act as the undertaker at a funeral. One day, perhaps sooner than expected, we'll find out. One thing, however, seemed to be certain – that it was the end of the long competitions career of the rear-drive Escort in motor sport. Will there ever be another car like it?

Appendices
Introduction

This is possibly the most important section of the book – a complete historical record of the events contested by 'The Works Escorts'.

At least, I hope it is complete! Even Ford, for all their efficient methods and their great competitions tradition, have had to compress and eliminate many of their old records. Finding, and annotating, all the facts has meant a lot of detective work.

On some occasions an outside specialist has been commissioned to build cars subsequently used by the works. Ford, themselves, have often built 'works' cars which have been on permanent loan to a private owner or team. So what is a 'works' Escort?

The list is impressive by any standard, but for the purposes of this book I have defined a 'works' Escort as:

A car built by Ford for a works driver to use in competition.

A car built on Ford's behalf, taken over by them, for a works driver to use.

A car built by Ford for officially-backed teams and drivers to use.

A car built on Ford's behalf, for officially-backed teams and drivers to use.

Each car to be registered and owned by Ford (unless used in un-registered condition for track events).

Each car to be used for serious competition – racing, rallying, rallycross or similar events.

On many occasions, Ford have supplied 'preparation kits' to far-flung subsidiaries, who have produced their own 'works replicas'. These do not appear in my lists.

Compiling an event-by-event record of factory-backed activities over the year has been a mammoth task. I have had to make certain limitations, merely to keep the table down to manageable length.

I agonised over the way I should define the identity of a particular car, and in spite of the fact that many machines were re-shelled, or even re-created, over the years, I chose the registration number/chassis plate method. There seems to be no other logical or understandable method of doing this ...

The David Sutton/Eatons/Rothmans Escorts
As explained in the main text, I have covered the career of the cars maintained at Acton by David Sutton's business, mainly because some of the drivers were always contracted to Ford, but also because Boreham lent help, both material and personal, to the team while it was in World Championship rallying until the end of 1981.

241

A

The Works
Escorts listed

Unless I applied some very strict rules, this list of cars could have been enormously bigger, and much more confusing. Both Boreham and Cologne have operated a great number of Escorts over the years, and these are all, I hope, listed below. However, both departments have also controlled cars used for testing, practice only, development, press use, and even merely for publicity. These have not been listed.

The Shellsport 'Celebrity' Escorts which race at Brands Hatch, as one example, were always 'owned' by Boreham, and appear in their fleet holdings, but do not figure in my survey.

As every motoring enthusiast knows, modern competition cars receive new engines frequently, many new components before every event, and even new body shells from time to time.

This makes my task of defining a car very difficult. Theoretically it is quite impossible to say when one particular car ceases to be the original machine. I worried about my definitions for some time, and had to conclude that it was incredibly complicated. Therefore, to keep things as logical as possible, I have defined a particular car as the life history of a registration number and/or its chassis plate.

There are many well known cases, of course, where a works Escort has been badly damaged in a racing or rallying accident. In these cases a completely new body shell would always be needed, but as many as possible of the original components would be rebuilt into the new shell. Thus a well-known car might, effectively, be 'reborn'.

I have listed the International events entered by each car while directly under Boreham or Cologne control. Some cars, however, were works-prepared but loaned to Ford organisations in other countries. In every case, these cars were used for a particular national or international championship; I have listed their use, but (because they were not usually under Boreham's control) not the individual results.

Events of only national status (such as RAC Rally Championship events) are not detailed, but cars which competed in a series are noted accordingly.

Inevitably, from an organisation which is looking forward, and slightly neglects its past, the records may not be complete. There might be a few gaps; I hope not.

Registration Number	Chassis number	First registered	Events entered	Crew	Result
XTW 368F (TC)	Pilot build No 4	23-11-67	Rallycross and original tests	Barry Lee	–
			– sold to Barry Lee, October 1970		
XTW 372F (TC)	BB48HB14109	9-2-68	Loaned to Roger Taylor for racing, 1968	Roger Taylor	–
			– sold to Mr A Taylor, February 1969		
XTW 378F (TC)	BB48HB14115	9-2-68	Loaned to Roger Taylor for racing 1968	Roger Taylor	–
			– sold to Mr A Taylor, February 1969		
XOO 243F (TC)	BB48GM11979	10-1-68	1969 Acropolis	Clark/Porter	2nd
			– sold to David Sutton, October 1969		
XOO 254F (TC)	BB48GF26931	16-1-68	1968 Tulip	Clark/Porter	1st
			1968 Acropolis	Clark/Porter	1st
			– sold to Vince Woodman, June 1971		
XOO 262F (TC)	BB48GP32578	18-1-68	1968 Circuit of Ireland	Clark/Porter	1st
			1968 Scottish	Clark/Porter	1st
			– sold to Roger Clark, August 1968		
XOO 341F (1300GT)	BB48GM06419	6-2-68	1968 and 1969 racing season, by Broadspeed	Chris Craft (mainly) and others	–
			– sold to Broadspeed, December 1969		
XOO 342F (1300GT)	BB48GP18165	6-2-68	1968 and 1969 racing season, by Broadspeed	John Fitzpatrick (mainly) and others	–
			– sold to Broadspeed, December 1969		
XOO 343F (1300GT)	BB48GP18169	6-2-68	1968 and 1969 racing season, Broadspeed back-up car	– various	–
			– sold to David Johnson, Keighley, in September 1972		
XOO 344F (TC)	BB48GM05157	6-2-68	1968 racing season for Alan Mann team	Frank Gardner, Peter Arundell and others	–
			– sold to Barry Pearson, Doncaster, February 1969		
XOO 345F (TC)	BB48GM05160	6-2-68	None – 1968 Alan Mann car, written off in test crash	–	–
			– written off March 1968, officially scrapped September 1969		
XOO 346F (TC)	BB48GM11978	6-2-68	1968 Alan Mann racing car, 1969 Frami racing car (on loan)	– various	–
			– sold to Stan Clark Cars, October 1971		

Registration Number	Chassis number	First registered	Events entered	Crew	Result
XOO 347F (TC)	BB48GP18167	6-2-68	Loaned to several race teams 1968/69/70	– various	–
			– sold to Alec Poole, Dublin, in August 1973		
XOO 348F (TC)	BB48HB39281	6-2-68	1968/69 Alan Mann racing car	– Gardner, Arundell and others	–
			– sold to Wylies of Glasgow, September 1972		
XOO 349F (TC)	BB48HB39279	6-2-68	1968/69 Alan Mann racing car	Frank Gardner	–
			Note: 1968 British Championship winning car		
			– sold to VWM Motors, Bristol, in July 1972		
XOO 350F (GT)	BB48HB40739	6-2-68	Loaned to Superspeed for 1968 racing season	Mike Young and others	–
			– sold to Superspeed Conversions, Ilford, August 1969		
XOO 354F (TC)	BB48GP32582	6-2-68	1969 Alpine	Mikkola/ Wood	DNF
			– sold to Chris Sclater, November 1970		
XOO 355F (TC)	BB48GP32579	6-2-68	1968 San Remo	Andersson/ Davenport	3rd
			1968 Tulip	Andersson/ Davenport	2nd
			1968 Acropolis	Andersson/ Davenport	9th
			1968 Gulf London	Andersson/ Davenport	2nd
			– stolen in Greece, May 1969, recovered by police, then finally sold to John Condellis, Ford Dealer, Athens, October 1969		
XOO 376F (1300GT)	BB48HB14113	9-2-68	1968 loan to Vince Woodman for racing	Vince Woodman	–
			– sold to Woodman, December 1969		
AL029 (Belgian No) (TC)	BB48GP32580	–	1968 Tulip	Staepelaere/ Aerts	DNF
			1968 Vltava	Staepelaere/ Aerts	3rd
			1968 Spanish	Staepelaere/ Aerts	3rd
			1968 Geneva	Staepelaere/ Aerts	4th
			1968 Tour of Belgium	Staepelaere/ Aerts	1st
			1969 Routes du Nord	Staepelaere/ Fontaine	DNF
			1969 Rallye des Vosges	Staepelaere/ Aerts	DNF
			1969 Tulip	Staepelaere/ Aerts	1st

Registration number	Chassis number	First registered	Events entered	Crew	Result
			1969 Wiesbaden	Staepelaere/ Aerts	13th
			1969 12hr Ypres	Staepelaere/ Aerts	1st
			1969 Czech	Staepelaere/ Aerts	1st
			1969 Polish	Staepelaere/ Aerts	2nd
			1969 Spanish	Staepelaere/ Aerts	2nd
			1969 Tour of Belgium	Staepelaere/ Aerts	1st
			1970 12hr Ypres	Staepelaere/ Aerts	1st
			1970 Vltava	Staepelaere/ Aerts	1st
			1970 Donau	Staepelaere/ Aerts	DNF
			1970 Three Cities	Staepelaere/ Aerts	3rd
			1970 Spanish	Staepelaere/ Aerts	3rd
			1970 Tour of Belgium	Staepelaere/ Aerts	1st

– sold to Ford Belgium in 1969, but still controlled by Boreham until end 1970

Registration number	Chassis number	First registered	Events entered	Crew	Result
YVW 591F (TC)	BB49HA21892	2-5-68	1968 Austrian Alpine	Soderstrom/ Palm	1st
			1968 Acropolis	Soderstrom/ Palm	4th
			1968 Gulf London	Soderstrom/ Palm	DNF
			1968 1000 Lakes	Soderstrom/ Palm	3rd
			1969 Acropolis	Andersson/ Palm	DNF
			1969 Tour de Corse	Mikkola/ Palm	6th

– sold to Clarke and Simpson, London, in November 1970

Registration number	Chassis number	First registered	Events entered	Crew	Result
YVW 592F (TC)	BB49HA21885	2-5-68	1968 and 1969 Rallycross loan	Barry Lee	–

– sold to Barry Lee, in October 1970

Registration number	Chassis number	First registered	Events entered	Crew	Result
AHK 901F (TC)	BB49HA21883	24-5-68	1968 1000 Lakes	Mikkola/ Jarvi	1st
			1969 Acropolis	Mikkola/ Wood	DNF
			1970 SMILE rally	Clark/Freud	5th
			1970 Arctic	Mikkola/ Suonio	1st

– also used by Hannu Mikkola in Finland, 1969/70
– sold to Clarke and Simpson, in March 1971

Registration number	Chassis number	First registered	Events entered	Crew	Result
AHK 935F (TC)	BB49HC19626	1-7-68	1968 1000 Lakes	Andersson/ Davenport	DNF

– sold to Service Garage, Barnsley (Eric Jackson) in February 1970

Registration Number	Chassis number	First registered	Events entered	Crew	Result
AHK 938F (TC)	BB49HK09552	18-7-68	1968 RAC	Makinen/ Easter	DNF
			— sold to Clarke and Simpson, February 1969		
AVX 574G (TC)	BB48GP26930	15-8-68	1968 Alpine	Clark/Porter	DNF
			— sold to Coventry Service Station, Ilford, after rallycross use by Barry Lee on their behalf, in October 1970		
AVX 578G (TC)	BB49HL20345	27-8-68	1968 Alpine	Soderstrom/ Palm	DNF
			— then rallycross use by Rod Chapman		
			— sold as scrap to Rod Chapman, in December 1973		
AVX 579G (TC)	BB49HL20346	27-8-68	1968 Alpine	Andersson/ Davenport	DNF
			1969 Monte	Andersson/ Palm	DNF
			— sold to Ateliers Sport-Auto, France, in January 1971		
BEV 781G (TC)	BB49HT35068	4-12-68	1969 Monte	Mikkola/ Porter	32nd
			1969 Swedish	Andersson/ Palm	DNF
			1969 Sestriere	Andersson/ Liz Nystrom	2nd
			1969 San Remo	Clark/Porter	10th
			1969 Austrian Alpine	Mikkola/ Wood	1st
			1969 Scottish	Miss Smith/ Miss Watson	6th
			— sold to Chris Sclater, in August 1969		
BEV 782G (TC)	BB49HT35069	4-12-68	1969 Monte	Piot/Todt	4th
			1969 San Remo	Mikkola/ Wood	DNF
			1969 Circuit of Ireland	Clark/Porter	1st
			1969 Welsh	Andersson/ Palm	1st
			1969 Scottish	Clark/Porter	DNF
			1969 RAC	Mikkola/ Wood	DNF
			— sold to Beacon Hill Garage, Wickham Bishops, Essex, in August 1973		
ETW 880G (1850GT)	BB49JG05378	23-7-69	1969 World Cup Recce	— various	—
			1969 Rally of Incas	Fall/Palm	1st
			— sold to Fischer Y Cia Limited, Guatemala, December 1970		
ETW 881G (TC)	BB49JG05379	23-7-69	1969 1000 Lakes	Mikkola/ Jarvi	1st
			— then rallycross to Rod Chapman	Rod Chapman	
			— sold to Rod Chapman, in August 1971		

Registration number	Chassis number	First registered	Events entered	Crew	Result
ETW 882G (TC)	BB49JG05380	23-7-69	1969 Alpine	Clark/Porter	DNF
			1970 Acropolis	Andersson/ Porter	3rd
			1970 Total	Fall/Liddon	DNF
			1971 Ethiopian Highland	Fall/Liddon	DNF
			– sold to Amropa Motors, Addis Ababa, Ethiopa, in 1971		
ETW 883G (TC)	BB49JG05381	23-7-69	1969 Alpine	Piot/Todt	DNF
			1970 Acropolis	Piot/Todt	4th
			1970 TAP	Fall/Liddon	DNF
			– scrapped at Boreham in August 1972		
ETW 884G (TC)	BB49JG05382	23-7-69	1969 Alpine	Andersson/ Davenport	DNF
			– then rallycross loan to Rod Chapman		
			– sold as scrap to Rod Chapman, in November 1973		
ETW 885G (TC)	BB49JG05383	12-7-69	1969 RAC	Clark/Porter	6th
			– car won by Sgt Eaton of BFPO 39, as a result of a *Daily Mirror* RAC Rally competition, in December 1969		
EVX 248H (TC)	BB49JA35012	27-10-69	1970 racing season by Broadspeed	Chris Craft and (once) Jackie Stewart	–
			– car sold to Broadspeed in February 1971		
EVX 256H (1300GT)	BB48JE15098	5-1-70	1970 racing season by Broadspeed	John Fitzpatrick and others	–
			– sold to Broadspeed in February 1971		
EVX 257H (1300GT)	BB48JE15099	5-1-70	Broadspeed back-up car in 1970	–	–
			– sold to Broadspeed, in February 1971		
FEV 1H (1850GT)	BB49JC39545	1-10-69	1970 World Cup	Mikkola/ Palm	1st
			– car retained by Ford Motor Co Ltd		
FEV 2H (1830GT)	BB49JC39546	1-10-69	1970 World Cup	Greaves/Fall	6th
			– sold to Jimmy Greaves, in March 1971		
FEV 3H (1850GT)	BB49JC39547	1-10-69	1970 World Cup	Clark/Poole	DNF
			– sold to Rod Chapman, after rallycross use, as scrap, in March 1974		
FEV 4H (1850GT)	BB49JC39548	1-10-69	1970 World Cup	Makinen Staepelaere	5th
			– sold to Ford Germany, for exhibition, in August 1973		
FEV 5H (TC)	BB49JC39549	1-10-69	1970 Monte	Mikkola/ Palm	DNF
			1970 Circuit of Ireland	Clark/Porter	1st

Registration number	Chassis number	First registered	Events entered	Crew	Result
			1970 Austrian Alpine	Piot/Todt	3rd
			1970 1000 Lakes	Mikkola Palm	1st
			1970 TAP	Clark/Porter	DNF
			1970 Tour de Corse	Piot/Porter	6th
			1971 Midco, Kenya	Clark/Liddon	1st
			1971 – East African events	– various	–
			– sold to Vic Preston, Nairobi, in March 1972		
FEV 6H (TC)	BB49JC39550	1-10-69	1970 Monte	Makinen/ Liddon	7th
			1970 Swedish	Makinen/ Porter	DNF
			1970 Finnish Snow	Makinen/ Keskitalo	1st
			1970 Austrian Alpine	Andersson/ Porter	DNF
			1970 Danube	Fall/Liddon	DNF
			1971 – East African events	– various	–
			– sold to Joginder Singh, Nairobi, in March 1972		
FEV 7H (TC)	BB49JC39551	1-10-69	1970 Monte	Piot/Todt	DNF
			1970 – French championship events	Piot and Ford France	–
			1970 TAP	Piot/Todt	DNF
			– sold to Clarke and Simpson, in March 1971		
FEV 8H (TC)	BB49JC39552	1-10-69	1970 Monte	Clark/Porter	5th
			1970 Swedish	Mikkola/ Palm	DNF
			1970 Finnish Snow	Mikkola/ Suonio	3rd
			1970 Scottish	Clark/Porter	DNF
			1970 1000 Lakes	Makinen/ Liddon	2nd
			– sold to Clarke and Simpson, in August 1971		
FTW 42H (TC)	BB49JC39554	1-10-69	1969 RAC	Andersson/ Palm	4th
			– sold to Clarke and Simpson, October 1970		
FTW 44H (TC)	BB49JC39556	1-10-69	For 1970 Ford France domestic season	Piot	–
			– sold to Jimmy Bullough, in November 1970		
FTW 46H (1850GT)	BB49JC39558	1-10-69	1970 World Cup – later used in rallycross by Rod Chapman	Aaltonen/ Liddon Rod Chapman	3rd –
			– sold to Rod Chapman, in March 1974		

Registration Number	Chassis number	First registered	Events entered	Crew	Result
FTW 47H (1850GT)	BB49JC39559	1-10-69	1970 World Cup – then used for London-Sydney Marathon recce 1971	Malkin/ Hudson-Evans Tony Ambrose	DNF
			– sold to Roger Clark Cars Ltd, in July 1972		
FTW 48H (1850GT)	BB49JC39560	1-10-69	1970 World Cup	Zasada/ Wachowski	8th
			– sold to Spencer Cars Ltd, Essex, in July 1972		
GNO 415H (TC)	BB49KL21866	6-2-70	1970 Cyprus	Mikkola/ Palm	DNF
			– sold to Withers of Winsford, in July 1972		
GNO 424H (TC)	BB49KL11061	9-2-70	1971 Safari du Congo	Staepelaere/ Byttebier	DNF
			– sold to David Sutton, in May 1972		
KHK 597J (RS1600)	BBATKR14978	30-9-70	1970 RAC	Clark/Porter	DNF
			1971 Hankiralli	Makinen/ Keskitalo	DNF
			1971 British events	Clark (mainly)	–
			– sold to Withers of Winsford, in April 1972		
KHK 598J (TC, later RS)	BBATKR14979	30-9-70	1970 RAC	Makinen/ Liddon	DNF
			1971 Safari	Preston/Smith	6th
			1971 German	Kleint/ Klapproth	DNF
			1971 Cyprus	Kirmitsis/ Lawrence	1st
			1971 RAC	Cowan/Syer	13th
			1972 Hong Kong	Clark/Porter	2nd
			– still held by Ford Motor Co Ltd, in Exhibition department		
KHK 599J (TC)	BBATKR14980	30-9-70	1970 RAC	Mikkola/ Palm	DNF
			– sold to Ford South Africa, in January 1971		
KOO 650J (Mexico)	BB49KM18132	8-10-70	– loaned to Mrs Gill Fortescue-Thomas for racing	Gill Fortescue-Thomas	–
			– sold to Terry Drury Racing, in May 1973		
KOO 653J (Mexico)	BB49KM18133	8-10-70	– loaned to Mrs Gill Fortescue-Thomas for racing	Gill Fortescue-Thomas	–
			– sold to Terry Drury Racing, in April 1973		
LVX 941J (RS1600)	BFATLC59901	1-2-71	1971 Ford-France rallying programme	Piot (mainly)	–
			1971 Routes du Nord	Piot/Porter	DNF

Registration Number	Chassis number	First registered	Events entered	Crew	Result
			1971 Lyon-Charbonnieres	Piot/Porter	2nd
			1971 Criterium Alpin	Piot/Porter	DNF
			1971 Circuit de Touraine	Piot	DNF
			1971 Alpine	Piot/Porter	3rd
			1971 Ronde Cevenole	Piot	3rd
			1971 Netherlands	Staepelaere/ Symens	1st
			1971 Tour of Belgium	Staepelaere/ Aerts	DNF
			1971 Criterium des Cevennes	Piot/Porter	25th
			1972 start season for Roger Clark		
			1972 Welsh	Clark/Porter	1st
			1973 Welsh	Hill/Wood	DNF

— sold to Roger Clark Cars, July 1973

Registration Number	Chassis number	First registered	Events entered	Crew	Result
LVX 942J (TC, then RS1600)	BFATLC59902	16-3-71	1971 Safari	Joginder Singh/ Jaswant Singh	14th
			1971 East African events	Joginder Singh	—
			1972 Scottish	Clark/Porter	2nd
			1972 Manx	Clark/Porter	1st
			1972 RAC	Clark/Mason	1st
			1973 Welsh	Clark/Porter	1st
			1973 Scottish	Clark/Porter	1st
			1973 Manx	Clark/Porter	DNF
			1972 and 1973 British events for Roger Clark	Roger Clark	—

— this car helped Clark to RAC Championships in 1972 and 1973
— sold to Hamiltons of Belfast, November 1973

Registration Number	Chassis number	First registered	Events entered	Crew	Result
LVX 943J (TC)	BFATLC59903	16-3-71	1971 Safari	Makinen/ Liddon	20th
			1971 Mt Elgon, Kenya	Preston/ Smith	1st
			1971 East African events	Preston	—

— this car won 1971 East African series for Vic Preston Junior
— sold to Rod Chapman, in June 1972

Registration Number	Chassis number	First registered	Events entered	Crew	Result
LVX 944J (TC)	BFATLC59904	16-3-71	1971 Safari	Clark/ Staepelaere	24th
			1971 Rally of Incas	Mikkola/ Palm	DNF
			1972/73 – in Uruguay		

— sold to Clarke and Simpson, in March 1974

Registration Number	Chassis number	First registered	Events entered	Crew	Result
LVX 945J (TC)	BFATLC59905	16-3-71	1971 Safari	Mikkola/ Palm	DNF

— sold to Clarke and Simpson, in January 1973

Registration Number	Chassis number	First registered	Events entered	Crew	Result
LVX 946J (TC)	BFATLC59906	16-3-71	1971 Safari	Hillyar/Aird	4th
			– sold to Sears Roebuck Corporation, in September 1972		
LVX 947J (RS1600)	BFATLC99918	7-4-71	1971 racing season by Ford Belgium	Bourgoignie and others	–
			1972 racing season by Boreham	Gerry Birrell and others	–
			– sold to Ron Douglas Racing, in April 1973		
LVX 948J (TC)	BFATLC99919	7-4-71	1971 racing season by Ford Sweden	–	–
			– sold to Auto Laminen, Finland, in 1972		
LVX 949J (RS)	BFATLC99920	7-4-71	1971 and 1972 racing by Ford Holland and Sony	– various	–
			– sold to Beacon Hill Garage, Essex, in June 1973		
LVX 950J (RS)	BFATLC99921	7-4-71	1972 and 1973 Swiss racing seasons	Rudy Heibling	–
			– sold to Rudy Heibling, Switzerland, in May 1974		
LVX 951J (RS)	BFATLC99922	7-4-71	1971 and 1972 Ford Holland racing programme	– various	–
			– sold to Terry Drury Racing, May 1973		
LVX 952J (RS)	BFATLC99923	7-4-71	1971 and 1972 Danish racing programme	– various	–
			– sold to Ford Denmark, January 1974		
LVX 953J (RS)	BFATLC99924	7-4-71	1972 1000 Lakes	Makinen/ Liddon	2nd
			1972 Tour of Belgium	Staepelaere/ 'Valliant'	1st
			1973 Scottish	Cowan/Syer	3rd
			– sold to Mogil Motors, Scotland, in September 1973		
LVX 981J (RS)	BFATLE31192	6-4-71	Used by Boreham as alloy-engine test car	–	–
			– sold to Terry Drury Racing, June 1973		
MEV 34J (RS)	BB49KMO2275	5-4-71	1971 Broadspeed British programme ('registered' as RS1600 for publicity)	John Fitzpatrick	–
			– written off early 1972, then sold as scrap to Broadspeed in June 1972		

Registration number	Chassis number	First registered	Events entered	Crew	Result
MEV 35J (RS)	BFATLC12928	14-1-71	1971 Swedish	Makinen/ Palm	DNF
			1971 Lyon Charbonnieres	Glemser/ Kaiser	3rd
			1971 Welsh	Clark/Phillips	DNF
			1971 Scottish	Clark/Porter	Non start
			1971 12hr Ypres	Staepelaere/ Aerts	2nd
			1971 British rally programme for:	Roger Clark	–

– sold to Hamilton Ltd, Belfast, in November 1971

Registration number	Chassis number	First registered	Events entered	Crew	Result
MEV 36J (RS)	BFATLC12929	14-1-71	1971 Tunturiralli	Mikkola/ Ahava	DNF
			1971 Hankiralli	Mikkola/ Suonio	DNF
			1971 1000 Lakes	Mikkola/ Palm	DNF
			1971 Finnish programme for:	Hannu Mikkola	–
			1972 Arctic	Makinen/ Salonen	2nd
			1972 Finnish programme for:	Hannu Mikkola/Timo Makinen	–
			1973 Acropolis	Sparrow/ Liddon	DNF
			1973 12hr Ypres	Staepelaere/ 'Valliant'	DNF
			1973 Cyprus	Kirmitsis/ Davenport	3rd
			1973 Tour de Corse	Chausseuil/ Baron	4th

– sold to Billy Coleman, Cork, in June 1974

Registration number	Chassis number	First registered	Events entered	Crew	Result
PVX 398K (RS)	BBATLM59962	12-11-71	1971 RAC	Makinen/ Liddon	5th
			1972 Hong Kong	Makinen/ Liddon	1st

– sold to Harpers, Hong Kong, February 1972

Registration number	Chassis number	First registered	Events entered	Crew	Result
PVX 399K (RS)	BBATLM59963	12-11-71	1971 RAC	Mikkola/ Palm	4th
			1972 Hong Kong	Moorat/ Fleming	3rd

– sold to Harpers, Hong Kong, February 1972

Registration number	Chassis number	First registered	Events entered	Crew	Result
PVX 400K (RS)	BBATLM59964	12-11-71	1971 RAC	Clark/Porter	11th
			1972 Scottish	Cowan/Syer	6th
			1972 Olympia	Glemser/ Kaiser	DNF
			1972 RAC	Makinen/ Liddon	DNF

– sold to Grimstead and Sons, Essex, in August 1973

Registration number	Chassis number	First registered	Events entered	Crew	Result
REV 119K (RS)	BBATLP59901	11-1-72	1972 Monte	Piot/Todt	5th
			1972 Safari	Hillyar/Birley	4th
			1972 Scottish	Mikkola/ Cardno	1st

– sold to Mark Birley, London, in July 1972

Registration number	Chassis number	First registered	Events entered	Crew	Result
REV 120K (RS)	BBATLP59902	11-1-72	1972 Monte	Makinen/ Liddon	DNF
			1972 and 1973 – loan to Hamilton of Belfast	Adrian Boyd	–
			– sold to Hamilton Ltd, Belfast, October 1973		
REV 128K (1300GT)	BBATMB11108	14-3-72	1972 British racing by Broadspeed	Vince Woodman	
			– sold to Broadspeed, in July 1973		
Unreg. (RS)	BBATMB59901	–	1972 racing by Norman Reeves Motors	Dave Brodie	–
			– sold to Norman Reeves Motors, July 1973		
RWC 455K (RS)	BBATMR59901	6-3-72	1972 Safari	Mikkola/ Palm	1st
			– then retained by Ford for exhibition purposes		
			– sold to A D R Motors, Chesterfield, June 1976		
RWC 456K (RS)	BBATMR59902	6-3-72	1972 Safari	Makinen/ Liddon	8th
			1972 Acropolis	Mikkola/ Liddon	DNF
			1972 12hr Ypres	Staepelaere/ Aerts	1st
			1972 Olympia	Mikkola/ Porter	DNF
			1972 Cyprus	Kirmitsis/ Lawrence	DNF
			1972 RAC	Cowan/Syer	DNF
			– sold to Ron Douglas Racing, September 1973		
RWC 457K (RS)	BBATMR59903	6-3-72	1972 Safari	Singh/Sembi	DNF
			1972 Acropolis	Hillyar/Porter	DNF
			– sold to Chris Sclater in February 1973		
RWC 458K (RS)	BBATMR59904	6-3-72	1972 Safari	Preston/ Smith	3rd
			1972 East African programme	Preston	–
			– sold to Clarke and Simpson, in July 1973		
SPU 254K (RS)	BFATMG59901	1-5-72	1972/73/74 racing programme Denmark and Belgium	– various	–
			1975 Circuit of Ireland	Clark/Porter	DNF
SPU 255K (RS)	BFATMG59902	1-5-72	1973 British Saloon Car Championship series	Dave Brodie	–
			– written off July 1973, and sold to Norman Reeves Ltd, London		

Registration Number	Chassis number	First registered	Events entered	Crew	Result
VVX958L (RS)	BFATMS99922	23-11-72	1972 RAC	Mikkola/ Davenport	DNF
			– sold to L.P.A. Ltd, London, as part of Kleber-*Wheelbase* prize		
WWC 251L (RS)	BFATMT99901	10-1-73	1973 Monte	Makinen/ Liddon	11th
			1973 Arctic	Makinen/ Salonen	1st
			1973 Finnish programme for	Makinen/ Mikkola	–
			1973 RAC	Alen/ Kivimaki	3rd
			– sold to Clarke and Simpson, January 1974		
WWC 252L (RS)	BFATMT99902	10-1-73	1973 Monte	Mikkola/ Porter	4th
			1973 Ford France programme for	Guy Chausseuil	–
			– sold to Hamilton Ltd, Belfast, in February 1974		
XNO 286L (Mexico)	BFATNJ00468	16-2-73	1973/74 British events for HRH Prince Michael	Prince Michael	–
			– sold to Marshall Wingfield Ltd, London, in January 1975		
XWC 563L (Mexico)	BFATML00211	16-3-73	1973 racing for Gill Fortescue-Thomas	Gill Fortescue Thomas	–
			– sold to Rod Chapman, February 1974		
XPU 216L (RS)	BBAFNM99901	2-4-73	1973 Safari	Clark/Porter	DNF
			1973 Scottish	Pond/Miss Cobb	7th
			1973 RAC	Brookes/ Brown	DNF
			1974 World Cup	Cowan/Syer	15th*
			– sold to Derby Road Garage, Notts, in November 1974		
XPU 217L (RS)	BBAFNM99902	2-4-73	1973 Safari	Preston/ Smith	14th
			1973 Heatway	Marshall/ McWatt	2nd
			– sold to Ford New Zealand, in May 1974		
XPU 218L (RS)	BBAFNM99904	2-4-73	1973 Safari	Mikkola/ Davenport	DNF
			1973 Heatway	Mikkola/ Porter	1st
			– sold to Ford New Zealand, in May 1974		
XPU 219L (RS)	BBAFNM99903	2-4-73	1973 Safari	Makinen/ Liddon	DNF
			1973 Scottish	Mikkola/ Davenport	2nd
			1973 Manx	Preston/White	DNF
			1973 RAC	Preston/White	DNF

Registration number	Chassis number	First registered	Events entered	Crew	Result
			1974 Arctic	Alen/ Kivimaki	4th
			1974 Welsh	Alen/ Davenport	1st
			1974 12hr Ypres	Staepelaere/ 'Jimmy'	1st
			— sold to Peter Clarke Autos, Yorkshire, in November 1974		
XPU 220L (RS)	BBAFNM99905	2-4-73	1973 Safari	Shiyuka/ Gatende	DNF
			1973 East African events	— various	—
			1974 Safari	Preston/ Barnard	9th
			1974 1000 Lakes	Mikkola/ Davenport	1st
			— stolen in January 1975, never recovered!		
			* *Identity swapped with YEV 208L*		
YOO 331L (Mexico)	BJATNM99908	24-4-73	1973 British racing (RS1300 engine) for Gill Fortescue-Thomas	Gill Fortescue-Thomas	—
			— sold to Ford Australia, in 1975		
YEV 207L (RS)	BJATNA69901	17-7-73	1973 1000 Lakes	Makinen/ Liddon	1st
			1974 Arctic	Mikkola/ Davenport	DNF
			1974 Finnish programme for	Timo Makinen	—
			— sold to Clarke and Simpson, in November 1974		
YEV 208L (RS)	BJATNA69902	17-7-73	1973/74 World Cup Rally recce	Liddon/Jim Gavin	—*
			1974 RAC	Rockey/ Channon	11th
			1975 Circuit	Rockey/Scott	DNF
			1975 Welsh	Rockey/ Channon	2nd
			1975 Scottish	Rockey/ Channon	DNF
			1975 Manx	Rockey/Scott	DNF
			1975 RAC	Rockey/ Tucker	DNF
			— also British events on loan to Nigel Rockey —		
			— sold to Nigel Rockey, February 1976		
AOO 674L (RS2000)	BFNTNB70120	20-6-73	Testing and British events	Clark	—
			1974 RAC	Benson Ford Jnr/Kaplan	DNF
			1975 Finnish programme	— various	—
			1975 1000 Lakes	Miss Avomeri/ Miss Valtaharju	DNF
			— sold to Clarke and Simpson, October 1975		

Identity swapped with XPU 216L

Registration number	Chassis number	First registered	Events entered	Crew	Result
OOO 96M (RS)	BJATND69901	7-11-73	1973 RAC	Clark/Mason	2nd
			1974 Welsh	Clark/Porter	DNF
			1974 Manx	Clark/Porter	3rd
			1974 RAC	Clark/Mason	7th
			1975 Circuit	Coleman/ Phelan	1st
			1975 Scottish	Taylor/ Fleming	10th
			1974 British programme for	Roger Clark	–
			– sold to Withers of Winsford, September 1975		
OOO 97M (RS)	BJATND69902	7-11-73	1973 RAC	Mikkola/ Davenport	DNF
			1974 loan to Kleber for award to James Rae	James Rae	–
			– sold to Clarke and Simpson, February 1975		
OOO 98M (RS)	BJATND69903	7-11-73	1973 RAC	Makinen/ Liddon	1st
			1974 Arctic	Miss Heinonen /Miss Saaristo	DNF
			1975 Arctic	Makinen/ Salonen	3rd
			1974 Finnish programme for	Timo Makinen	–
			– sold to J Kynsilehto, Finland, in February 1975		
PVX 445M (RS2000)	BFATPS00348	18-3-74	1974 Tour of Britain	Clark/Porter	1st
			– sold to North Manchester Eng Co Ltd, November 1974		
PVX 446M (RS2000)	BFATPS00349	18-3-74	1974 Tour of Britain	Marshall/ White	2nd
			– sold to Paul Appleby, Sussex, in December 1974		
SNO 666M (RS)	BFATPU69901	5-6-74	1974 1000 Lakes	Makinen/ Liddon	2nd
			1975 Arctic	Makinen/ Salonen	DNF
			1975 Finnish programme for	Timo Makinen	–
			1975 1000 Lakes	Vatanen/ Phillips	DNF
			– sold to David Sutton (Cars) Ltd, October 1975		
SYW 946M (RS)	BFATPT99901	3-4-74	1974 RAC	Alen/White	DNF
			– sold to Ford New Zealand in 1975		
SYW 947M (RS)	BFATPT99902	3-4-74	1974 RAC	Mikkola/ Davenport	DNF
			– sold to Ford Australia in 1975		
GVX 833N (RS2000)	BFATPB00392	5-11-74	1974/5 loan to Russell Brookes	Russell Brookes	–
			– sold to Russell Brookes, May 1975		

Registration number	Chassis number	First registered	Events entered	Crew	Result
GVX 883N (RS)	BFATPA69901	12-11-74	1974 RAC	Makinen/ Liddon	1st
			1975 Boucles de Spa	Staepelaere/ 'Valliant'	1st
			1975 Nacht der Kemper	Staepelaere/ 'Valliant'	1st
			1975 Circuit Ardennes	Staepelaere/ 'Valliant'	1st
			1975 12hr de l'Est	Staepelaere/ 'Valliant'	7th
			1975 Criterium dé Tourraine	Staepelaere/ 'Valliant'	7th
			1975 Criterium Lucien Bianchi	Staepelaere/ 'Valliant'	2nd
			1975 24hr Ypres	Staepelaere/ 'Valliant'	4th
			— sold to Galindo and Cia, Bolivia, December 1975		
HHJ 700N (RS1800)	BFATRE69901	10-4-75	1975 Welsh	Clark/Porter	1st
			1975 Scottish	Clark/Porter	1st
			1975 British programme for	Roger Clark	—
			1976 Mintex	Sclater/ Liddon	5th
			— sold to Chris Sclater, in April 1976		
HHJ 701N (RS1800)	BFATRE69902	10-4-75	On loan to Billy Coleman 1975/76		
			1975 Welsh	Coleman/ Davenport	DNF
			1975 Scottish	Coleman O'Sullivan	3rd
			1975 Donegal	Coleman/ Scott	3rd
			1975 Manx	Coleman/ O'Sullivan	3rd
			1975 RAC	Coleman O'Sullivan	6th
			1976 Mintex	Coleman/ O'Sullivan	DNF
			1976 Welsh	Coleman/ O'Sullivan	DNF
			— sold to Malcolm Wilson, in December 1976		
HHJ 702N (RS1800)	BFATRL69901	7-5-75	On loan to Russell Brookes		
			1975 Welsh	Brookes/ Brown	5th
			1975 Scottish	Brookes/ Brown	2nd
			1975 Manx	Brookes/ Brown	DNF
			1975 RAC	Brookes/ Brown	DNF
			1976 Mintex	Brookes/ Brown	2nd
			— sold to David Stokes, January 1977		

Registration Number	Chassis number	First registered	Events entered	Crew	Result
HHJ 703N (RS1800)	BFATRL69902	7-5-75	1975 Scottish	Makinen/ Liddon	5th
			1975 1000 Lakes	Makinen/ Liddon	3rd
			1976 Safari	Hillyar/Hart	DNF
			– sold to David Sutton (Cars) Ltd., 1977		
HHJ 704N (RS1800)	BFATRK69902	12-2-75	On loan to Alec Poole for 1976 ETC racing		
			– sold to Alec Poole Ltd., 1977		
HHJ 705N (RS1800)	BFATRK69901	12-2-75	On loan to Ford Holland for rallycross 1975 To Rod Chapman for rallycross 1976	– Rod Chapman	– –
			– sold to Rod Chapman, 1977		
JJN 974N (RS1800)	BFATPG69901	2-6-75	1975 Taurus	Staepelaere/ 'Valliant'	1st
			1975 12hr van Ronse	Staepelaere/ 'Valliant'	2nd
			1975 Omloop van Haspenguow	Staepelaere/ 'Valliant'	1st
			1975 Omloop van Vlaanderen	Staepelaere/ 'Valliant'	2nd
			1976 Boucles de Spa	Staepelaere/ 'Valliant'	DNF
			1976 Nacht der Kempen	Staepelaere/ 'Valliant'	1st
			1976 12hr de l'Est	Staepelaere/ 'Valliant'	1st
			1976 Tulip	Staepelaere/ 'Valliant'	3rd
			1976 Omloop van Haspenguow	Staepelaere/ 'Valliant'	1st
			1976 Criterium Lucien Bianchi	Staepelaere/ 'Valliant'	1st
			1976 Donegal	Coleman/ Scott	DNF
			1976 12hr Ypres	Staepelaere/ 'Valliant'	DNF
			1976 Taurus	Staepelaere/ 'Valliant'	1st
			1976 Limburgia	Staepelaere/ 'Valliant'	3rd
			1976 12 Hours van Ronse	Staepelaere/ 'Valliant'	DNF
			1976 12 Hours de Charleroi	Staepelaere/ 'Valliant'	1st
			1976 Omloop van Vlaanderen	Staepelaere/ 'Valliant'	DNF
			1977 Nacht der Kempen	Staepelaere/ Bessem	1st
			1977 Antwerpen-Liege-Antwerpen	Staepelaere/ Franssen	1st
			1977 12 Heures de l'Est	Staepelaere/ Bessem	3rd

Registration number	Chassis number	First registered	Events entered	Crew	Result
			1977 Omloop van Haspenguow	Staepelaere/ Bessem	1st
			1977 Criterium L. Bianchi	Staepelaere/ Franssen	2nd
			1977 Tulip	Staepelaere/ Bessem	1st
			1977 Eindhoven-Liege-Eindhoven	Staepelaere/ Bessem	1st
			1977 24 Uren van Ieper	Staepelaere/ Franssen	DNF
			1977 Limburgia	Staepelaere/ Bessem	1st
			1977 12 Uren van Ronse	Staepelaere/ Bessem	DNF
			1977 De Drie Zustersteden	Staepelaere/ Bessem	1st
			1977 OAMC-Rally Austria	Staepelaere/ Franssen	1st
			1977 Kohle und Stahl	Staepelaere/ Bessem	1st
			1977 Warchau Rally Poland	Staepelaere/ Bessem	DNF
			1978 Boucles de Spa	Staepelaere/ Franssen	DNF
			1978 Tour du Luxembourg	Staepelaere/ Franssen	1st
			1978 Kempen-rally	Staepelaere/ Franssen	1st
			1978 Circuit des Ardennes	Staepelaere/ Bessem	1st
			1978 12 Heures de l'Est	Staepelaere/ Franssen	3rd
			1978 Criterium L. Bianchi	Staepelaere/ Franssen	1st
			1978 Tulip	Staepelaere/ Bessem	3rd
			1978 Omloop van Haspenguow	Staepelaere/ Bessem	1st
			1978 Poland	Staepelaere/ Franssen	1st
			1978 Bosphorus (Turkey)	Staepelaere/ Franssen	1st
			– sold to Ford Motor Co., Belgium, 1978		
JPU 401N (**1600 Sport**)	BBATRC32936	24-3-75	1975/76 Mexico racing car	Gordon Bruce, then Ari Vatanen	–
			– sold to Canlec Ltd., Birmingham, 1977		
KHK 982N (**RS1800**)	BFATRY69903	10-6-75	1975 Tour de France	Makinen/ Liddon	DNF
			1975 San Remo	Makinen/ Liddon	DNF
			1976 Monte	Makinen/ Liddon	DNF
			1976 Hankiralli	Vatanen/ Putkonen	DNF

259

Registration number	Chassis number	First registered	Events entered	Crew	Result
			1976 1000 Lakes	Makinen/ Liddon	4th
			1976 RAC	Lampinen/ Wood	DNF
			1977 Mintex	Dawson/ Marriott	5th
			1977 Circuit of Ireland	Dawson/ Spokes	4th
			1977 Burmah	Dawson/ Pegg	3rd
			1977 Manx	Dawson/ Pegg	3rd
			1977 RAC	Dawson/ Marriott	5th

– and other events in Andy Dawson's domestic British programme, 1977
– sold to Andy Dawson Auto. Developments Ltd., 1977

Registration number	Chassis number	First registered	Events entered	Crew	Result
KHK 983N (RS1800)	BFATRY69904	10-6-75	1975 Antibes	Clark/Porter	DNF
			1975 Manx	Clark/Porter	1st
			1975 San Remo	Clark/Porter	DNF
			1976 Monte	Clark/Porter	5th
			1976 Galway	Coleman/ Porter	1st
			1976 Firestone	Clark/Porter	DNF
			1976 Circuit of Ireland	Coleman/ O'Sullivan	1st

– sold to David Sutton (Cars) Ltd., 1977

Registration number	Chassis number	First registered	Events entered	Crew	Result
LAR 800P (RS1800)	BFATRM69902	5-11-75	1975 RAC	Clark/Mason	2nd
			1976 Mintex	Clark/Porter	DNF
			1976 Welsh	Clark/Porter	3rd
			1976 Scottish	Clark/Porter	2nd
			1976 Manx	Clark/Porter	DNF
			1976 RAC	Hettema/ Billet	DNF
			– and 1976 programme for	Roger Clark	

– sold to Tanner Couch Ltd., New Zealand, 1977

Registration number	Chassis number	First registered	Events entered	Crew	Result
LAP 801P (RS1800)	BFATRM69903	5-11-75	1975 RAC	Makinen/ Liddon	1st
			1976 programme for	Ari Vatanen	–
			1976 Mintex	Vatanen/ Bryant	3rd
			1976 Welsh	Vatanen/ Bryant	1st
			1976 Scottish	Vatanen/ Bryant	DNF
			1976 Manx	Vatanen/ Bryant	1st

– sold to Vic Preston Ltd., Nairobi, Kenya, 1977

Registration number	Chassis number	First registered	Events entered	Crew	Result
LVW 690P (RS1800)	BFATRJ69901	8-9-75	1975 RAC	Vatanen/ Bryant	DNF
			1976 Morocco	Makinen/ Liddon	DNF
			1976 Southern Cross	Makinen/ Liddon	DNF

– sold to Ford New Zealand, October 1976

Registration Number	Chassis number	First registered	Events entered	Crew	Result
MTW 200P (RS1800)	BFATRP69904	10-12-75	1976 Firestone	Makinen/ Liddon	2nd
			1976 Total	Makinen/ Liddon	1st
			1976 RAC	Waldegard/ Thorzelius	3rd
			1977 San Remo	Vatanen/ Bryant	DNF
			1978 Portugal	Nicolas/ Laverne	3rd
			– sold to David Sutton (Cars) Ltd., May 1979		
MTW 201P (RS1800)	BFATRP69905	10-12-75	1976 Morocco	Clark/Porter	DNF
			1976 Southern Cross	Clark/Porter	14th
			– sold to Ford New Zealand, October 1976		
NOO 894P (RS2000)	BFATSR02930	2-3-76	1976 Tour of Britain	Clark/Porter	DNF
			– sold to Peter Clarke Autos, Yorkshire, September 1976		
NOO 895P (RS2000)	BFATSR02931	2-3-76	1976 Tour of Britain	HRH Prince Michael/ Clarkson	11th
			– sold to David Sutton (Cars) Ltd., 1977		
OVX 430P (RS2000)	BFATSG41291	15-6-76	1976 Tour of Britain	Makinen/ Liddon	DNF
			1976 1000 Lakes	Saaristo/ Alanen	9th
			1976 RAC	Saaristo/ Francis	27th
			– sold to Vic Preston Ltd., Kenya, 1977		
OVX 431P (RS2000)	BFATSG41288	15-6-76	1976 Tour of Britain	Vatanen/ Bryant	1st
			1976 1000 Lakes	Hamalainen/ Vihervaara	DNF
			1976 RAC	Hamalainen/ Vihervaara	DNF
			– sold to Withers of Winsford Ltd., 1977		
ODA 622R (RS1800)		1-8-76	1976 Circuit of Ireland	Brookes/ Brown	2nd
			1976 Welsh	Brookes/ Crellin	14th
			1976 Scottish	Brookes/ Brown	1st
			1976 Manx	Brookes/ Brown	DNF
			1976 RAC	Brookes/ Brown	DNF
			1977 Arctic	Brookes/ Brown	DNF
			1977 Tulip	Brookes/ Bryant	3rd
			1977 Scottish	Cowan/ McNeil	DNF
			– and other events in Russell Brookes' domestic British programme, 1976 and 1977		

Registration number	Chassis number	First registered	Events entered	Crew	Result
			– sold to Jeff Churchill, 1977		
			– Note: This car actually carried HHJ 702N plates for its first five International events.		
POO 489R (RS1800)	BFATSE69901	5-8-76	1976 1000 Lakes	Vatanen/Aho	DNF
			1976 RAC	Vatanen/ Bryant	DNF
			1977 Arctic	Vatanen/ Aho	1st
			– then used in Vatanen's domestic Finnish programme, 1977		
			1977 1000 Lakes	Hamalainen/ Tiukkanen	1st
			– then used by Vatanen in Finnish programme in 1978		
			1978 1000 Lakes	Miss Korpi/ Miss Heinio	Ladies' Prize/ 28th
			– sold to Tony Maslen, May 1979		
POO 504R (RS1800)	BBATSS69902	21-9-76	1976 RAC	Makinen/ Liddon	DNF
			1977 Portugal	Vatanen/ Bryant	DNF
			1977 Acropolis	Vatanen/ Aho	DNF
			1977 1000 Lakes	Vatanen/ Aho	DNF
			– then Vatanen's domestic programme, late 1977		
			1978 Mintex	Mikkola/ Hertz	DNF
			1978 Welsh	Mikkola/ Hertz	1st
			1978 Scottish	Mikkola/ Hertz	1st
			1978 Burmah (E)	Mikkola/ Hertz	1st
			1978 Manx (E)	Mikkola/ Hertz	DNF
			1979 Portugal	Mikkola/ Hertz	1st
			1979 Quebec (R)	Vatanen/ Richards	3rd
			1979 RAC	Brookes/ White	2nd
			– sold to Ron Hudson, February 1980		
POO 505R (RS1800)	BBATSS69901	21-9-76	1976 RAC	Clark/ Pegg	1st
			1977 Galway	Clark/ Porter	1st
			1977 Portugal	Clark/ Porter	DNF
			1977 Acropolis	Clark/ Porter	2nd
			1977 Donegal	Clark/ Porter	DNF
			1977 Tour de Corse	Brookes/ Holmes	DNF

Registration Number	Chassis number	First registered	Events entered	Crew	Result
			1978 Circuit of Ireland	Clark/ Porter	4th
			– then test car at Boreham, then:		
			1979 Portugal	Waldegard/ Thorzelius	2nd
			1979 Quebec (R)	Waldegard/ Thorzelius	1st
			1979 RAC	Clark/ Wilson	DNF
			– sold to Jeff Churchill, May 1980		
STW 128R **(RS1800)**	BBATTJ69901	1-2-77	1976 Manx	Coleman/ Liddon	DNF
			1976 RAC	Coleman/ O'Sullivan	6th
			1977 Sachs Winterrallye	Hainbach/ Linzen	2nd
			1977 Sachs-Rallye Trifels	Hainbach/ Linzen	DNF
			1977 Rallye Weser-Ems	Hainbach/ Linzen	1st
			1977 Saarland Rallye	Hainbach/ Linzen	1st
			1977 Metz-Rallye	Hainbach/ Linzen	1st
			1977 Rallye Hessen	Hainbach/ Linzen	DNF
			1977 Rallye Vorderpfalz	Hainbach/ Linzen	DNF
			1977 Hunsruck Rallye	Hainbach/ Linzen	1st
			1977 Rallye Westfalen Lippe	Hainbach/ Linzen	1st
			1977 Sachs Rallye Baltic	Hainbach/ Linzen	DNF
			1977 RAC	Hainbach/ Linzen	20th
			– sold to Reinhard Hainbach, 1978		
			– Note: This car actually carried HHJ 701N plates for its first two International events.		
STW 129R **(RS1800)**	BBATTJ69902	1-2-77	1977 Mintex	Brookes/ Brown	DNF
			1977 Circuit of Ireland	Brookes/ Brown	1st
			1977 Welsh	Brookes/ Brown	DNF
			1977 Scottish	Brookes/ Brown	3rd
			1977 Burmah	Brookes/ Brown	2nd
			1977 Manx	Brookes/ Brown	DNF
			1977 RAC	Brookes/ Brown	3rd
			1978 Mintex	Brookes/ Brown	2nd
			1978 Tulip	Brookes/ Bryant	1st

Registration number	Chassis number	First registered	Events entered	Crew	Result
			1978 Scottish	Brookes/ Brown	7th
			1978 Burmah	Brookes/ Bryant	2nd
			1978 Cyprus	Kirmitsis/ Adams	2nd
			1979 Mintex	Brookes/ White	4th
			1979 Welsh	Brookes/ White	2nd
			1979 Scottish	Brookes/ White	10th
			1979 RAC	Carr/Gocentas	10th

– and other events in Russell Brookes' domestic British programme in 1977/1978/1979
– sold to Hannu Mikkola, February 1980

Registration number	Chassis number	First registered	Events entered	Crew	Result
STW 130R (RS1800)	BBATTJ69903	1-2-77	1977 Portugal	Waldegard/ Thorzelius	2nd
			1977 Acropolis	Waldegard/ Thorzelius	1st
			1977 1000 Lakes	Waldegard/ Thorzelius	3rd
			1977 RAC	Hamalainen/ Scott	6th
			1978 Mille Pistes	Nicolas/ Laverne	DNF
			1979 New Zealand (R)	Vatanen/ Richards	3rd

(Ran as IZ8320 in this event)
– sold to Ford New Zealand, July 1979

Registration number	Chassis number	First registered	Events entered	Crew	Result
STW 200R RS1800)	BBATTM69901	1-3-77	1977 East African Safari	Clark/ Porter	DNF
			1977 Quebec	Clark/ Porter	3rd
			1977 RAC	Clark/Pegg	4th
			1978 Circuit of Ireland	Mikkola/ Hertz	DNF
			1978 Criterium Alpin	Nicolas/ Laverne	2nd
			1978 Scottish	Samson/ Samson	8th
			1978 Antibes	Nicolas/ Laverne	8th
			1978 Ypres	Staepelaere/ Franssen	2nd
			1978 Vorderplatz	Hainbach/ Linzen	2nd
			1978 Hunsruck	Hainbach/ Linzen	DNF
			1978 Burmah	Carr/Gocentas	6th
			1978 Kurkessen	Hainbach/ Linzen	1st
			1978 Tour de France	Nicolas/ Laverne	DNF
			1978 Cyprus	Clark/Porter	1st

– sold to B. Neville, Ireland, April 1980

Registration number	Chassis number	First registered	Events entered	Crew	Result
STW 201R (**RS1800**)	BBATTM69902	1-3-77	1977 East African Safari	Waldegard/ Thorzelius	1st

– Safari car 'de-registered', and placed in Ford museum. Rebuilt car's history, as follows:

			1978 1000 Lakes	Mikkola/ Hertz	DNF
			1979 Sweden	Mikkola/ Hertz	5th
			1979 Cyprus (R)	Vatanen/ Richards	1st

– sold to David Sutton (Cars) Ltd., March 1980

Registration number	Chassis number	First registered	Events entered	Crew	Result
STW 202R (**RS1800**)	BBATTM69903	1-3-77	1977 East African Safari	Vatanen/ Aho	DNF
			1977 Quebec	Vatanen/ Aho	DNF
			1977 RAC	Vatanen/ Bryant	DNF
			1978 Arctic	Vatanen/ Aho	1st
			1978 Swedish	Vatanen/ Aho	5th
			1978 Hankiralli	Vatanen/ Aho	DNF
			1978 Portugal	Vatanen/ Bryant	DNF
			1978 1000 Lakes	Hamalainen/ Koronen	8th

– sold to David Sutton (Cars) Ltd., November 1978

Registration number	Chassis number	First registered	Events entered	Crew	Result
STW 203R (**RS1800**)	BBATTM69904	1-3-77	1977 East African Safari	Preston/ Lyall	DNF

– sold to Vic Preston Ltd., Kenya, 1977

Registration number	Chassis number	First registered	Events entered	Crew	Result
TWC 235R (**RS1800**)	BBATTB69902	12-5-77	1979 Welsh	Donald/ Tucker	9th

– this was a recce car in 1977 and 1978, along with TWC 234R. 235R was only used once, as detailed, and 234R was never used, on an international rally
– sold to Bjorn Waldegard, March 1980

Registration number	Chassis number	First registered	Events entered	Crew	Result
VHK 47S (**RS1800**)	BBATTA69907	9-8-77	1977 Mintex	Taylor/ Jensen	DNF
			1977 Welsh	Taylor/ Jensen	5th
			1977 Scottish	Taylor/ Jensen	DNF
			1977 Burmah	Taylor/ Short	DNF
			1978 Galway	Taylor/ Short	1st
			1979 Monte Carlo	Mikkola/ Hertz	5th

– and John Taylor's domestic British programme, 1977 – 1978
– sold to Pubblimo corporation, February 1980

Registration number	Chassis number	First registered	Events entered	Crew	Result
VHK 74S (RS1800)	BBATTC69901	27-9-77	1977 San Remo	Waldegard/ Thorzelius	5th
			1977 Corsica	Nicolas/ Laverne	DNF
			1978 Circuit of Ireland	Brookes/ Brown	1st
			1978 Welsh	Brookes/ Brown	5th
			1978 Manx	Brookes/ Bryant	DNF
			1979 Monte Carlo	Waldegard/ Thorzelius	2nd

– sold to Pubblimo corporation, February 1980

Registration number	Chassis number	First registered	Events entered	Crew	Result
WTW 567S (RS1800)	BBATTC69902	9-11-77	1977 RAC	Waldegard/ Thorzelius	1st
			1978 Swedish	Waldegard/ Thorzelius	1st
			1978 Portugal	Waldegard/ Thorzelius	DNF
			1978 South Sweden	Waldegard/ Thorzelius	1st
			1979 Sweden (R)	Vatanen/ Richards	DNF
			1979 Portugal (R)	Vatanen/ Bryant	DNF
			1979 Acropolis (R)	Waldegard/ Thorzelius	1st
			1979 1000 Lakes	Waldegard/ Billstam	3rd

– sold to J. Hagman, Sweden, January 1980

Registration number	Chassis number	First registered	Events entered	Crew	Result
WTW 568S (RS1800)	BBATTC69903	9-11-77	1978 Swedish	Mikkola/ Hertz	2nd
			1978 Hankiralli	Mikkola/ Hertz	DNF
			1978 Portugal	Mikkola/ Hertz	2nd
			1978 1000 Lakes	Vatanen/ Aho	DNF
			1978 RAC (E)	Waldegard/ Thorzelius	2nd
			1979 New Zealand	Mikkola/ Hertz	1st

(– ran as JB780 in the latter event)
– sold to Ford New Zealand, July 1979

Registration number	Chassis number	First registered	Events entered	Crew	Result
WTW 569S (RS1800)	BBATTC69904	9-11-77	1978 Mintex	Clark/Porter	4th
			1978 Welsh	Clark/Porter	2nd
			1978 Scottish	Clark/Porter	3rd
			1978 Burmah	Clark/Porter	3rd
			1978 Manx	Clark/Porter	4th
			1979 Sweden	Waldegard/ Thorzelius	2nd
			1979 Acropolis	Iaveris/ Stefanis	5th
			1979 RAC (E)	Mikkola/ Hertz	1st

– retained for back-to-back testing against RS1700T project cars, 1980 to 1983. Sold to Malcolm Wilson, 1983

For the 1978 Lombard-RAC Rally, when the competitions department at Boreham was immobilised by a company-wide strike over pay, the 'works' effort was divided into three 'mini-dealer-teams'. Only one car was a recognisable 'works' machine. The cars, crews and results achieved, were as follows:

1978 RAC
Run by David Sutton (Cars) Ltd:
SJN 830R (E), Mikkola/Hertz, 1st.
MLD 999P, Vatanen/Bryant, DNF.
Run by Russell Brookes/Andrews Heat for Hire:
UNY 956S, Brookes/Tucker, 3rd.
WTW 568S (E), Waldegard/Thorzelius, 2nd.
Run by Haynes of Maidstone/John Taylor:
OKK 380P, Clark/Wilson, DNF.
SKK 625R, Taylor/Short, 7th.

Notes: SJN 830R contained parts of a famous Boreham car, but was otherwise not directly connected to any known 'identity'.
MLD 999P was retained by David Sutton, used mainly as a Rothmans or Eatons Yale practice car, or for minor events, and finally resurfaced as an RS2000 for Ivory Coast in 1981!
UNY 956S was a brand-new Boreham car, partly built for the rally, sold off to Jeff Churchill as the strike began, 'lease-lent' to Russell Brookes, and returned to Churchill afterwards.
WTW 568S was a Boreham car, 'sold' off to Thomas Motors before the rally, 're-purchased' afterwards, and subsequently re-prepared, shipped out to New Zealand where, re-registered as JB870, Hannu Mikkola used it to win the 1979 Rally of New Zealand.
OKK 380P and SKK 625R were both regular John Taylor/Haynes of Maidstone Cars, used by him before and after this event. These machines qualify in my book as 'semi-works' Escorts.

Registration number	Chassis number	First registered	Events entered	Crew	Result
FEV 1T	BBATWE81065	15-5-79	1979 Acropolis (R)	Mikkola/ Hertz	DNF
(RS1800)			1979 1000 Lakes	Mikkola/ Hertz	DNF
			– sold to Malcolm Wilson, 1980		
GVX 488T	BBATWE81063	15-5-79	1979 Acropolis (R)	Clark/Porter	DNF
(RS1800)			1979 1000 Lakes (R)	Vatanen/ Richards	2nd
			1979 RAC (R)	Vatanen/ Richards	4th
			– sold to Autobetrieb, Worms, Germany, 1980		
GVX 489T	BBATWE81064	15-5-79	1979 Circuit of Ireland	Brookes/ White	DNF
(RS1800)			1979 Ypres	Brooks/ Bryant	DNF
			1979 Manx	Brookes/ White	1st
			1979 Ulster	Brookes/ White	DNF
			– sold to Brendan Neville, Ireland, 1980		
GJN 126T	BBATWL92658	7-6-79	1979 RAC (E)	Waldegard/ Thorzelius	9th
(RS1800)			– sold to David 'Piggy' Thompson, 1980		

From the autumn of 1978, the David Sutton organisation grew closer and progressively closer to Boreham. In 1978, as listed, they ran Hannu Mikkola's car on Boreham's behalf, and in 1979 they ran their own cars, with factory drivers, in British events. The factory officially withdrew from rallying at the end of 1979, but retained the services of some drivers. In 1980 and 1981, the Sutton team ran extensive programmes, with cars built at Acton, West London, and with Eatons and Rothmans finance. Details of the 1979-1981 Sutton programmes are listed below. (E) denotes an Eatons Yale sponsored car, (R) a Rothmans sponsored car.

MLD 999P
(RS1800)
1979 Scottish (E), Waldegard/Thorzelius, DNF.
– then re-created as a single-cam RS2000 for:
1981 Ivory Coast (R), Taylor/Spiller, DNF
Sold to: Pekka Hokkanen, Finland.

STW 201R (ex-Boreham 'works' car)
(RS1800)
1980 Cyprus (R), Clark/Wilson, 1st.
1981 Mintex (R), Wilson/Harryman, 6th.
1981 Circuit of Ireland (R), Wilson/Harryman, DNF.
1981 Welsh (R), Wilson/Harryman, 5th.
1981 Scottish (R), Wilson/Harryman, 3rd.
1981 Manx (R), Wilson/Harryman, 3rd.
1981 RAC (R), Wilson/Harryman, DNF.
Sold to: Motoguzzi UK Ltd. (Clew Hughes).

GVX 489T (an ex-Boreham 'works' car, owned by Brendan Neville, in Southern Ireland)
(RS1800)
1980 Circuit of Ireland (E), Coleman/Neville, DNF.

UYY 256S
(RS1800)
1979 Manx (E), Mikkola/Hertz, DNF.
1980 Portugal (R), Vatanen/Richards, DNF.
1980 Acropolis (R), Vatanen/Richards, 1st.
1980 1000 Lakes (R), Vatanen/Richards, 2nd.
1981 Mintex (R), Airikkala/Short, 1st.
1981 Costa Smeralda (R), Airikkala/Virtanen, 2nd.
1981 Elba (R), Airikkala/Virtanen, 4th.
1981 1000 Lakes (R), Airikkala/Virtanen, 5th.
1981 RAC (R), Airikkala/Short, 4th.
Sold to: Timo Makinen, Finland.

CLM 184T
(RS1800)
1979 Welsh (E), Mikkola/Hertz, 1st.
1979 Scottish (E), Mikkola/Hertz, 6th.
1981 Portugal (R), Wilson/Harryman, DNF.
1981 Acropolis (R), Wilson/Harryman, DNF.
1981 Cyprus (R), Wilson/Harryman, DNF.
Sold to: Newport Racing, USA (for Rod Millen to drive).

DKP 191T
(RS1800)
1981 Acropolis (R), Vatanen/Richards, 1st.

1981 1000 Lakes (R), Vatanen/Richards, 1st.
1981 San Remo (R), Vatanen/Richards, 7th.
Sold to: MCD Services (for Ari Vatanen's 1982 programme in the UK).

EUW 938V
(RS1800)
1980 Mintex (R), Vatanen/Richards, 2nd.
1980 Circuit (R), Vatanen/Richards, 2nd.
1980 Welsh (R), Vatanen/Richards, 1st.
1980 Scottish (R), Vatanen/Richards, 2nd.
1980 CS Rally (R), Vatanen/Richards, 2nd.
1980 Manx (R), Vatanen/Richards, 2nd.
1981 Maspalomas (R), Vatanen/Richards, 2nd.
1981 Welsh (R), Vatanen/Richards, 1st.
1981 Manx (R), Airikkala/Virtanen, DNF.
1981 Corte Ingles (R), Airikkala/Virtanen, 7th.
1981 Tenerife (R), Airikkala/Virtanen, DNF.
Sold to: Ford Autoindustry, Saarbrucken, West Germany.

EUW 939V
(RS1800)
1980 Mintex (E), Mikkola/Hertz, 1st.
1980 Welsh (E), Mikkola/Hertz, 2nd.
1980 Scottish (E), Mikkola/Hertz, 1st.
1980 RAC (E), Mikkola/Hertz, 2nd.
1981 Swedish (R), Vatanen/Richards, 2nd.
Sold to: Carlos Peres, Portugal.

EUC 958V
(RS1800)
1980 Portugal (R), Mikkola/Hertz, DNF.
1980 Acropolis (R), Mikkola/Hertz, DNF.
1980 San Remo (R), Mikkola/Hertz, 3rd.
1980 RAC (R), Makinen/Holmes, 6th.
1981 Sweden (R), Airikkala/Virtanen, 3rd.
1981 Welsh (R), Airikkala/Short, 4th.
1981 Scottish (R), Airikkala/Short, 5th.
1981 Brazil (R), Vatanen/Richards, 1st.
Still owned by David Sutton (Cars) Ltd.

PLY 829W
(RS1800)
1980 San Remo (R), Vatanen/Richards, 2nd.
1980 RAC (R), Vatanen/Richards, DNF.
1981 Monte Carlo (R), Vatanen/Richards, DNF.
1981 Portugal (R), Vatanen/Richards, DNF.
1981 Circuit of Ireland (R), Airikkala/Short, DNF.
Rally identity destroyed — not sold as rally car.

RRK 425W
(RS1800)
1981 Argentina (R), Vatanen/Richards, DNF.
1981 Ivory Coast (R), Vatanen/Richards, 9th.
Sold to: Harri Toivonen, Finland.

269

VLE 756X
(RS1800)
1981 RAC (R), Vatanen/Richards, 2nd.
Sold to: Carreras Rothmans, for permanent display.

B

The Works Escorts calendar ~ 1968 to 1981

What follows is a complete list of international events in which works or works-controlled Escorts have been entered. Of course, works cars have also contested – and won – hundreds of events with national status, but these results have been omitted. This is done merely to keep the list of achievements within bounds!

Once a works car was sold off by the factory or, from 1980 and 1981, by the David Sutton organisation, it no longer figures in this list. Nevertheless, I must point out that many pensioned-off machines have continued to have distinguished competitions careers in the hands of their private owners.

Date	Event	Driver/Co-driver	Model	Engine (cc)	Reg. No	Result
1968						
March	**San Remo**	Andersson/ Davenport	TC	1600	XOO 355F	3rd
April	**Circuit of Ireland**	Clark/Porter	TC	1600	XOO 262F	1st
	Silverstone *Daily Express*	Fitzpatrick	1300GT	1300	XOO 342F	2nd class
	Tulip	Clark/Porter	TC	1600	XOO 254F	1st
		Andersson/ Davenport	TC	1600	XOO 355F	2nd
		Staepelaere/ Aerts	TC	1600	ALO 29	DNF
May	**Zolder ETC**	Gardner	TC	1600	XOO 344F	1st
	Austrian Alpine	Soderstrom/ Palm	TC	1600	YVW 591F	1st
	Acropolis	Clark/Porter	TC	1600	XOO 254F	1st +
		Soderstrom/ Palm	TC	1600	YVW 591F	4th Team Prize
		Andersson/ Davenport	TC	1600	XOO 355F	9th
June	**Scottish**	Clark/Porter	TC	1600	XOO 262F	1st
July	**Gulf London**	Andersson/ Davenport	TC	1600	XOO 355F	2nd
		Soderstrom/ Palm	TC	1600	YVW 591F	DNF
	Nurburgring 6-Hour	Gardner/ Arundell	TC	1600	XOO 344F	DNF
		Glemser/ Neerpasch	TC	1600	XOO 349F	DNF
		Craft/Clark	1300GT	1300	XOO 341F	9th + Class 1st
		Fitzpatrick/ Taylor	1300GT	1300	XOO 342F	10th + Class 2nd
	Vltava	Staepelaere/ Aerts	TC	1600	ALO 29	3rd
	Brands Hatch (GP Meeting)	Gardner	TC	1600	XOO 349F	1st
		Clark	TC	1600	XOO 346F	DNF
		Fitzpatrick	1300GT	1300	XOO 342F	3rd + Class
		Craft	1300GT	1300	XOO 341F	12th
August	**1000 Lakes**	Mikkola/Jarvi	TC	1600	AHK 901F	1st
		Soderstrom/ Palm	TC	1600	YVW 591F	3rd
		Andersson/ Davenport	TC	1600	AHK 935F	DNF
	Zandvoort ETC	Gardner	TC	1600	XOO 344F	DNF
September	**Alpine**	Clark/Porter	TC	1600	AVX 574G	DNF
		Andersson/ Davenport	TC	1600	AVX 579G	DNF
		Soderstrom/ Palm	TC	1600	AVX 578G	DNF

Date	Event	Driver/Co-driver	Model	Engine (cc)	Reg. No	Result
	Spanish	Staepelaere/ Aerts	TC	1600	ALO 29	3rd
	Geneva	Staepelaere/ Aerts	TC	1600	ALO 29	4th
	Eigenthal ETC	Gardner	TC	1600	XOO 344F	6th + Class 1st
	Jarama ETC	Gardner	TC	1600	XOO 344F	11th + Class 1st
October	Brands Hatch	Gardner	TC	1600	XOO 348F	1st
		Craft	1300GT	1300	XOO 341F	Class 1st
		Fitzpatrick	1300GT	1300	XOO 342F	Class 3rd
November	Tour of Belgium	Staepelaere/ Aerts	TC	1600	ALO 29	1st
	RAC Rally	Makinen/Easter	TC	1600	AHK 938F	DNF
1969 January	Monte Carlo	Piot/Todt	TC	1600	BEV 782G	4th
		Andersson/ Palm	TC	1600	AVX 579G	DNF
		Mikkola/Porter	TC	1600	BEV 781G	32nd
February	Routes du Nord	Staepelaere/ Fontaine	TC	1600	ALO 29	DNF
	Swedish	Andersson/ Palm	TC	1600	BEV 781G	DNF
	Sestriere	Andersson/Liz Nystrom	TC	1600	BEV 781G	2nd
March	San Remo	Mikkola/Wood	TC	1600	BEV 782G	DNF
		Clark/Porter	TC	1600	BEV 781G	10th
	Brands Hatch Race of Champions meeting	Fitzpatrick	1300GT	1300	XOO 342F	DNF
		Craft	1300GT	1300	XOO 341F	DNF
		Gardner	TC	1600	XOO 349F	3rd
	Silverstone	Fitzpatrick	1300GT	1300	XOO 342F	5th, 1st Class
	Int. Trophy meeting	Craft	1300GT	1300	XOO 341F	DNF
		Gardner	TC	1600	XOO 349F	1st
April	Circuit of Ireland	Clark/Porter	TC	1800	BEV 782G	1st
	Rallye des Vosges	Staepelaere/ Aerts	TC	1600	ALO 29	DNF
May	Tulip	Staepelaere/ Aerts	TC	1600	ALO 29	1st
	Welsh	Andersson/ Palm	TC	1800	BEV 782G	1st
	Austrian Alpine	Mikkola/Wood	TC	1600	BEV 781G	1st
	Wiesbaden	Staepelaere/ Aerts	TC	1600	ALO 29	13th
	Acropolis	Clark/Porter	TC	1600	XOO 243F	2nd
		Andersson/ Palm	TC	1600	YVW 591F	DNF
		Mikkola/Wood	TC	1600	AHK 901F	DNF

273

Date	Event	Driver/Co-driver	Model	Engine (cc)	Reg No	Result
June	Scottish	Clark/Porter	TC	1600	BEV 782G	DNF
		Miss Smith/Miss Watson	TC	1600	BEV 781G	6th
	12hr Ypres	Staepelaere/ Aerts	TC	1600	ALO 29	1st
	European Touring Challenge – Brands Hatch	Fitzpatrick/ Taylor	1300GT	1300	XOO 342F	2nd, 1st Class
July	Czech	Staepelaere/ Aerts	TC	1600	ALO 29	1st
	Polish	Staepelaere/ Aerts	TC	1600	ALO 29	2nd
	Silverstone – GP meeting	Fitzpatrick	1300GT	1300	XOO 342F	6th, 2nd Class
		Craft	1300GT	1300	XOO 341F	5th, 1st Class
		Gardner	TC	1600	XOO 349F –,	3rd Class
August	1000 Lakes	Mikkola/Jarvi	TC	1600	ETW 881G	1st
September	Alpine	Clark/Porter	TC-V6	2300	ETW 882G	DNF
		Mikkola/Wood	TC	1800	XOO 354F	DNF
		Andersson/ Davenport	TC	1800	ETW 884G	DNF
		Piot/Todt	TC	1800	ETW 883G	DNF
	Brands Hatch – 'Guards' meeting	Fitzpatrick	1300GT	1300	XOO 342F	2nd Class
		Craft	1300GT	1300	XOO 341F	6th, 1st Class
		Gardner	TC	1600	XOO 349F	DNF
October	Rally of Incas	Fall/Palm	TC	1600	ETW 880G	1st
	Spanish	Staepelaere/ Aerts	TC	1600	ALO 29	2nd
	Brands Hatch – Show 200 meeting	Fitzpatrick	1300GT	1300	XOO 342F	6th, 1st Class
		Craft	1300GT	1300	XOO 341F	2nd Class
		Gardner	TC	1600	XOO 349F	1st
November	Tour of Belgium	Staepelaere/ Aerts	TC	1600	ALO 29	1st
	RAC Rally	Clark/Porter	TC	1600	ETW 885G	6th
		Mikkola/Wood	TC	1600	BEV 782G	DNF
		Andersson/ Palm	TC	1600	FTW 42H	4th
	Tour de Corse	Mikkola/Palm	TC-V6	2300	YVW 591F	6th
1970 January	SMILE Rally	Clark/Freud	TC	1600	AHK 901F	5th
	Monte Carlo	Clark/Porter	TC	1600	FEV 8H	5th
		Makinen/Liddon	TC	1600	FEV 6H	7th
		Mikkola/Palm	TC	1600	FEV 5H	DNF
		Piot/Todt	TC	1600	FEV 7H	DNF
February	Arctic	Mikkola/Suonio	TC	1600	AHK 901F	1st
	Routes du Nord	Piot/Todt	TC	1600	FTW 44H	12th

Date	Event	Driver/Co-driver	Model	Engine (cc)	Reg No	Result
	Swedish	Makinen/Porter	TC	1600	FEV 6H	DNF
		Mikkola/Palm	TC	1600	FEV 8H	DNF
	Finnish Snow	Makinen/Keskitalo	TC	1600	FEV 6H	1st
		Mikkola/Suonio	TC	1600	FEV 8H	3rd
March	**Brands – Race of Champions meeting**	Craft	TC	1600	EVX 248H	2nd
		Fitzpatrick	1300GT	1300	EVX 256H	28th
	Circuit of Ireland	Clark/Porter	RS1600	1800	FEV 5H	1st
April	**Silverstone – Int. Trophy meeting**	Craft	TC	1600	EVX 248H	4th
		Fitzpatrick	1300GT	1300	EVX 256H	6th
April/ May	**World Cup Rally**	Mikkola/Palm	1850	1850*	FEV 1H	1st
		Greaves/Fall	1850	1850*	FEV 2H	6th
		Clark/Poole	1850	1850*	FEV 3H	DNF
		Makinen/Staepelaere	1850	1850*	FEV 4H	5th
		Aaltonen/Liddon	1850	1850*	FTW 46H	3rd
		Malkin/Hudson-Evans	1850	1850*	FTW 47H	DNF
		Zasada/Wachowski	1850	1850*	FTW 48H	8th
May	**Austrian Alpine**	Andersson/Porter	TC	1600	FEV 6H	DNF
		Piot/Todt	TC	1600	FEV 5H	3rd
	Acropolis	Andersson/Porter	TC	1600	ETW 882G	3rd
		Piot/Todt	TC	1600	ETW 883G	4th
June	**Scottish Tourist Trophy 12 Hr Ypres**	Clark/Porter	RS1600	1800	FEV 8H	DNF
		Stewart/Craft	TC	1600	EVX 248H	DNF
		Fitzpatrick	GT	1300	EVX 256H	29th
		Staepelaere/Aerts	TC	1600	ALO 29	1st

* 1850 cc pushrod engine. Cars really prototype 'Mexicos'.

Date	Event	Driver/Co-driver	Model	Engine (cc)	Reg No	Result
July	**Vltava (Czech)**	Staepelaere/Aerts	TC	1600	ALO 29	1st
	Donau	Staepelaere/Aerts	TC	1600	ALO 29	DNF
	Danube	Fall/Liddon	TC	1600	FEV 6H	DNF
	GP Meeting – Brands Hatch	Craft	TC	1600	EVX 248H	11th
		Fitzpatrick	GT	1300	EVX 256H	4th, Class 1st
August	**1000 Lakes**	Mikkola/Palm	TC	1800	FEV 5H	1st
		Makinen/Liddon	TC	1800	FEV 8H	2nd
September	**Three Cities**	Staepelaere/Aerts	TC	1600	ALO 29	3rd
	Total	Fall/Liddon	TC	1600	ETW 882G	DNF

Date	Event	Driver/Co-driver	Model	Engine (cc)	Reg No	Result
October	**Spanish**	Staepelaere/ Aerts	TC	1600	ALO 29	3rd
	Rothmans Cyprus	Mikkola/Palm	TC	1800	GNO 415H	DNF
	TAP	Clark/Porter	RS1600	1800	FEV 5H	DNF
		Piot/Todt	TC	1600	FEV 7H	DNF
		Fall/Liddon	TC	1600	ETW 883G	DNF
	Brands Hatch	Fitzpatrick	TC	1600	EVX 256H	1st
November	**Tour de Corse**	Piot/Porter	TC	1800	FEV 5H	6th
	Tour of Belgium	Staepelaere/ Aerts	TC	1600	ALO 29	1st
	RAC	Clark/Porter	RS1600	1800	KHK 597J	DNF
		Makinen/Liddon	TC	1800	KHK 598J	DNF
		Mikkola/Palm	TC	1800	KHK 599J	DNF
1971 February	**Routes du Nord**	Piot/Porter	RS1600	1800	LVX 941J	DNF
	Swedish	Makinen/Palm	RS1600	1800	MEV 35J	DNF
	Tunturiralli	Mikkola/Ahava	RS1600	1800	MEV 36J	DNF
	Midco, Kenya	Clark/Liddon	TC	1800	FEV 5H	1st
March	**Hankiralli**	Mikkola/Suonio	RS1600	1800	MEV 36J	DNF
		Makinen/ Keskitalo	RS1600	1800	KHK 597J	DNF
	Lyon – Charbonnières	Piot/Porter	RS1600	1800	LVX 941J	2nd
		Glemser/Kaiser	RS1600	1800	MEV 35J	3rd
	Circuit de Touraine	Piot	RS1600	1800	LVX 941J	DNF
	Ethiopian Highland	Fall/Liddon	TC	1600	ETW 882G	DNF
	Monza 4 hour	Fitzpatrick/Mass	RS1600	1800		4th
	Brands – Race of Champions	Fitzpatrick	RS1600	1800	MEV 34J	1st
April	**Safari**	Clark/ Staepelaere	TC	1800	LVX 944J	24th
		Mikkola/Palm	TC	1800	LVX 945J	DNF
		Makinen/Liddon	TC	1800	LVX 943J	20th
		Joginder/ Jaswant Singh	TC	1800	LVX 942J	16th
		Hillyar/Aird	TC	1800	LVX 946J	4th
		Preston/Smith	TC	1800	KHK 598J	6th
	Salzburgring	Fitzpatrick	RS1600	1800		1st Class
May	**Welsh**	Clark/Phillips	RS1600	1800	MEV 35J	DNF
	Criterium Alpin	Piot/Porter	RS1600	1800	LVX 941J	DNF
	Brno	Fitzpatrick	RS1600	1800		DNF
	Silverstone – Int. Trophy meeting	Fitzpatrick	RS1600	1800	MEV 34J	3rd
June	**Alpine**	Piot/Porter	RS1600	1800	LVX 941J	3rd

Date	Event	Driver/Co-driver	Model	Engine (cc)	Reg. No	Result
	Scottish	Clark/Porter	RS1600	1800	MEV 35J	Non-start
	12hr Ypres	Staepelaere Aerts	RS1600	1800	MEV 35J	2nd
	Mt. Elgon, Kenya	Preston/Smith	TC	1800	LVX 943J	1st
July	**Nurburgring 6hr**	Fitzpatrick/ Mazet	RS1600	1800		DNF
	Silverstone – GP meeting	Fitzpatrick	RS1600	1800	MEV 34J	7th
	Spa 24hr	Fitzpatrick/ Mazet	RS1600	1800		DNF
		Crabtree/Taylor	RS1600	1800	MEV 34J	DNF
August	**Zandvoort**	Fitzpatrick	RS1600	1800		DNF
	1000 Lakes	Mikkola/Palm	RS1600	1800	MEV 36J	DNF
	Ronde Cevenole	Piot	RS1600	1800	LVX 941J	3rd
September	**German**	Kleint/Klapproth	RS1600	1800	KHK 598J	DNF
	Netherlands	Staepelaere/ Symens	RS1600	1800	LVX 941J	1st
	Ricard 2 x 6hr	Fitzpatrick/ Mazet	RS1600	1800		DNF
October	**Cyprus**	Kirmitsis/ Lawrence	RS1600	1800	KHK 598J	1st
	Safari du Congo	Staepelaere/ Byttebier	RS1600	1800	GNO 424H	DNF
	Rally of Incas	Mikkola/Palm	RS1600	1800	LVX 944J	DNF
	Jarama	Fitzpatrick/Mass	RS1600	1800		1st
	Brands Hatch	Fitzpatrick	RS1600	1800	MEV 34J	DNF
November	**Tour of Belgium**	Staepelaere/ Aerts	RS1600	1800	LVX 941J	DNF
	Criterium des Cevennes	Piot/Porter	RS1600	1800	LVX 941J	25th
	RAC	Cowan/Syer	RS1600	1800	KHK 598J	13th
		Makinen/Liddon	RS1600	1800	PVX 398K	5th
		Mikkola/Palm	RS1600	1800	PVX 399K	4th
		Clark/Porter	RS1600	1800	PVX 400K	11th
1972 January	**Monte Carlo**	Makinen/Liddon	RS1600	1800	REV 120K	DNF
		Piot/Todt	RS1600	1800	REV 119K	5th
February	**Hong Kong**	Clark/Porter	RS1600	1800	KHK 598J	2nd
		Makinen/Liddon	RS1600	1800	PVX 398K	1st
		Moorat/Fleming	RS1600	1800	PVX 399K	3rd
	Arctic	Makinen/Salonen	RS1600	1800	MEV 36J	2nd
March	**Race of Champions Brands Hatch**	Woodman	1300GT	1300	REV 128K	5th, Class 1st
	Monza 4 hour	Birrell/ Bourgoignie	RS1600	1800	LVX 947J	3rd, Class 1st

Date	Event	Driver/Co-Driver	Model	Engine (cc)	Reg No	Result
April	**Safari**	Mikkola/Palm	RS1600	1800	RWC 455K	1st
		Makinen/Liddon	RS1600	1800	RWC 456K	8th
		Preston/Smith	RS1600	1800	RWC 458K	3rd
		Singh/Sembi	RS1600	1800	RWC 457K	DNF
		Hillyar/Birley	RS1600	1800	REV 119K	4th
	Salzburgring	Birrell	RS1600	1800	LVX 947J	7th
	Silverstone –	Woodman	1300GT	1300	REV 128K	DNF
	Int. Trophy					
	Welsh	Clark/Porter	RS1600	1800	RVX 941J	1st
	Brno	Birrell	RS1600	1800	LVX 947J	5th
	Acropolis	Mikkola/Liddon	RS1600	1800	RWC 456K	DNF
		Hillyar/Porter	RS1600	1800	RWC 457K	DNF
June	**Scottish**	Cowan/Syer	RS1600	1800	PVX 400K	6th
		Mikkola/Cardno	RS1600	1800	REV 119K	1st
		Clark/Porter	RS1600	1800	LVX 942J	2nd
	12hr Ypres	Staepelaere/ Aerts	RS1600	1800	RWC 456K	1st
July	**Nurburgring**	Menzel	RS1600	1800	LVX 947J	DNF
	Spa 24hr	Menzel/ Matthews	RS1600	1800	LVX 947J	26th
	Brands – GP meeting	Woodman	1300GT	1300	REV 128K	DNF
August	**Olympia**	Mikkola/Porter	RS1600	1800	RWC 456K	DNF
		Glemser/Kaiser	RS1600	1800	PVX 400K	DNF
	1000 Lakes	Makinen/Liddon	RS1600	2000	LVX 953J	2nd
September	**Cyprus**	Kirmitsis/ Lawrence	RS1600	1800	RWC 456K	DNF
	Manx	Clark/Porter	RS1600	2000	LVX 942J	1st
October	**Brands Hatch**	Hoyer	RS1600	2000	LVX 947J	5th
November	**Tour of Belgium**	Staepelaere/ 'Valliant'	RS1600	2000	LVX 953J	1st
	RAC	Makinen/Liddon	RS1600	2000	PVX 400K	DNF
		Clark/Mason	RS1600	2000	LVX 942J	1st
		Mikkola/ Davenport	RS1600	1800	VVX 958L	DNF
		Cowan/Syer	RS1600	1800	RWC 456K	DNF
1973 January	**Monte Carlo**	Makinen/Liddon	RS1600	2000	WWC 251L	11th
		Mikkola/Porter	RS1600	2000	WWC 252L	4th
February	**Arctic**	Makinen/Salonen	RS1600	2000	WWC 251L	1st
March	**Brands – Race of Champions**	Brodie	RS1600	2000	SPU 255K	2nd, Class 1st
		Mrs. Fortescue-Thomas	GT	1300*	YOO 331L	DNF
April	**Safari**	Clark/Porter	RS1600	2000	XPU 216L	DNF
		Preston/Smith	RS1600	2000	XPU 217L	14th
		Mikkola/ Davenport	RS1600	2000	XPU 218L	DNF

Date	Event	Driver/Co-driver	Model	Engine (cc)	Reg No	Result
		Makinen/Liddon	RS1600	2000	XPU 219L	DNF
		Shiyuka/ Gatende	RS1600	2000	XPU 220L	DNF
	Silverstone – Int. Trophy	Brodie	RS1600	2000	SPU 255K	4th
	Monza 4 hour	Brodie/ Bourgoignie	RS1600	2000	SPU 255K	DNF
May	Welsh	Clark/Porter	RS1600	2000	LVX 942J	1st
		Hill/Wood	RS1600	2000	LVX 941J	DNF
	Acropolis	Sparrow/Liddon	RS1600	2000	MEV 36J	DNF
June	Scottish	Clark/Porter	RS1600	2000	LVX 942J	1st
		Cowan/Syer	RS1600	2000	LVX 953J	3rd
		Mikkola/ Davenport	RS1600	2000	XPU 219L	2nd
		Pond/Miss Cobb	RS1600	2000	XPU 216L	7th

* Fitted with 1300 version of BDA engine.

Date	Event	Driver/Co-driver	Model	Engine (cc)	Reg No	Result
	12 hr Ypres	Staepelaere/ 'Valiant'	RS1600	2000	MEV 36J	DNF
	Mantorp Park, Sweden	Brodie/ Bourgoignie	RS1600	2000	SPU 255K	DNF
July	Heatway Rally	Mikkola/Porter	RS1600	2000	XPU 218L	1st
		Marshall/McWatt	RS1600	2000	XPU 217L	2nd
	Silverstone –	Brodie	RS1600	2000	SPU 255K	DNF
	GP meeting	Mrs Fortescue-Thomas	GT	1300*	YOO 331L	7th
August	1000 Lakes	Makinen/Liddon	RS1600	2000	YEV 207L	1st
September	Manx	Clark/Porter	RS1600	2000	LVX 942J	DNF
		Preston/White	RS1600	2000	XPU 219L	DNF
	Cyprus	Kirmitsis/ Davenport	RS1600	2000	MEV 36J	3rd
October	Brands Hatch	Hoyer	GT	1300*	YOO 331L	10th
November	Tour of Belgium	Chausseuil/ Baron	RS1600	2000	WWC 252L	DNF
	RAC	Clark/Mason	RS1600	2000	OOO 96M	2nd
		Mikkola/ Davenport	RS1600	2000	OOO 97M	DNF
		Makinen/Liddon	RS1600	2000	OOO 98M	1st
		Alen/Kivimaki	RS1600	2000	WWC 251L	3rd
		Preston/White	RS1600	2000	XPU 219L	DNF
		Brookes/Brown	RS1600	2000	XPY 216L	DNF
		HRH Prince Michael/Clarkson	Mexico	1600	XNO 286L	DNF
	Tour de Corse	Chausseuil/Baron	RS1600	2000	MEV 36J	4th
		Gamet/Huret	RS1600	2000	WWC 252L	DNF
1974 February	Arctic	Mikkola/ Davenport	RS1600	2000	YEV 207L	DNF
		Makinen/Salonen	RS1600	2000	OOO 98M	3rd
		Alen/Kivimaki	RS1600	2000	XPU 219L	4th

Date	Event	Driver/Co-driver	Model	Engine (cc)	Reg No	Result
March	**Monza 4 hour**	Heyer/Kautz	RS1600	2000		5th, Class 1st

* Fitted with 1300 version of BDA engine.

Date	Event	Driver/Co-driver	Model	Engine (cc)	Reg No	Result
April	**East African Safari**	Preston/Barnard	RS1600	2000	XPU 220L	9th
	Salzburgring 4 hous	Heyer/Kautz	RS1600	2000		4th, Class 1st
May	**UDT World Cup Rally**	Cowan/Syer	RS2000	2000	XPU 216L	15th
	Welsh	Clark/Porter	RS1600	2000	OOO 96M	DNF
		Alen/Davenport	RS1600	2000	XPU 219L	1st
	Vallelunga 500 km	Heyer/Krebs	RS1600	2000		3rd, Class 1st
June	**Scottish**	Clark/Porter	RS1600	2000	OOO 96M	Last minute cancell- ation of event
		Makinen/ Fleming	RS1600	2000	SNO 666M	
		Mikkola/ Davenport	RS1600	2000	XPU 220L	
		Alen/Mason	RS1600	2000	XPU 219L	
	Ypres 12 hr	Staepelaere/ 'Jimmy'	RS1600	2000	XPU 219L	1st
July	**Tour of Britain**	Clark/Porter	RS2000	2000	PVX 445M	1st
		Marshall/White	RS2000	2000	PVX 446M	2nd
	Nurburgring 6 hour	Heyer/Ludwig	RS1600	2000		1st
		Mass/Krebs/ Appel	RS1600	2000		3rd
August	**1000 Lakes**	Mikkola/ Davenport	RS1600	2000	XPU 220L	1st
		Makinen/Liddon	RS1600	2000	SNO 666M	2nd
	Zandvoort 4-hour	Heyer/Ludwig	RS1600	2000		7th, Class 1st
	Total Rally	Clark/Mason	RS1600	2000	SYW 946M	DNF
September	**Manx**	Clark/Porter	RS1600	2000	OOO 96M	3rd
October	**Jarama 4 hour**	Hezemans/Mohr	RS1600	2000		2nd, Class 1st
November	**RAC Rally**	Clark/Mason	RS1600	2000	OOO 96M	7th
		Makinen/Liddon	RS1600	2000	GVX 883N	1st
		Mikkola/ Davenport	RS1600	2000	SYW 947M	DNF
		Alen/White	RS1600	2000	SYW 946M	DNF
		Benson Ford Jr./ Kaplan	RS2000	2000	AOO 674L	DNF
		Rockey/ Channon	RS1600	2000	YEV 208L	11th
		Brookes/Brown	RS2000	2000	GVX 833N	DNF

1975

Date	Event	Driver/Co-driver	Model	Engine (cc)	Reg No	Result
January	**Arctic**	Makinen/Salonen	RS1600	2000	SNO 666M	DNF
		Miss Heinonen/ Miss Saaristo	RS1600	2000	OOO 98M	DNF

Date	Event	Driver/Co-driver	Model	Engine (cc)	Reg. No	Result
February	**Boucles de Spa**	Staepelaere/ 'Valliant'	RS1600	2000	GVX 883N	1st
	Mintex	Brookes/Brown	RS2000	2000	GVX 833N	8th
March	**Nacht der Kempen**	Staepelaere/ 'Valliant'	RS1600	2000	GVX 883N	1st
	Circuit Ardennes	Staepelaere/ 'Valliant'	RS1600	2000	GVX 883N	1st
	Monza 4 hr	Heyer/Finotto	RS1600	2000	Unreg.	2nd
	Circuit of Ireland	Clark/Porter	RS1600	2000	SPU 254K	DNF
		Coleman/Phelan	RS1600	2000	OOO 96M	1st
		Rockey/Scott	RS1600	2000	YEV 208L	DNF
		Brookes/Brown	RS2000	2000	GVX 833N	5th
April	**12 hour de l'Est (Belgium)**	Staepelaere/ 'Valliant'	RS1600	2000	GVX 883N	7th
	Criterium de Tourraine	Staepelaere/ 'Valliant'	RS1600	2000	GVX 883N	7th
May	**Welsh**	Clark/Porter	RS1800	2000	HHJ 700N	1st
		Coleman/ Davenport	RS1800	2000	HHJ 701N	DNF
		Brookes/Brown	RS1800	2000	HHJ 702N	5th
		Rockey/ Channon	RS1600	2000	YEV 208L	2nd
	Criterium Lucien Bianchi	Staepelaere/ 'Valliant'	RS1600	2000	GVX 883N	2nd
June	**Scottish**	Clark/Porter	RS1800	2000	HHJ 700N	1st
		Coleman/ O'Sullivan	RS1800	2000	HHJ 701N	3rd
		Brookes/Brown	RS1800	2000	HHJ 702N	2nd
		Makinen/Liddon	RS1800	2000	HHJ 703N	5th
		Taylor/Fleming	RS1600	2000	OOO 96M	10th
		Rockey/ Channon	RS1600	2000	YEV 208L	DNF
	24 hr Ypres	Staepelaere/ 'Valliant'	RS1600	2000	GVX 883N	4th
	Donegal	Coleman/Scott	RS1800	2000	HHJ 701N	3rd
	Antibes	Clark/Porter	RS1800	2000	KHK 983N	DNF
July	**Nurburgring 6 hour**	Heyer	RS1800	2000	Unreg.	DNF
August	**Taurus (Hungary)**	Staepelaere/ 'Valliant'	RS1800	2000	JJN 974N	1st
	1000 Lakes	Makinen/Liddon	RS1800	2000	HHJ 703N	3rd
		Vatanen/Phillips	RS1600	2000	SNO 666M	DNF
		Miss Avomeri/ Miss Valtaharju	RS2000	2000	AOO 674L	DNF
September	**Tour de France**	Makinen/Liddon	RS1800	2000	KHK 982N	DNF
	12 hour van Ronse	Staepelaere/ 'Valliant'	RS1800	2000	JJN 974N	2nd
	Omloop van Haspenguow	Staepelaere/ 'Valliant'	RS1800	2000	JJN 974N	1st

Date	Event	Driver/Co-driver	Model	Engine (cc)	Reg No	Result
	Manx	Clark/Porter	RS1800	2000	KHK 983N	1st
		Coleman/O'Sullivan	RS1800	2000	HHJ 701N	3rd
		Brookes/Brown	RS1800	2000	HHJ 702N	DNF
		Rockey/Scott	RS1800	2000	YEV 208L	DNF
October	Omloop van Vlaanderen	Staepelaere/'Valliant'	RS1800	2000	JJN 974N	2nd
	San Remo	Clark/Porter	RS1800	2000	KHK 983N	DNF
		Makinen/Liddon	RS1800	2000	KHK 982N	DNF
	Kyalami 1000 km	Heyer/Hennige	RS1800	2000	Unreg.	1st
November	RAC	Clark/Mason	RS1800	2000	LAR 800P	2nd
		Makinen/Liddon	RS1800	2000	LAR 801P	1st
		Vatanen/Bryant	RS1800	2000	LVW 690P	DNF
		Coleman/O'Sullivan	RS1800	2000	HHJ 701N	6th
		Brookes/Brown	RS1800	2000	HHJ 702N	DNF
		Rockey/Tucker	RS1600	2000	YEV 208L	DNF
1976 January	Monte Carlo	Clark/Porter	RS1800	2000	KHK 983N	5th
		Makinen/Liddon	RS1800	2000	KHK 982N	DNF
February	Boucles de Spa	Staepelaere/'Valliant'	RS1800	2000	JJN 974N	DNF
	Galway	Coleman/Porter	RS1800	2000	KHK 983N	1st
	Mintex	Clark/Porter	RS1800	2000	LAR 800P	DNF
		Vatanen/Bryant	RS1800	2000	LAR 801P	3rd
		Brookes/Brown	RS1800	2000	HHJ 702N	2nd
		Coleman/O'Sullivan	RS1800	2000	HHJ 701N	DNF
		Sclater/Liddon	RS1800	2000	HHJ 700N	5th
March	Nacht der Kempen	Staepelaere/'Valliant'	RS1800	2000	JJN 974N	1st
	Hankiralli	Vatanen/Putkonen	RS1800	2000	KHK 982N	DNF
	Firestone	Clark/Porter	RS1800	2000	KHK 983N	DNF
		Makinen/Liddon	RS1800	2000	MTW 200P	2nd
	Monza 4 hr	Finotto/Muller	RS1800	2000	Unreg.	DNF
		Poole	RS1800	1866	HHJ 704N	DNF
April	12 hr de l'Est	Staepelaere/'Valliant'	RS1800	2000	JJN 974N	1st
	Safari	Hillyar/Hart	RS1800	2000	HHJ 703N	DNF
	Circuit of Ireland	Coleman/O'Sullivan	RS1800	2000	KHK 983N	1st
		Brookes/Brown	RS1800	2000	ODA 622R	2nd
	Tulip	Staepelaere/'Valliant'	RS1800	2000	JJN 974N	3rd
May	Mugello	Poole/Cochesa	RS1800	1866	HHJ 704N	6th
	Welsh	Clark/Porter	RS1800	2000	LAR 800P	3rd
		Vatanen/Bryant	RS1800	2000	LAR 801P	1st
		Brookes/Crellin	RS1800	2000	ODA 622R	14th
		Coleman/O'Sullivan	RS1800	2000	HHJ 701N	DNF

Date	Event	Driver/Co-driver	Model	Engine (cc)	Reg No	Result
	Brno	Finotto	RS1800	1866	Unreg.	DNF
		Poole/Handley	RS1800	1866	HHJ 704N	3rd
	Omloop van Haspenguow	Staepelaere/'Valliant'	RS1800	2000	JJN 974N	1st
	Criterium Lucien Bianchi	Staepelaere/'Valliant'	RS1800	2000	JJN 974N	1st
June	**Scottish**	Clark/Porter	RS1800	2000	LAR 800P	2nd
		Vatanen/Bryant	RS1800	2000	LAR 801P	DNF
		Brookes/Brown	RS1800	2000	ODA 622R	1st
	Donegal	Coleman/Scott	RS1800	2000	JJN 974N	DNF
	12 hr Ypres	Staepelaere/'Valliant'	RS1800	2000	JJN 974N	DNF
	Morocco	Clark/Porter	RS1800	2000	MTW 201P	DNF
		Makinen/Liddon	RS1800	2000	LVW 690P	DNF
July	**Nurburgring 4 hour**	Scheckter	RS1800	1866	HHJ 704N	DNF
	Tour of Britain	Clark/Porter	RS2000	2000	NOO 894P	DNF
		Makinen/Liddon	RS2000	2000	OVX 430P	DNF
		Vatanen/Bryant	RS2000	2000	OVX 431P	1st
		HRH Prince Michael/Clarkson	RS2000	2000	NOO 895P	11th
	Total	Makinen/Liddon	RS1800	2000	MTW 200P	1st
August	**Taurus**	Staepelaere/'Valliant'	RS1800	2000	JJN 974N	1st
	1000 Lakes	Makinen/Liddon	RS1800	2000	KHK 982N	4th
		Vatanen/Aho	RS1800	2000	POO 489R	DNF
		Saaristo/Alanen	RS2000	2000	OVX 430P	9th 1st Gp 1
		Hamalainen/Vihervaara	RS2000	2000	OVX 431P	DNF
	Limburg	Staepelaere/'Valliant'	RS1800	2000	JJN 974N	3rd
September	**12 hr Ronse**	Staepelaere/'Valliant'	RS1800	2000	JJN 974N	DNF
	Manx	Clark/Porter	RS1800	2000	LAR 800P	DNF
		Vatanen/Bryant	RS1800	2000	LAR 801P	1st
		Coleman/Liddon	RS1800	2000	STW 128R	DNF
		Brookes/Brown	RS1800	2000	ODA 622R	DNF
	Tourist Trophy	Poole/Handley	RS1800	1866	HHJ 704N	9th
October	**Jarama**	Poole/Handley	RS1800	1866	HHJ 704N	DNF
	12 hr Charleroi	Staepelaere/'Valliant'	RS1800	2000	JJN 974N	1st
	Omloop van Vlaanderen	Staepelaere/'Valliant'	RS1800	2000	JJN 974N	DNF
	Southern	Clark/Porter	RS1800	2000	MTW 201P	14th
	Cross	Makinen/Liddon	RS1800	2000	LVW 690P	DNF
November	**Kyalami**	Heyer/Ludwig	RS1800	2000	Unreg.	2nd
	1000 km	Schenken/Hezemans	RS1800	2000	Unreg.	DNF

Date	Event	Driver/Co-driver	Model	Engine (cc)	Reg No	Result
	RAC	Makinen/Liddon	RS1800	2000	POO 504R	DNF
		Clark/Pegg	RS1800	2000	POO 505R	1st
		Vatanen/Bryant	RS1800	2000	POO 489R	DNF
		Waldegard/ Thorzelius	RS1800	2000	MTW 200P	3rd
		Saaristo/Francis	RS2000	2000	OVX 430P	27th
		Hamalainen/ Vihervaara	RS2000	2000	OVX 431P	DNF
		Lampinen/Wood	RS1800	2000	KHK 982N	DNF
		Hettema/Billet	RS1800	2000	LAR 800P	DNF
		Coleman/ O'Sullivan	RS1600	2000	STW 128R	6th
		Brookes/Brown	RS1800	2000	ODA 622R	DNF
1977						
February	Arctic	Vatanen/Aho	RS1800	2000	POO 489R	1st
		Brookes/Brown	RS1800	2000	ODA 622R	DNF
	Galway	Clark/Porter	RS1800	2000	POO 505R	1st
	Mintex	Dawson/Marriott	RS1800	2000	KHK 982N	5th
		Brookes/Brown	RS1800	2000	STW 129R	DNF
		Taylor/Jensen	RS1800	2000	VHK 47S	DNF
	Sachs-Winterrallye	Hainbach/Linzen	RS1800	2000	STW 128R	2nd
March	Portugal	Waldegard/ Thorzelius	RS1800	2000	STW 130R	2nd
		Clark/Porter	RS1800	2000	POO 505R	DNF
		Vatanen/Bryant	RS1800	2000	POO 504R	DNF
	Sachs Rallye Trifels	Hainbach/Linzen	RS1800	2000	STW 128R	DNF
	Nacht der Kempen	Staepelaere/ Bessem	RS1800	2000	JJN 974N	1st
	Antwerpen-Liege-Antwerpen	Staepelaere/ Franssen	RS1800	2000	JJN 974N	1st
April	East African Safari	Clark/Porter	RS1800	2000	STW 200R	DNF
		Waldegard/ Thorzelius	RS1800	2000	STW 201R	1st
		Vatanen/Aho	RS1800	2000	STW 202R	DNF
		Preston/Lyall	RS1800	2000	STW 203R	DNF
	Circuit of Ireland	Dawson/Spokes	RS1800	2000	KHK 982N	4th
		Brookes/Brown	RS1800	2000	STW 129R	1st
	Rallye Weser-Ems	Hainbach/ Linzen	RS1800	2000	STW 128R	1st
	Saarland Rallye	Hainbach/ Linzen	RS1800	2000	STW 128R	1st
	12 Heures de l'Est	Staepelaere/ Bessem	RS1800	2000	JJN 974N	3rd
	Omloop van Haspenguow	Staepelaere/ Bessem	RS1800	2000	JJN 974N	1st
May	Tulip	Staepelaere/ Bessem	RS1800	2000	JJN 974N	1st
		Brookes/Bryant	RS1800	2000	ODA 622R	3rd
	Welsh	Brookes/Brown	RS1800	2000	STW 129R	DNF
		Taylor/Jensen	RS1800	2000	VHK 47S	5th
	Acropolis	Waldegard/ Thorzelius	RS1800	2000	STW 130R	1st

Date	Event	Driver/Co-driver	Model	Engine (cc)	Reg. No	Result
		Clark/Porter	RS1800	2000	POO 505R	2nd
		Vatanen/Aho	RS1800	2000	POO 504R	DNF
	Criterium L.Bianchi	Staepelaere/Franssen	RS1800	2000	JJN 974N	2nd
	Metz Rallye	Hainbach/Linzen	RS1800	2000	STW 128R	DNF
	Rallye Hessen	Hainbach/Linzen	RS1800	2000	STW 128R	DNF
June	Scottish	Brookes/Brown	RS1800	2000	STW 129R	3rd
		Cowan/McNeil	RS1800	2000	ODA 622R	DNF
		Taylor/Jensen	RS1800	2000	VHK 47S	DNF
	Donegal	Clark/Porter	RS1800	2000	POO 505R	DNF
	Eindhoven-Liege-Eindhoven	Staepelaere/Bessem	RS1800	2000	JJN 974N	1st
	24 Uren van Ieper	Staepelaere/Franssen	RS1800	2000	JJN 974N	DNF
July	Rallye Vorderpfalz	Hainbach/Linzen	RS1800	2000	STW 128R	DNF
	Hunsruck Rallye	Hainbach Linzen	RS1800	2000	STW 128R	1st
August	1000 Lakes	Waldegard/Thorzelius	RS1800	2000	STW 130R	3rd
		Vatanen/Aho	RS1800	2000	POO 504R	DNF
		Hamalainen/Tiukkanen	RS1800	2000	POO 489R	1st
	Burmah	Dawson/Pegg	RS1800	2000	KHK 982N	3rd
		Brookes/Brown	RS1800	2000	STW 129R	2nd
		Taylor/Short	RS1800	2000	VHK 47S	DNF
	Rallye Westfalen Lippe	Hainbach/Linzen	RS1800	2000	STW 128R	1st
	Limburgia	Staepelaere/Bessem	RS1800	2000	JJN 974N	1st
September	Quebec	Clark/Porter	RS1800	2000	STW 200R	3rd
		Vatanen/Aho	RS1800	2000	STW 202R	DNF
	Manx	Dawson/Pegg	RS1800	2000	KHK 982N	3rd
		Brookes/Brown	RS1800	2000	STW 129R	DNF
	Sachs Rallye Baltic	Hainbach/Linzen	RS1800	2000	STW 128R	DNF
	12 Uren van Ronse	Staepelaere/Bessem	RS1800	2000	JJN 974N	DNF
	De Drie Zustersteden	Staepelaere/Bessem	RS1800	2000	JJN 974N	1st
October	San Remo	Waldegard/Thorzelius	RS1800	2000	VHK 74S	5th
		Vatanen/Bryant	RS1800	2000	MTW 200P	DNF
	OAMC Rallye Austria	Staepelaere/Franssen	RS1800	2000	JJN 974N	1st
	Kohle und Stahl	Staepelaere/Bessem	RS1800	2000	JJN 974N	1st
November	Tour de Corse	Brookes/Holmes	RS1800	2000	POO 505R	DNF
		Nicolas/Laverne	RS1800	2000	VHK 74S	DNF

Date	Event	Driver/Co-driver	Model	Engine (cc)	Reg No	Result
	RAC	Waldegard/ Thorzelius	RS1800	2000	WTW 567S	1st
		Clark/Pegg	RS1800	2000	STW 200R	4th
		Vatanen/Bryant	RS1800	2000	STW 202R	DNF
		Dawson/Marriott	RS1800	2000	KHK 982N	5th
		Brookes/Brown	RS1800	2000	STW 129R	3rd
		Hamalainen/ Scott	RS1800	2000	STW 130R	6th
		Hainbach/Linzen	RS1800	2000	STW 128R	20th
	Warchau Rally Poland	Staepelaere/ Bessem	RS1800	2000	JJN 974N	DNF
1978 February	**Arctic**	Vatanen/Aho	RS1800	2000	STW 202R	1st
	Swedish	Waldegard/ Thorzelius	RS1800	2000	WTW 567S	1st
		Mikkola/Hertz	RS1800	2000	WTW 568S	2nd
		Vatanen/Aho	RS1800	2000	STW 202R	5th
	Hankiralli	Mikkola/Hertz	RS1800	2000	WTW 568S	DNF
		Vatanen/Aho	RS1800	2000	STW 202R	DNF
	Mintex	Clark/Porter	RS1800	2000	WTW 569S	4th
		Mikkola/Hertz	RS1800	2000	POO 504R	DNF
		Brookes/Brown	RS1800	2000	STW 129R	2nd
	Galway	Taylor/Short	RS1800	2000	VHK 47S	1st
	Boucles de Spa	Staepelaere/ Franssen	RS1800	2000	JJN 974N	DNF
	Tour de Luxembourg	Staepelaere/ Franssen	RS1800	2000	JJN 974N	1st
March	**Kempenrally**	Staepelaere/ Franssen	RS1800	2000	JJN 974N	1st
	Circuit des Ardennes	Staepelaere/ Bessem	RS1800	2000	JJN 974N	1st
	Circuit of Ireland	Clark/Porter	RS1800	2000	POO 505R	4th
		Mikkola/Hertz	RS1800	2000	STW 200R	DNF
		Brookes/Brown	RS1800	2000	VHK 74S	1st
April	**Portugal**	Waldegard/ Thorzelius	RS1800	2000	WTW 567S	DNF
		Mikkola/Hertz	RS1800	2000	WTW 568S	2nd
		Vatanen/Bryant	RS1800	2000	STW 202R	DNF
		Nicolas/Laverne	RS1800	2000	MTW 200P	3rd
	12 Heures de l'Est	Staepelaere/ Franssen	RS1800	2000	JJN 974N	3rd
	Criterium L. Bianchi	Staepelaere/ Franssen	RS1800	2000	JJN 974N	1st
	Tulip	Staepelaere/ Bessem	RS1800	2000	JJN 974N	3rd
		Brookes/Bryant	RS1800	2000	STW 129R	1st
May	**Welsh**	Mikkola/Hertz	RS1800	2000	POO 504R	1st
		Clark/Porter	RS1800	2000	WTW 569S	2nd
		Brookes/Brown	RS1800	2000	VHK 74S	5th
	Criterium Alpin	Nicolas/ Laverne	RS1800	2000	STW 200R	2nd
	South Sweden	Waldegard/ Thorzelius	RS1800	2000	WTW 567S	1st

Date	Event	Driver/Co-driver	Model	Engine (cc)	Reg No	Result
June	**Scottish**	Mikkola/Hertz	RS1800	2000	POO 504R	1st
		Clark/Porter	RS1800	2000	WTW 569S	3rd
		Brookes/Brown	RS1800	2000	STW 129R	7th
		Samson/Samson	RS1800	2000	STW 200R	8th
	Omloop van Haspenguow	Staepelaere/Bessem	RS1800	2000	JJN 974N	1st
	Antibes	Nicolas/Laverne	RS1800	2000	STW 200R	8th
	Ypres	Staepelaere/Franssen	RS1800	2000	STW 200R	2nd
July	**Mille Pistes**	Nicolas/Laverne	RS1800	2000	STW 130R	DNF
	Vorderplatz	Hainbach/Linzen	RS1800	2000	STW 200R	2nd
August	**Hunsruck**	Hainbach/Linzen	RS1800	2000	STW 200R	DNF
	Burmah	Mikkola/Hertz	RS1800	2000	POO 504R	1st
		Brookes/Bryant	RS1800	2000	STW 129R	2nd
		Clark/Porter	RS1800	2000	WTW 569S	3rd
		Carr/Gocentas	RS1800	2000	STW 200R	6th
	1000 Lakes	Hamalainen/Koronen	RS1800	2000	STW 202R	8th
		Mikkola/Hertz(E)	RS1800	2000	STW 201R	DNF
		Vatanen/Aho	RS1800	2000	WTW 568S	DNF
		Miss Korpi/Miss Heinio	RS1800	2000	POO 489R	28th
September	**Kurkessen**	Hainbach/Linzen	RS1800	2000	STW 200R	1st
	Manx	Clark/Porter	RS1800	2000	WTW 569S	4th
		Mikkola/Hertz(E)	RS1800	2000	POO 404R	DNF
		Brookes/Bryant	RS1800	2000	VHK 74S	DNF (Disq)
	Tour de France	Nicolas/Laverne	RS1800	2000	STW 200R	DNF
	Cyprus	Clark/Porter	RS1800	2000	STW 200R	1st
		Kirmitsis/Adams	RS1800	2000	STW 129R	2nd
October	**Poland**	Staepelaere/Franssen	RS1800	2000	JJN 974N	1st
November	**Bosphorus (Turkey)**	Staepelaere/Franssen	RS1800	2000	JJN 974N	1st
	RAC	(All cars run for Boreham by 'mini-dealer-teams', due to company strike)				
		Mikkola/Hertz(E)	RS1800	2000	SJN 830R	1st
		Waldegard/Thorzelius(E)	RS1800	2000	WTW 568S	2nd
		Brookes/Tucker	RS1800	2000	UNY 956S	3rd
		Taylor/Short	RS1800	2000	SKK 625R	7th
		Clark/Wilson	RS1800	2000	OKK 380P	DNF
		Vatanen/Bryant	RS1800	2000	MLD 999P	DNF

1979

Date	Event	Driver/Co-driver	Model	Engine (cc)	Reg No	Result
January	**Monte Carlo**	Waldegard/Thorzelius	RS1800	2000	VHK 74S	2nd
		Mikkola/Hertz	RS1800	2000	VHK 47S	5th

287

Date	Event	Driver/Co-driver	Model	Engine (cc)	Reg No	Result
February	**Sweden**	Waldegard/ Thorzelius	RS1800	2000	WTW 569S	2nd
		Mikkola/Hertz	RS1800	2000	STW 201R	5th
		Vatanen/Richards	RS1800	2000	WTW 567S	DNF
	Mintex	Brookes/White	RS1800	2000	STW 129R	4th
March	**Portugal**	Mikkola/Hertz	RS1800	2000	POO 504R	1st
		Waldegard/ Thorzelius	RS1800	2000	POO 505R	2nd
		Vatanen/Bryant	RS1800	2000	WTW 567S	DNF
	Circuit of Ireland	Brookes/White	RS1800	2000	GVX 489T	DNF
May	**Welsh**	Mikkola/ Hertz(E)	RS1800	2000	CLM 184T	1st
		Brookes/White	RS1800	2000	STW 129R	2nd
		Donald/Tucker	RS1800	2000	TWC 235R	9th
	Acropolis	Waldegard/ Thorzelius(R)	RS1800	2000	WTW 567S	1st
		Iaveris/Stefanis	RS1800	2000	WTW 569S	5th
		Mikkola/Hertz(R)	RS1800	2000	FEV 1T	DNF
		Clark/Porter(R)	RS1800	2000	GVX 488T	DNF
June	**Scottish**	Mikkola/ Hertz(E)	RS1800	2000	CLM 184T	6th
		Brookes/White	RS1800	2000	STW 129R	10th
		Waldegard/ Thorzelius(E)	RS1800	2000	MLD 999P	DNF
July	**Ypres**	Brookes/White	RS1800	2000	GVX 489T	DNF
	Motogard (New Zealand)	Mikkola/Hertz	RS1800	2000	WTW 568S (Re-reg. JB780)	1st
		Vatanen/ Richards(R)	RS1800	2000	STW 130R (Re-reg. IZ8320)	3rd
August	**1000 Lakes**	Vatanen/ Richards(R)	RS1800	2000	GVX 488T	2nd
		Waldegard/ Billstam	RS1800	2000	WTW 567S	3rd
		Mikkola/Hertz	RS1800	2000	FEV 1T	DNF
September	**Quebec**	Waldegard/ Thorzelius(R)	RS1800	2000	POO 505R	1st
		Vatanen/ Richards(R)	RS1800	2000	POO 504R	3rd
	Manx	Brookes/White	RS1800	2000	GVX 489T	1st
		Mikkola/ Hertz(E)	RS1800	2000	UYY 256S	DNF
	Cyprus	Vatanen/ Richards(R)	RS1800	2000	STW 201R	1st
October	**Ulster**	Brookes/White	RS1800	2000	GVX 489T	1st
November	**RAC**	Mikkola/ Hertz(E)	RS1800	2000	WTW 569S	1st
		Brookes/White	RS1800	2000	POO 504R	2nd
		Vatanen/ Richards(R)	RS1800	2000	GVX 488T	4th

Date	Event	Driver/Co-driver	Model	Engine (cc)	Reg. No	Result
		Waldegard/ Thorzelius(E)	RS1800	2000	GJN 126T	9th
		Carr/Gocentas	RS1800	2000	STW 129R	10th
		Clark/Wilson	RS1800	2000	POO 505R	DNF

Note: From mid-1978, cars were regularly sponsored by Eaton's Yale, and by Rothmans. Such cars are denoted by an (E), and an (R), respectively, after the driver pairings. In a few cases, these entries were run on behalf of Boreham by the David Sutton team, sometimes with Sutton-prepared cars.

The David Sutton (Cars) Ltd., operation, 1980 and 1981

As already stated in the 'Cars' Appendix, the activities of these cars, in 1980 and 1981, is detailed here:

1980

Date	Event	Driver/Co-driver	Model	Engine (cc)	Reg. No	Result
February	**Mintex**	Mikkola/Hertz	RS1800	2000	EUW 939V	1st
		Vatanen/Richards	RS1800	2000	EUW 838V	2nd
March	**Portugal**	Mikkola/Hertz	RS1800	2000	EUC 958V	DNF
		Vatanen/Richards	RS1800	2000	UYY 256S	DNF
April	**Circuit of Ireland**	Vatanen/Richards	RS1800	2000	EUW 938V	2nd
		Coleman/Neville	RS1800	2000	GVX 489T	DNF
May	**Welsh**	Vatanen/Richards	RS1800	2000	EUW 938V	1st
		Mikkola/Hertz	RS1800	2000	EUW 939V	2nd
	Acropolis	Vatanen/Richards	RS1800	2000	UYY 256S	1st
		Mikkola/Hertz	RS1800	2000	EUC 958V	DNF
June	**Scottish**	Mikkola/Hertz	RS1800	2000	EUW 939V	1st
		Vatanen/Richards	RS1800	2000	EUW 938V	2nd
July	**CS (Spain)**	Vatanen/Richards	RS1800	2000	EUW 938V	2nd
August	**1000 Lakes**	Vatanen/Richards	RS1800	2000	UYY 256S	2nd
September	**Manx**	Vatanen/Richards	RS1800	2000	EUW 938V	2nd
	Cyprus	Clark/Wilson	RS1800	2000	STW 201R	1st
October	**San Remo**	Vatanen/Richards	RS1800	2000	PLY 829W	2nd
		Mikkola/Hertz	RS1800	2000	EUC 958V	3rd
November	**RAC**	Mikkola/Hertz	RS1800	2000	EUW 939V	2nd
		Makinen/Holmes	RS1800	2000	EUC 958V	6th
		Vatanen/Richards	RS1800	2000	PLY 829W	DNF

1981

Date	Event	Driver/Co-driver	Model	Engine (cc)	Reg. No	Result
January	**Monte Carlo**	Vatanen/Richards	RS1800	2000	PLY 829W	DNF
February	**Sweden**	Vatanen/Richards	RS1800	2000	EUW 939V	2nd
		Airikkala/ Virtanen	RS1800	2000	EUC 958V	3rd
	Mintex	Airikkala/Short	RS1800	2000	UYY 256S	1st
		Wilson/Harryman	RS1800	2000	STW 201R	6th

Date	Event	Driver/Co-driver	Model	Engine (cc)	Reg. No	Result
March	**Portugal**	Vatanen/Richards	RS1800	2000	PLY 829W	DNF
		Wilson/Harryman	RS1800	2000	CLM 184T	DNF
April	**Costa Smeralda**	Airikkala/Virtanen	RS1800	2000	UYY 256S	4th
	Circuit of Ireland	Airikkala/Short	RS1800	2000	PLY 829W	DNF
		Wilson/Harryman	RS1800	2000	STW 201R	DNF
	Maspalomas (Italy)	Vatanen/Richards	RS1800	2000	EUW 938V	2nd
	Elba	Airikkala Virtanen	RS1800	2000	UYY 256S	4th
May	**Welsh**	Vatanen/Richards	RS1800	2000	EUW 938V	1st
		Airikkala/Short	RS1800	2000	EUC 958V	4th
		Wilson/Harryman	RS1800	2000	STW 201R	5th
	Acropolis	Vatanen/Richards	RS1800	2000	DKP 191T	1st
		Wilson/Harryman	RS1800	2000	CLM 184T	DNF
June	**Scottish**	Wilson/Harryman	RS1800	2000	STW 201R	3rd
		Airikkala/Short	RS1800	2000	EUC 958V	5th
July	**Argentina (Codasur)**	Vatanen/Richards	RS1800	2000	RRK 425W	DNF
August	**Brazil**	Vatanen/Richards	RS1800	2000	EUC 958V	1st
	1000 Lakes	Vatanen/Richards	RS1800	2000	DKP 191T	1st
		Airikkala/Virtanen	RS1800	2000	UYY 256S	5th
September	**Manx**	Wilson/Harryman	RS1800	2000	STW 201R	3rd
		Airikkala/Virtanen	RS1800	2000	EUW 938V	DNF
	Cyprus	Wilson/Harryman	RS1800	2000	CLM 184T	DNF
October	**Corte Ingles (Canaries)**	Airikkala/Virtanen	RS1800	2000	EUW 938V	7th
	San Remo	Vatanen/Richards	RS1800	2000	DKP 191T	7th
	Tenerife	Airikkala/Virtanen	RS1800	2000	EUW 938V	DNF
	Ivory Coast	Vatanen/Richards	RS1800	2000	RRK 425W	9th
		Taylor/Spiller	RS2000	2000	MLD 999P	DNF
November	**RAC**	Vatanen/Richards	RS1800	2000	VLE 756X	2nd
		Airikkala/Short	RS1800	2000	UYY 256S	4th
		Wilson/Harryman	RS1800	2000	STW 201R	DNF

From this point the David Sutton operation split from Rothmans. In 1982, Sutton were to run an Audi Quattro, and Rothmans support was transferred to Opel.

Index

Note: Some names are so important to the story of the Works Escorts that they crop up on almost every page. For that reason alone, I have made no attempt to index Peter Ashcroft, Bill Barnett, Roger Clark, Walter Hayes, Mick Jones, Timo Makinen, Hannu Mikkola, Henry Taylor and Stuart Turner.

291